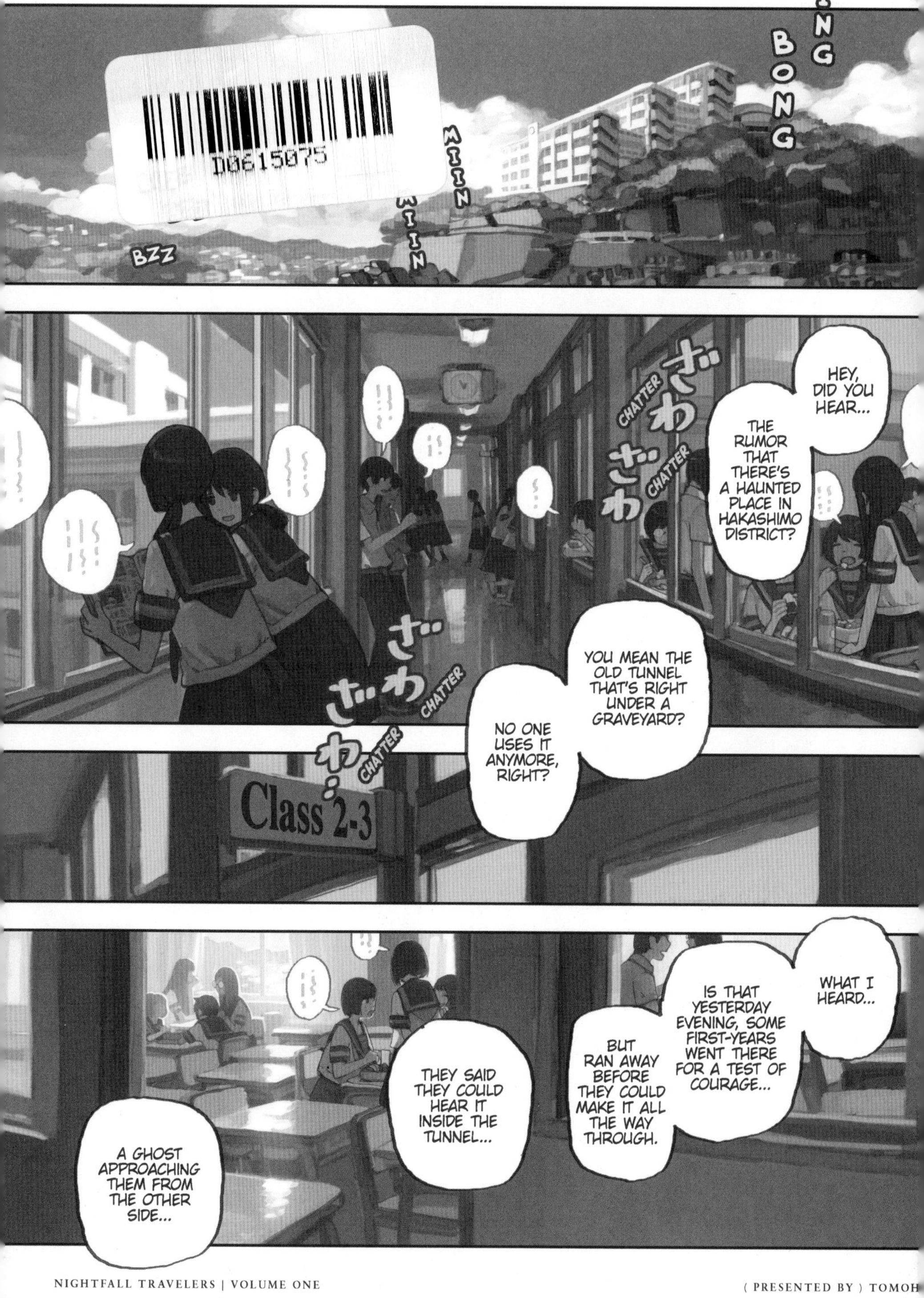
BING
BONG
MIIIN
MIIIN
BZZ
HEY, DID YOU HEAR...
THE RUMOR THAT THERE'S A HAUNTED PLACE IN HAKASHIMO DISTRICT?
ざわ ざわ
CHATTER CHATTER
YOU MEAN THE OLD TUNNEL THAT'S RIGHT UNDER A GRAVEYARD?
NO ONE USES IT ANYMORE, RIGHT?
ざわ ざわ ざわ
CHATTER CHATTER CHATTER
Class 2-3
WHAT I HEARD...
IS THAT YESTERDAY EVENING, SOME FIRST-YEARS WENT THERE FOR A TEST OF COURAGE...
BUT RAN AWAY BEFORE THEY COULD MAKE IT ALL THE WAY THROUGH.
THEY SAID THEY COULD HEAR IT INSIDE THE TUNNEL...
A GHOST APPROACHING THEM FROM THE OTHER SIDE...

Contents

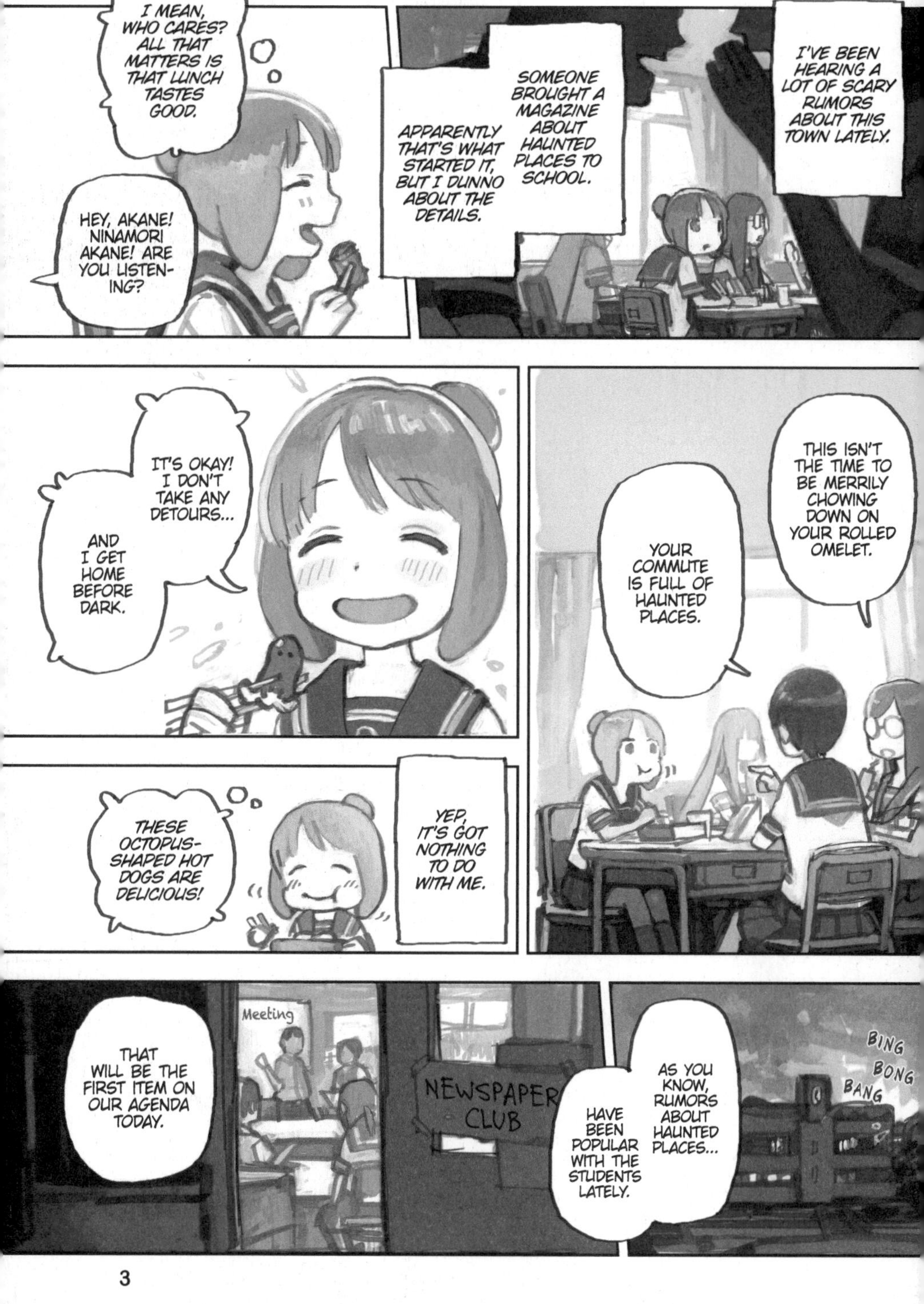
I'VE BEEN HEARING A LOT OF SCARY RUMORS ABOUT THIS TOWN LATELY.
SOMEONE BROUGHT A MAGAZINE ABOUT HAUNTED PLACES TO SCHOOL.
APPARENTLY THAT'S WHAT STARTED IT, BUT I DUNNO ABOUT THE DETAILS.
I MEAN, WHO CARES? ALL THAT MATTERS IS THAT LUNCH TASTES GOOD.
HEY, AKANE! NINAMORI AKANE! ARE YOU LISTENING?
THIS ISN'T THE TIME TO BE MERRILY CHOWING DOWN ON YOUR ROLLED OMELET.
YOUR COMMUTE IS FULL OF HAUNTED PLACES.
IT'S OKAY! I DON'T TAKE ANY DETOURS...
AND I GET HOME BEFORE DARK.
YEP, IT'S GOT NOTHING TO DO WITH ME.
THESE OCTOPUS-SHAPED HOT DOGS ARE DELICIOUS!
BING BONG BANG
AS YOU KNOW, RUMORS ABOUT HAUNTED PLACES...
HAVE BEEN POPULAR WITH THE STUDENTS LATELY.
NEWSPAPER CLUB
Meeting
THAT WILL BE THE FIRST ITEM ON OUR AGENDA TODAY.

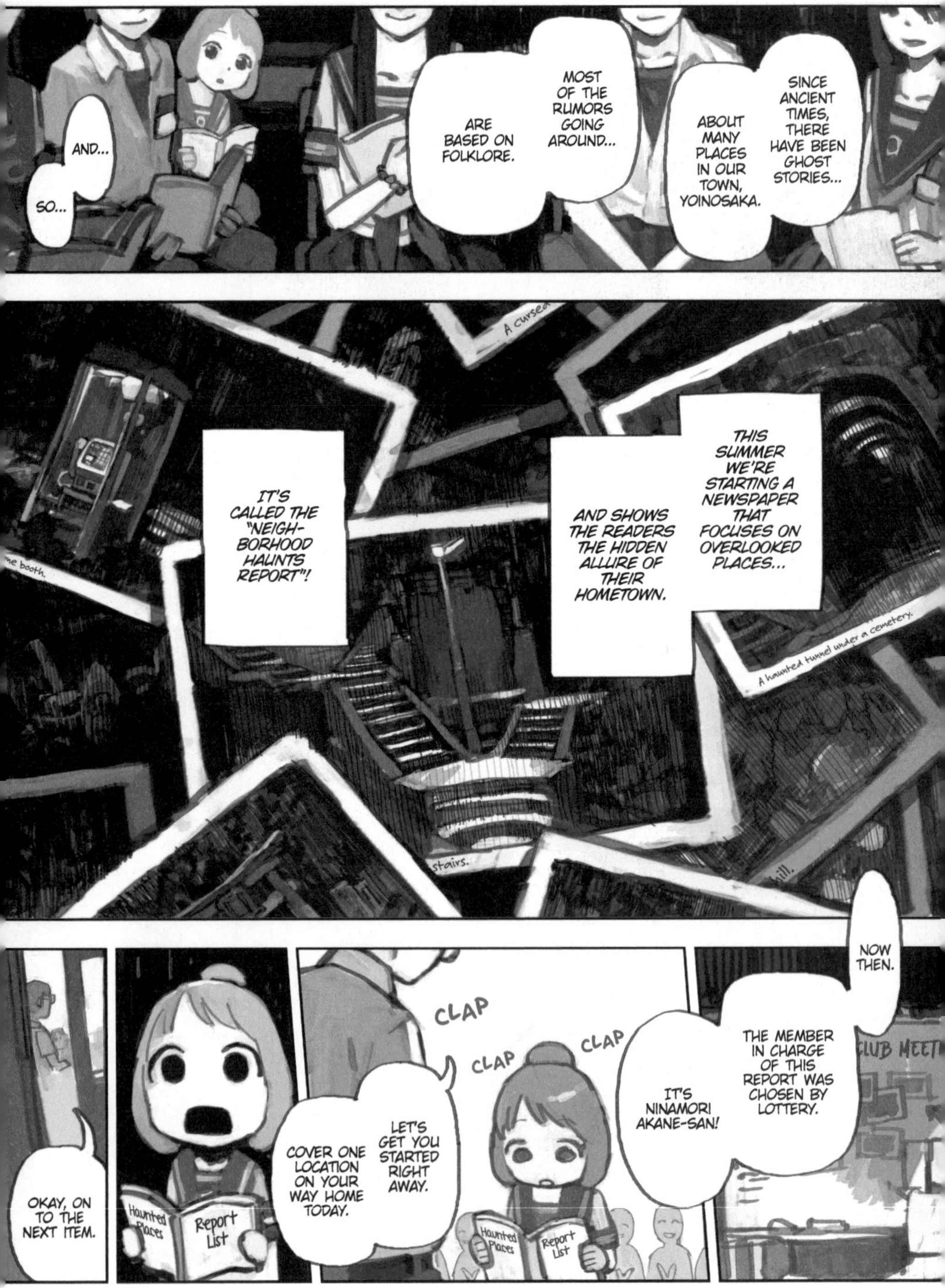
SINCE ANCIENT TIMES, THERE HAVE BEEN GHOST STORIES...
ABOUT MANY PLACES IN OUR TOWN, YOINOSAKA.
MOST OF THE RUMORS GOING AROUND...
ARE BASED ON FOLKLORE.
AND...
SO...
A cursed
THIS SUMMER WE'RE STARTING A NEWSPAPER THAT FOCUSES ON OVERLOOKED PLACES...
AND SHOWS THE READERS THE HIDDEN ALLURE OF THEIR HOMETOWN.
IT'S CALLED THE "NEIGH-BORHOOD HAUNTS REPORT"!
A haunted tunnel under a cemetery.
hill.
stairs.
NOW THEN.
THE MEMBER IN CHARGE OF THIS REPORT WAS CHOSEN BY LOTTERY.
IT'S NINAMORI AKANE-SAN!
CLAP
CLAP
CLAP
LET'S GET YOU STARTED RIGHT AWAY.
COVER ONE LOCATION ON YOUR WAY HOME TODAY.
Haunted Places
Report List
Haunted Places
Report List
OKAY, ON TO THE NEXT ITEM.

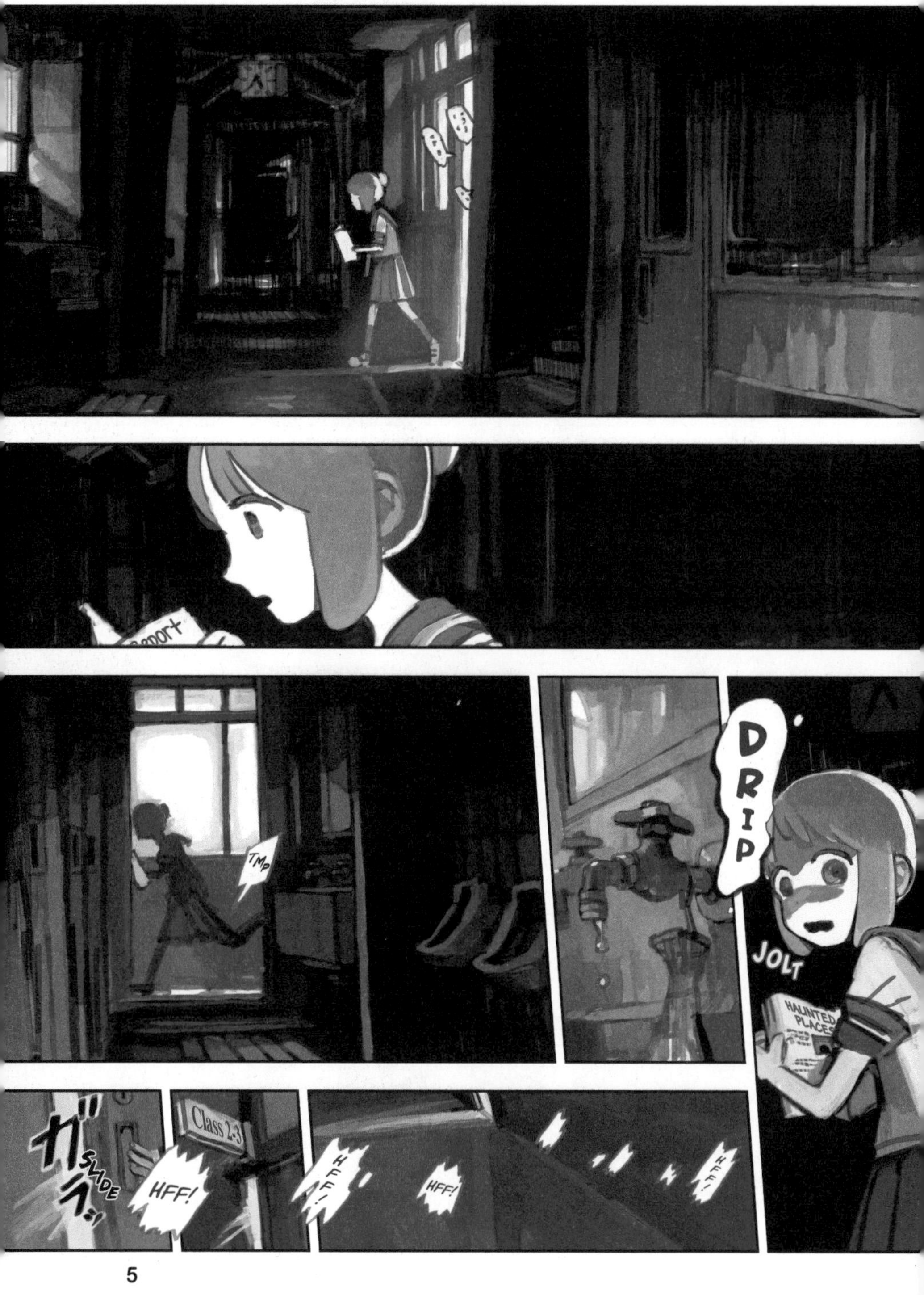

Report
DRIP
JOLT
HAUNTED PLACES
TMP
HFF!
HFF!
HFF!
Class 2-3
HFF!
ガラ
SLIDE

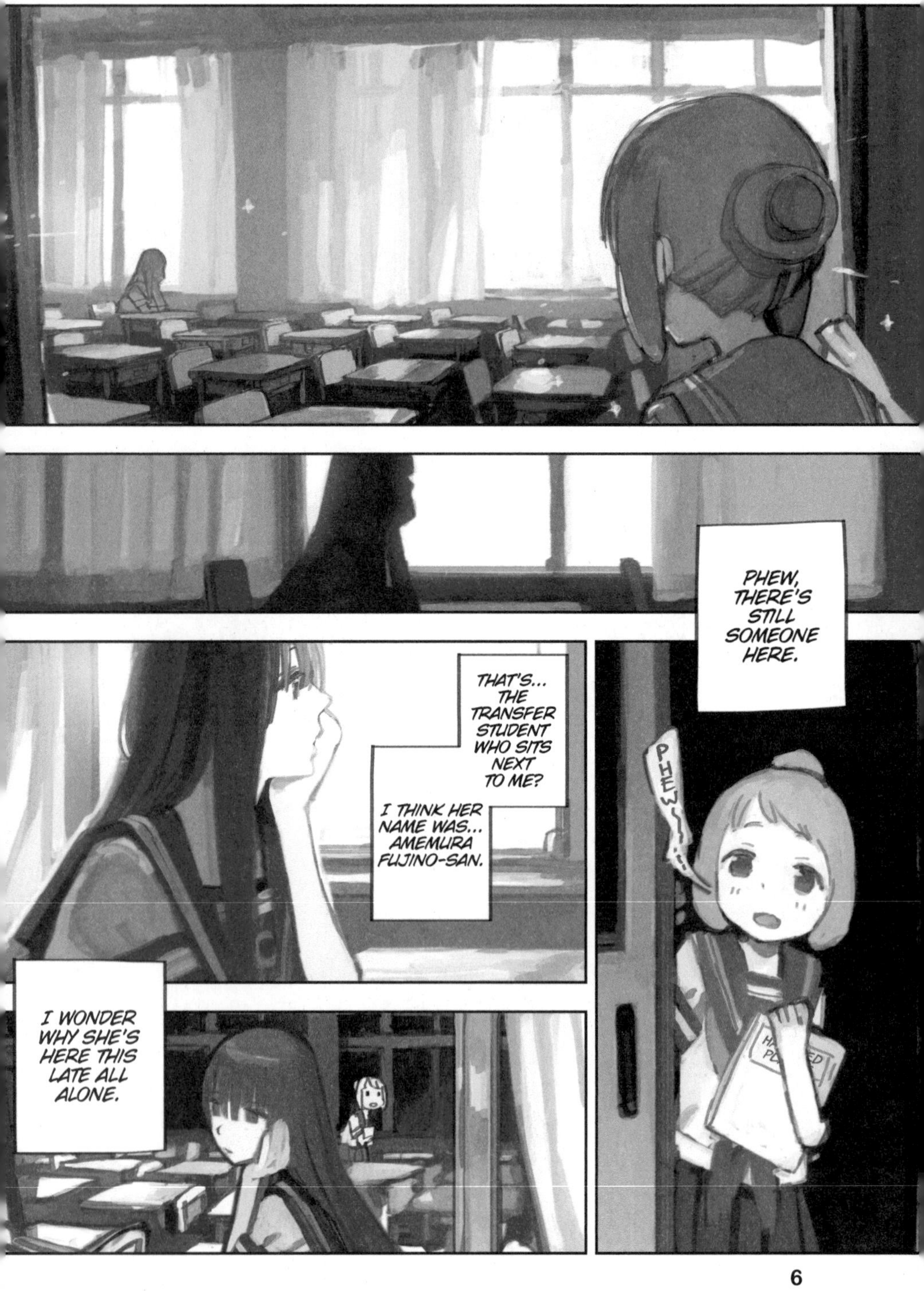
PHEW, THERE'S STILL SOMEONE HERE.
PHEW~
THAT'S... THE TRANSFER STUDENT WHO SITS NEXT TO ME?
I THINK HER NAME WAS... AMEMURA FUJINO-SAN.
I WONDER WHY SHE'S HERE THIS LATE ALL ALONE.

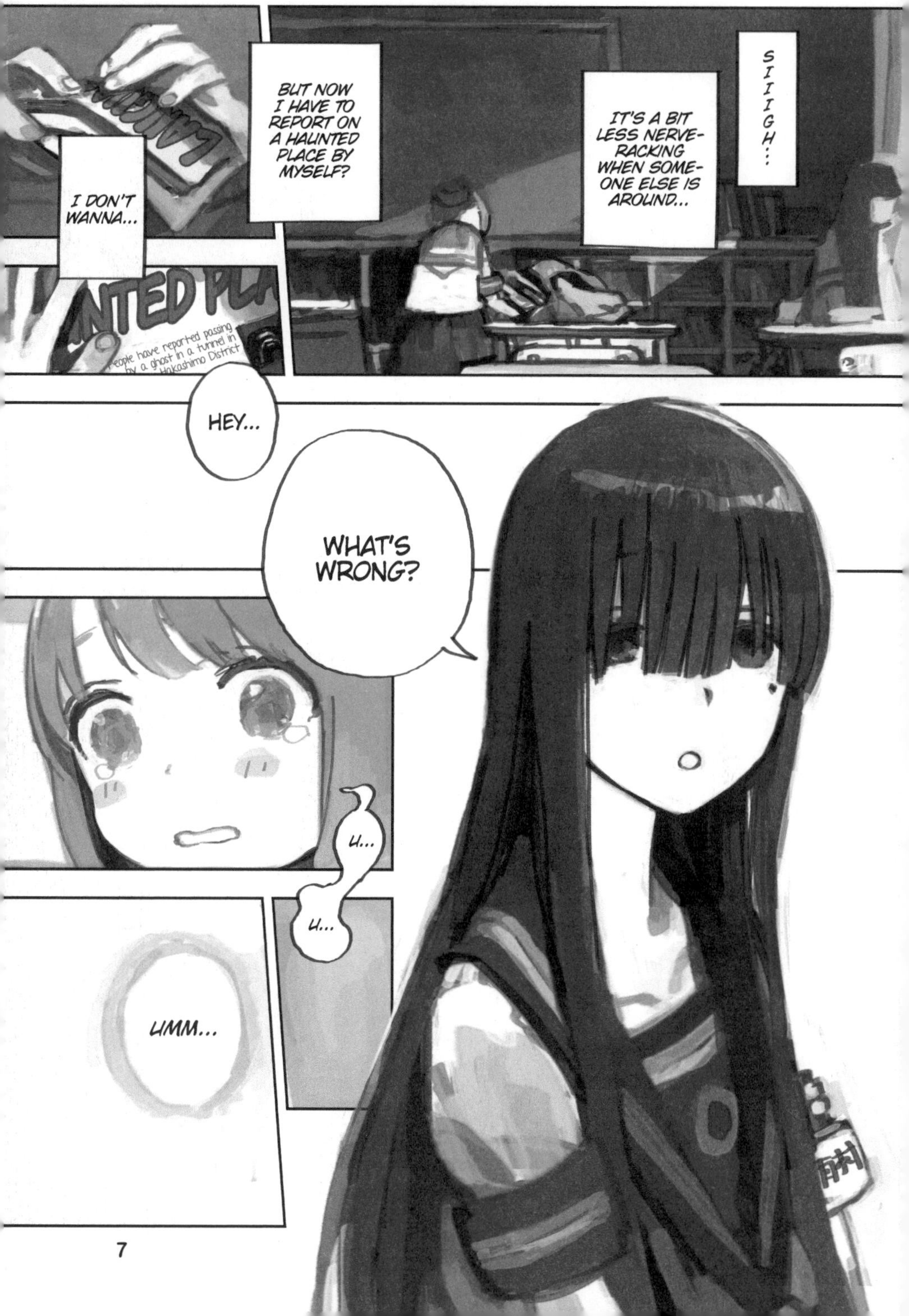
SIIIGH...
IT'S A BIT LESS NERVE-RACKING WHEN SOME-ONE ELSE IS AROUND...
BUT NOW I HAVE TO REPORT ON A HAUNTED PLACE BY MYSELF?
I DON'T WANNA...
NTED PLA
People have reported passing by a ghost in a tunnel in Hakashimo District
HEY...
WHAT'S WRONG?
U...
U...
UMM...

Chapter 1:
The Haunted Tunnel Under the Cemetery

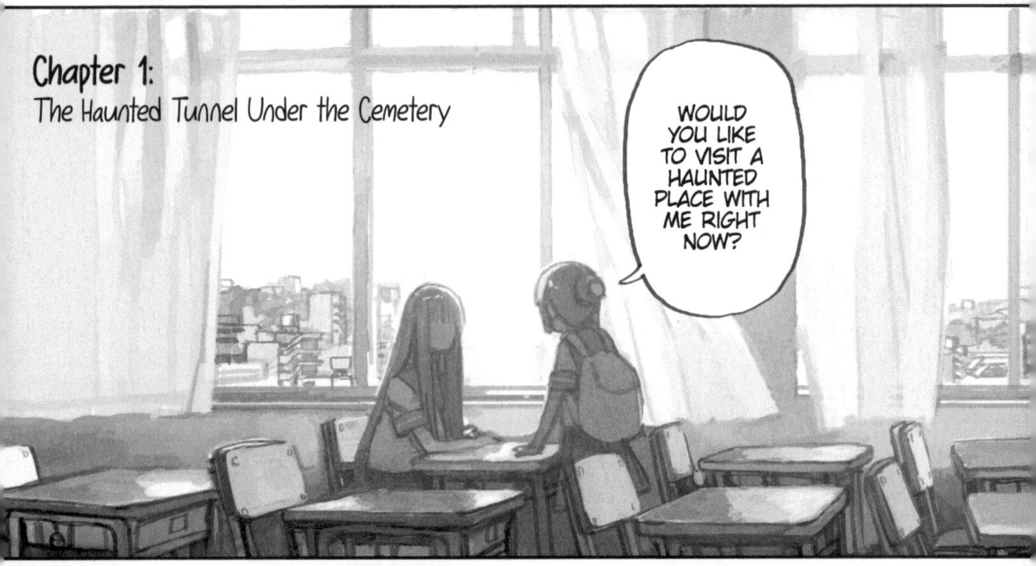
WOULD YOU LIKE TO VISIT A HAUNTED PLACE WITH ME RIGHT NOW?

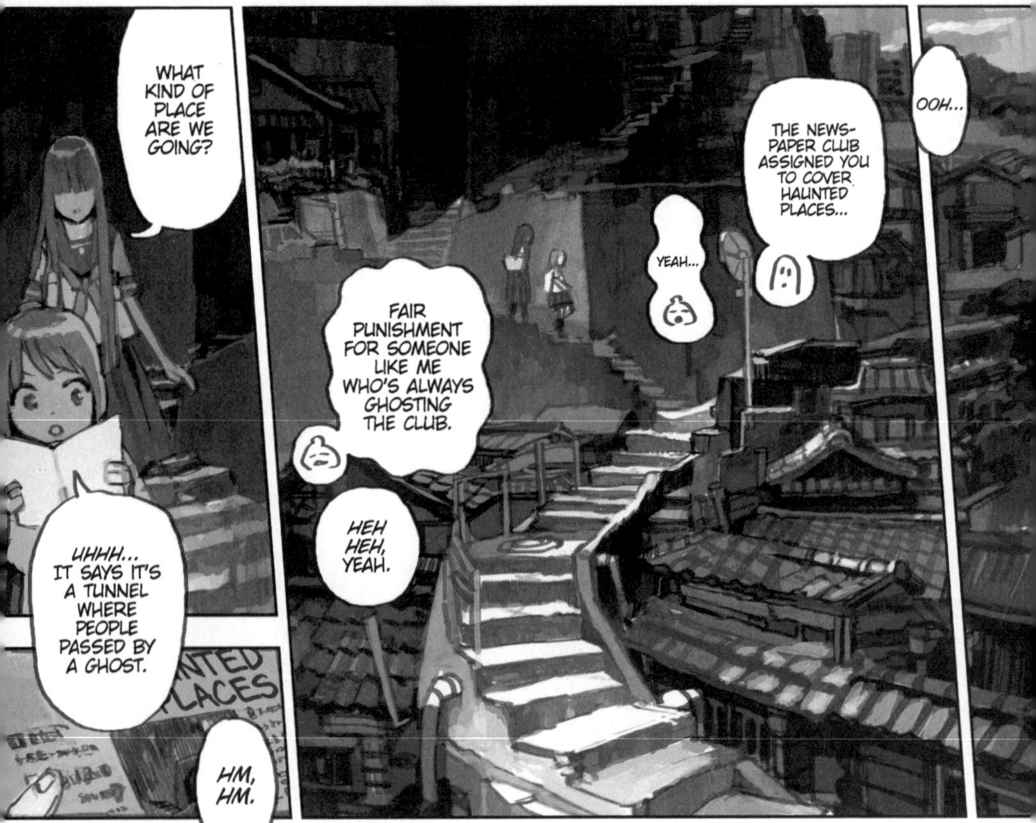
OOH...
THE NEWS-PAPER CLUB ASSIGNED YOU TO COVER HAUNTED PLACES...
YEAH...
FAIR PUNISHMENT FOR SOMEONE LIKE ME WHO'S ALWAYS GHOSTING THE CLUB.
HEH HEH, YEAH.
WHAT KIND OF PLACE ARE WE GOING?
UHHH... IT SAYS IT'S A TUNNEL WHERE PEOPLE PASSED BY A GHOST.
HM, HM.

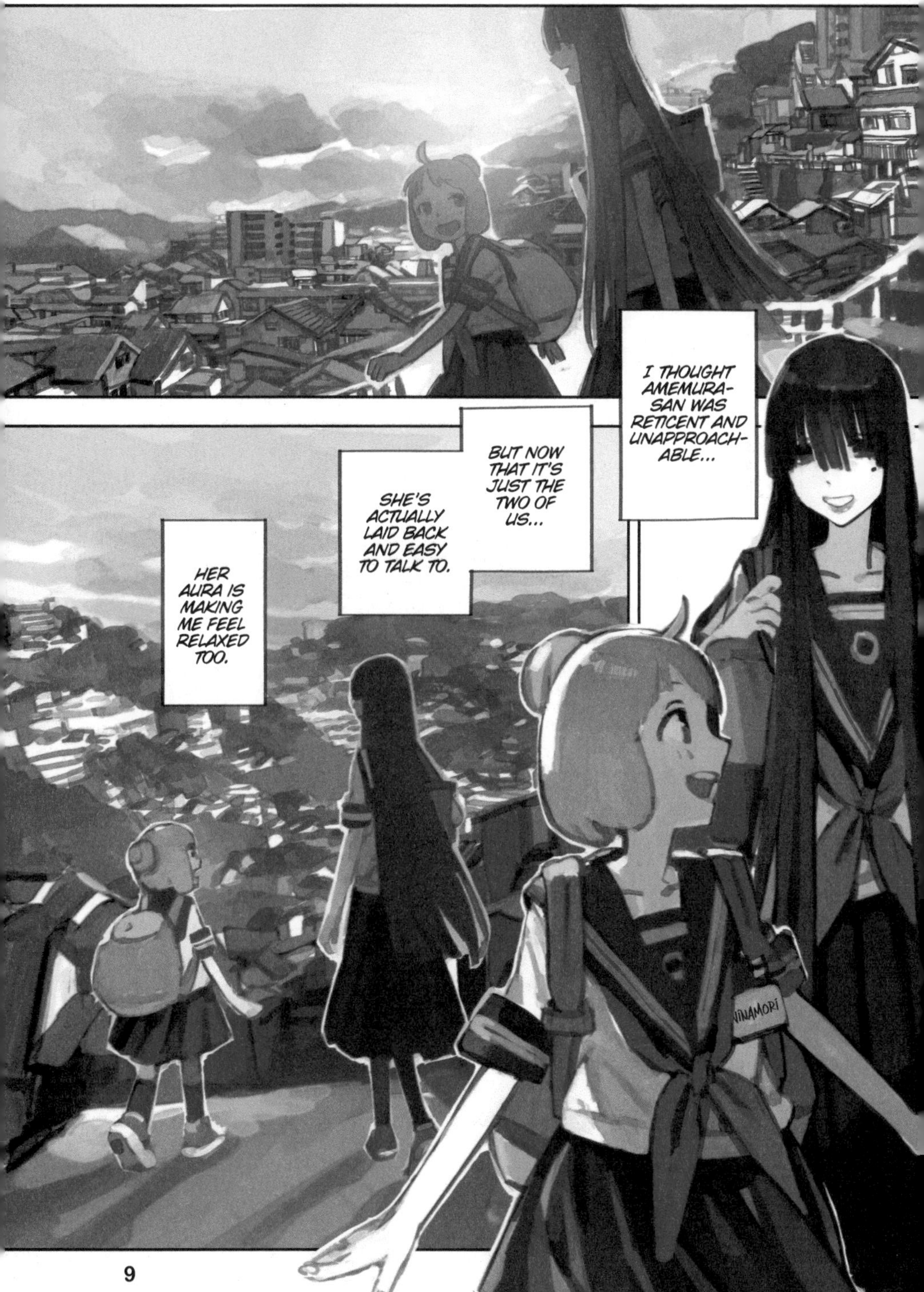
I THOUGHT AMEMURA-SAN WAS RETICENT AND UNAPPROACHABLE...
BUT NOW THAT IT'S JUST THE TWO OF US...
SHE'S ACTUALLY LAID BACK AND EASY TO TALK TO.
HER AURA IS MAKING ME FEEL RELAXED TOO.
NINAMORI

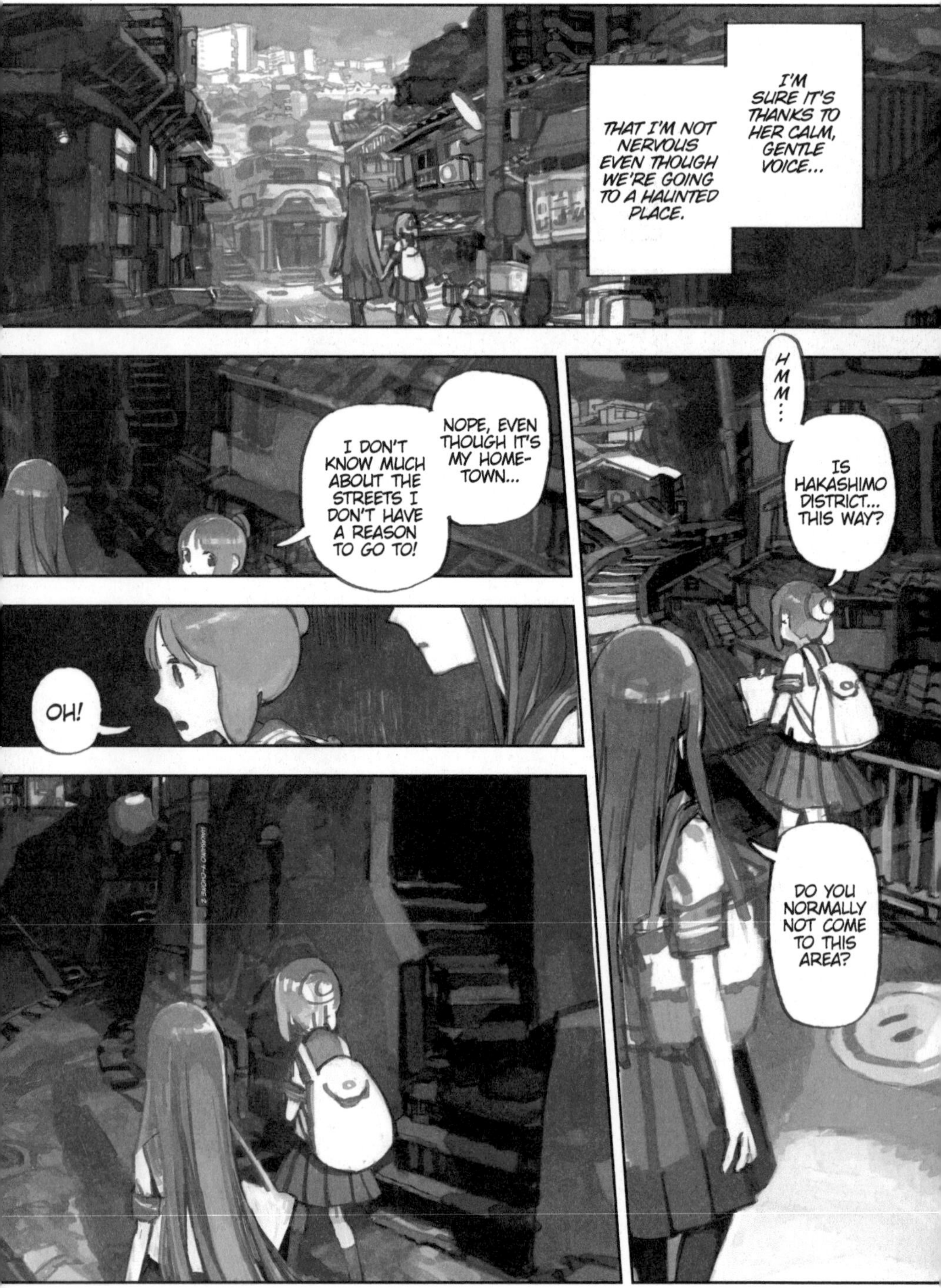
I'M SURE IT'S THANKS TO HER CALM, GENTLE VOICE...
THAT I'M NOT NERVOUS EVEN THOUGH WE'RE GOING TO A HAUNTED PLACE.
HMM...
IS HAKASHIMO DISTRICT... THIS WAY?
DO YOU NORMALLY NOT COME TO THIS AREA?
NOPE, EVEN THOUGH IT'S MY HOME-TOWN...
I DON'T KNOW MUCH ABOUT THE STREETS I DON'T HAVE A REASON TO GO TO!
OH!

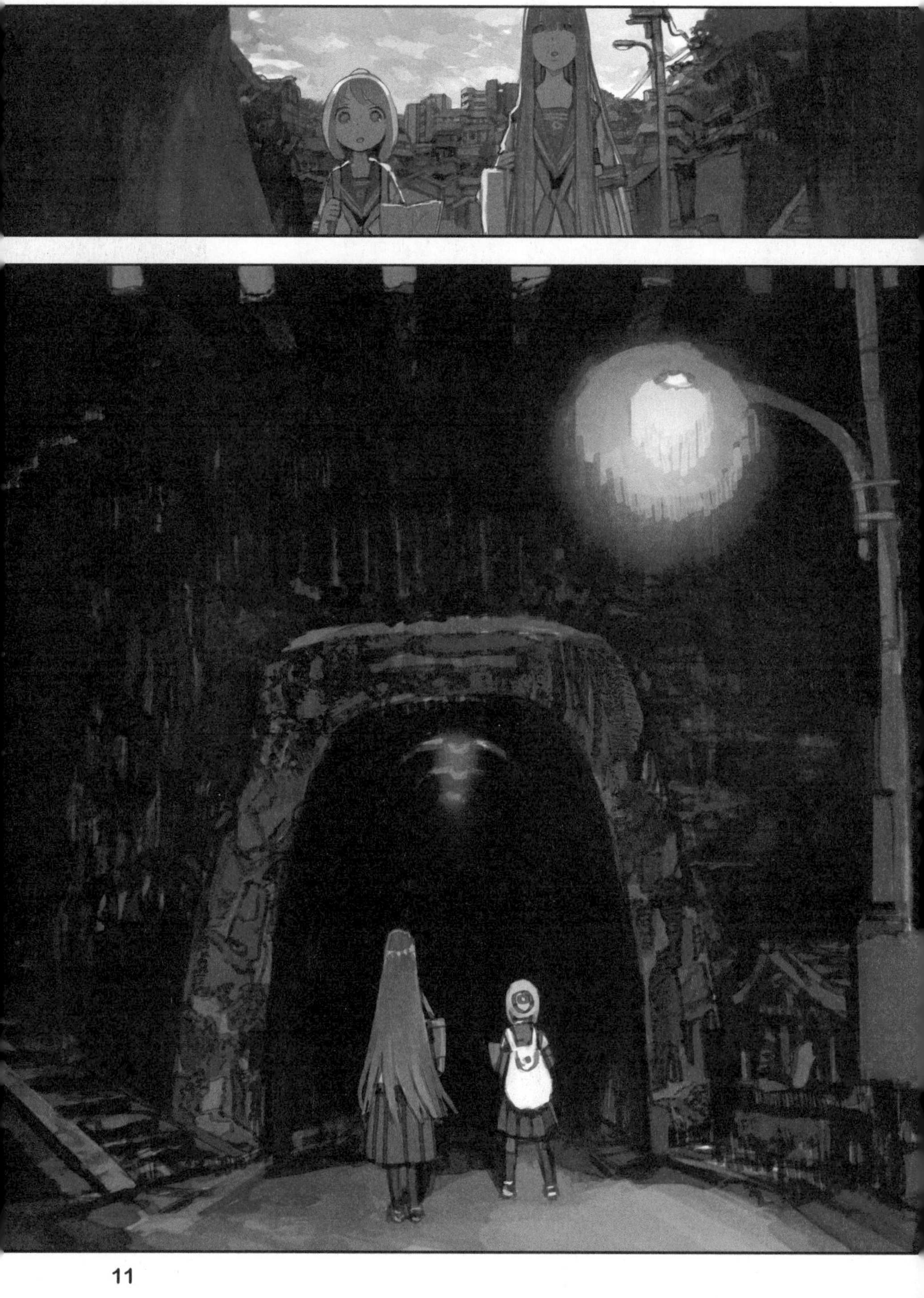

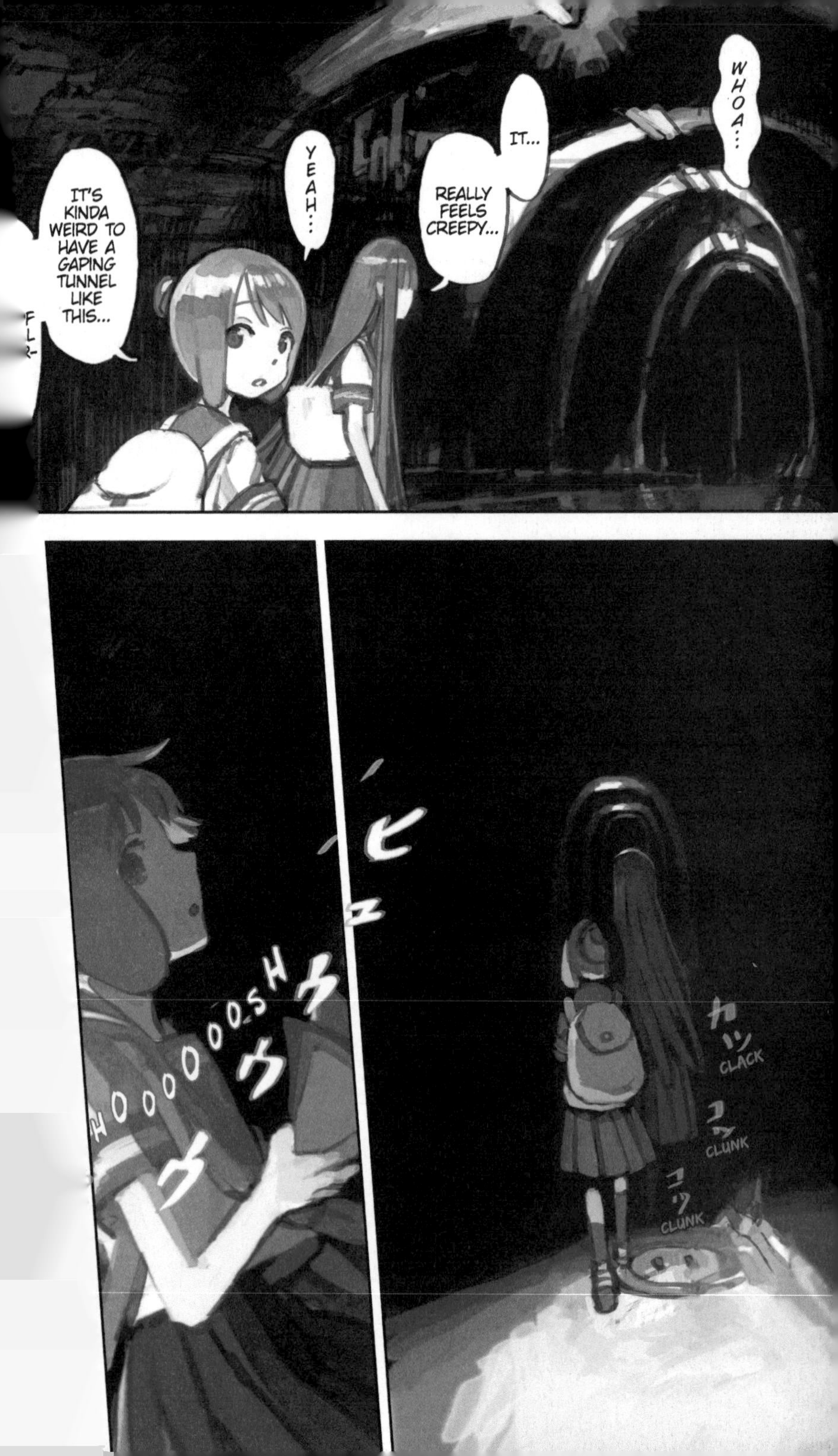
WHOA...
IT...
REALLY FEELS CREEPY...
YEAH...
IT'S KINDA WEIRD TO HAVE A GAPING TUNNEL LIKE THIS...
カッ
CLACK
コッ
CLUNK
コッ
CLUNK
ヒュウウウ
HOOOOOOOSH

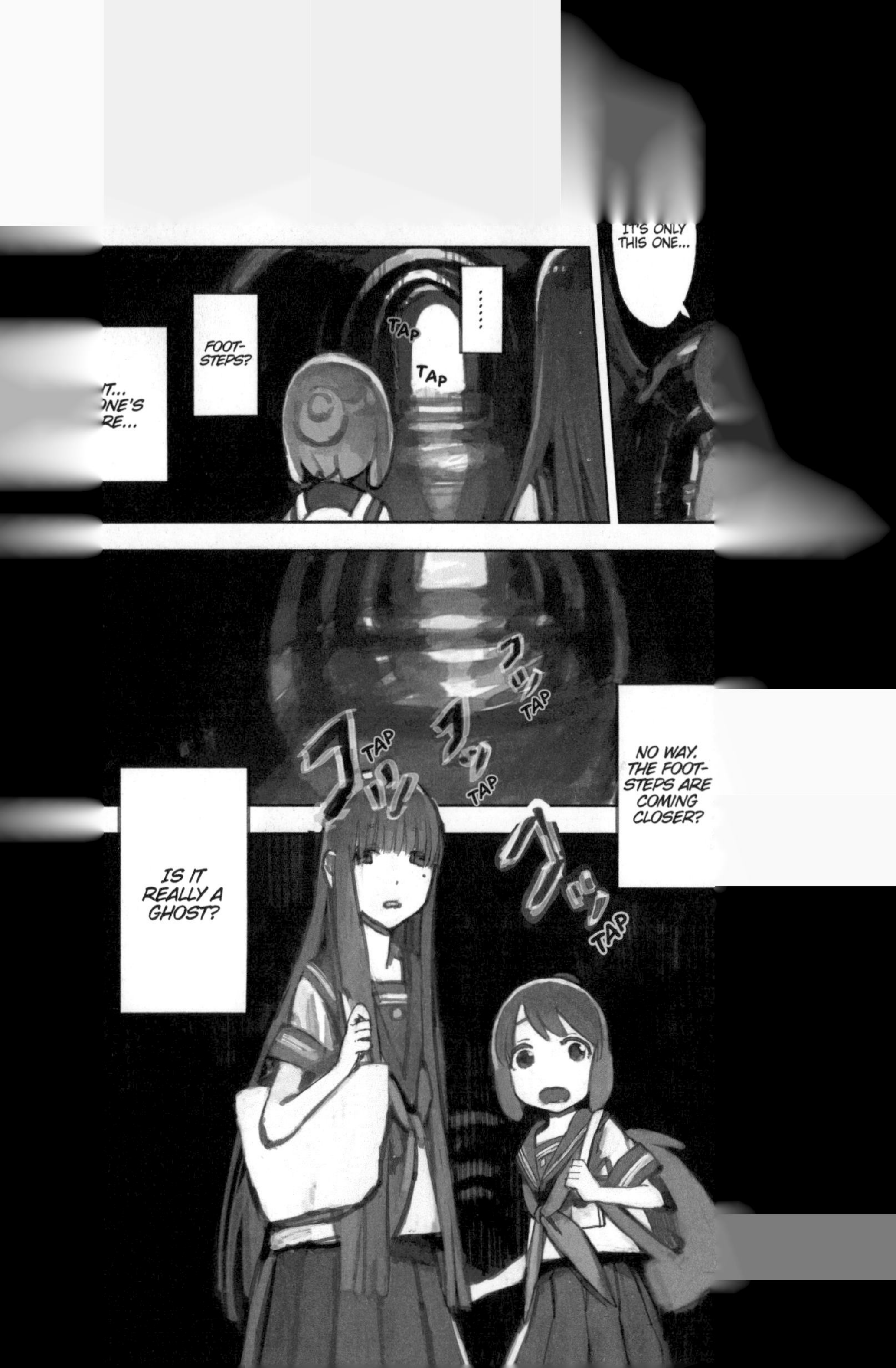
IT'S ONLY THIS ONE...
......
TAP
TAP
FOOT-STEPS?
TAP
TAP
TAP
NO WAY. THE FOOT-STEPS ARE COMING CLOSER?
IS IT REALLY A GHOST?
TAP

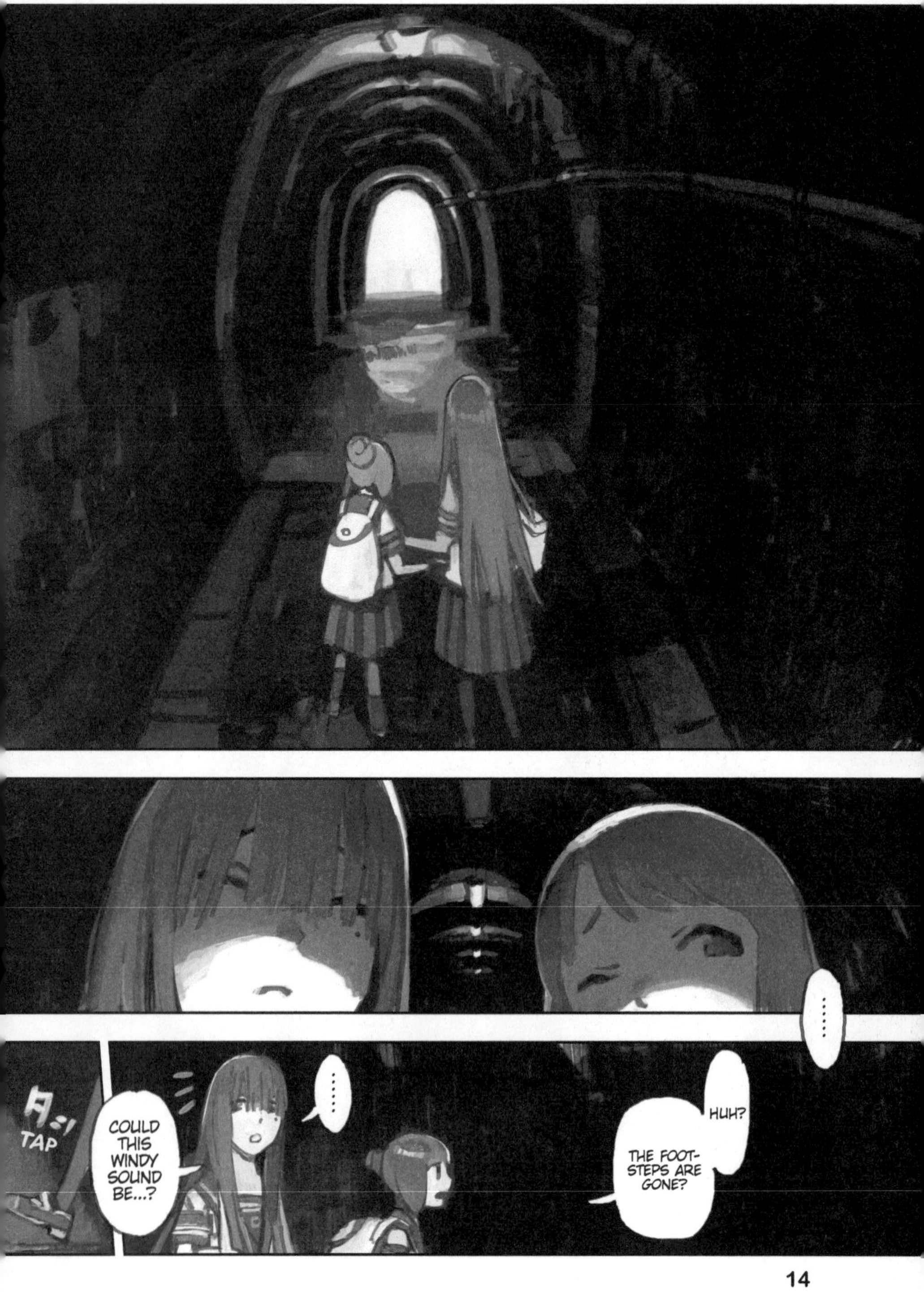
......
HUH?
THE FOOT-STEPS ARE GONE?
......
COULD THIS WINDY SOUND BE...?
TAP

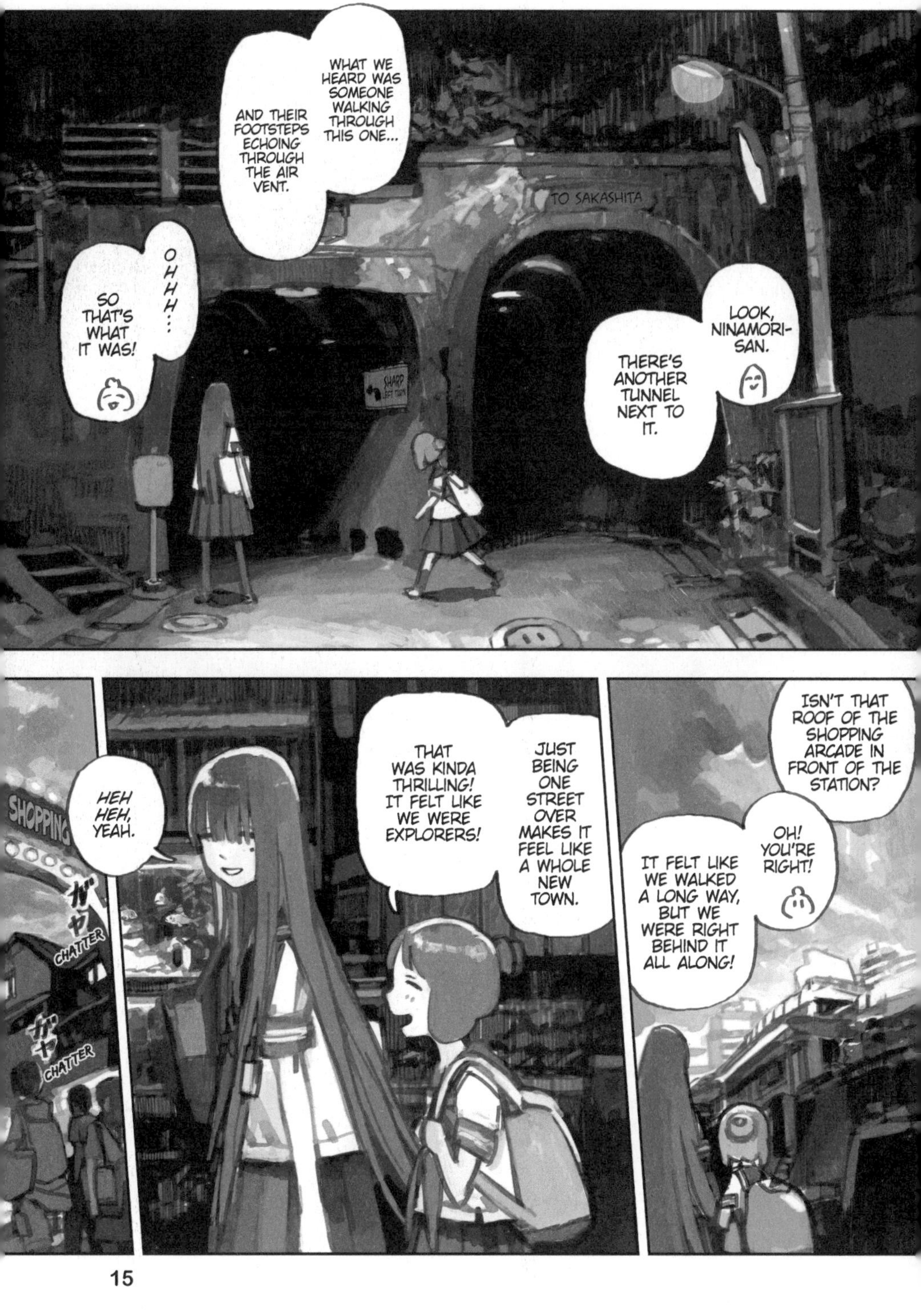
LOOK, NINAMORI-SAN.
THERE'S ANOTHER TUNNEL NEXT TO IT.
TO SAKASHITA
WHAT WE HEARD WAS SOMEONE WALKING THROUGH THIS ONE...
AND THEIR FOOTSTEPS ECHOING THROUGH THE AIR VENT.
OHHH...
SO THAT'S WHAT IT WAS!
ISN'T THAT ROOF OF THE SHOPPING ARCADE IN FRONT OF THE STATION?
OH! YOU'RE RIGHT!
IT FELT LIKE WE WALKED A LONG WAY, BUT WE WERE RIGHT BEHIND IT ALL ALONG!
JUST BEING ONE STREET OVER MAKES IT FEEL LIKE A WHOLE NEW TOWN.
THAT WAS KINDA THRILLING! IT FELT LIKE WE WERE EXPLORERS!
HEH HEH, YEAH.
SHOPPING
ガヤ CHATTER
ガヤ CHATTER

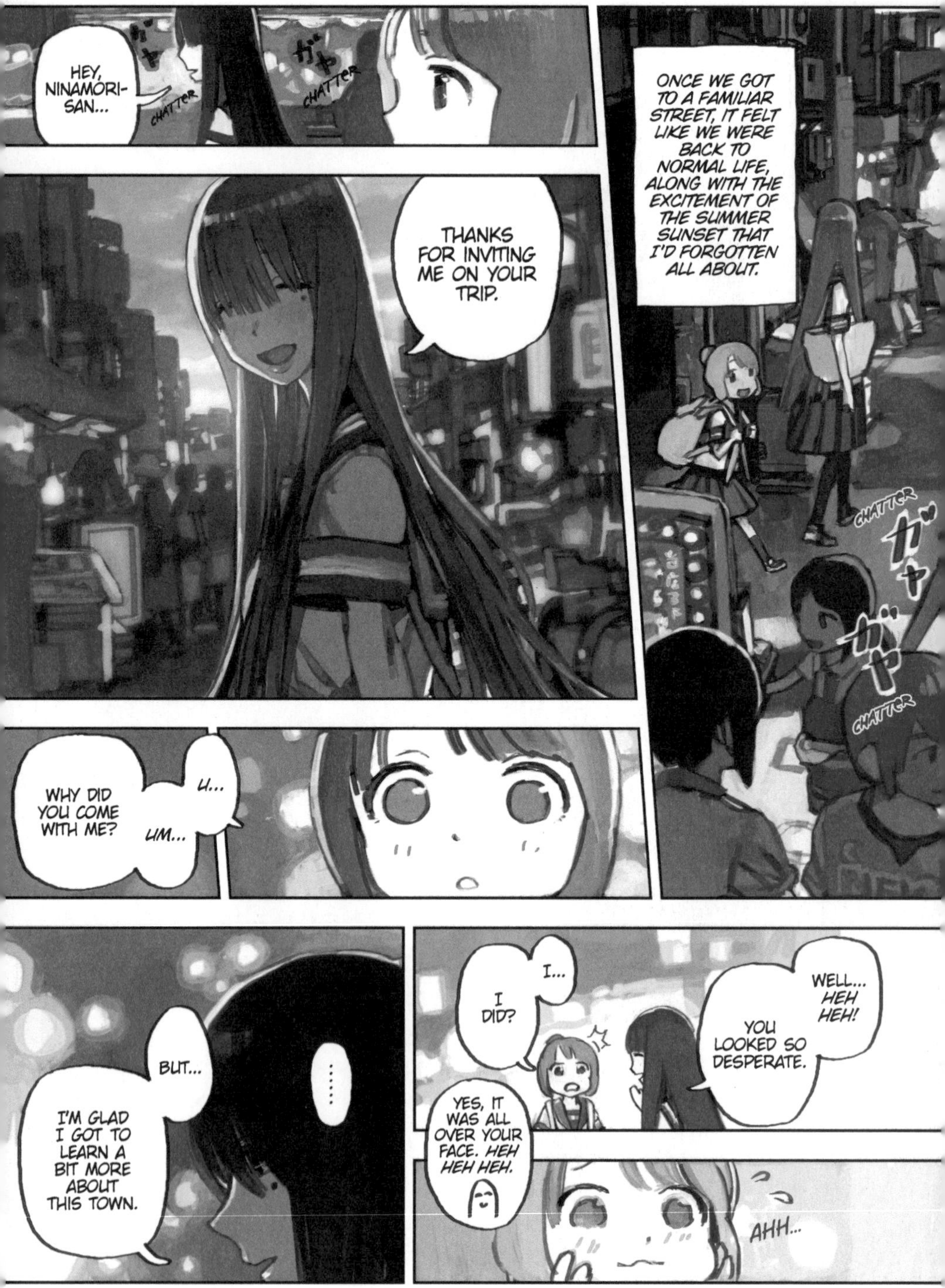
ONCE WE GOT TO A FAMILIAR STREET, IT FELT LIKE WE WERE BACK TO NORMAL LIFE, ALONG WITH THE EXCITEMENT OF THE SUMMER SUNSET THAT I'D FORGOTTEN ALL ABOUT.
CHATTER
CHATTER
CHATTER
CHATTER
HEY, NINAMORI-SAN...
THANKS FOR INVITING ME ON YOUR TRIP.
U...
UM...
WHY DID YOU COME WITH ME?
WELL... HEH HEH!
YOU LOOKED SO DESPERATE.
I...
I DID?
YES, IT WAS ALL OVER YOUR FACE. HEH HEH HEH.
AHH...
......
BUT...
I'M GLAD I GOT TO LEARN A BIT MORE ABOUT THIS TOWN.

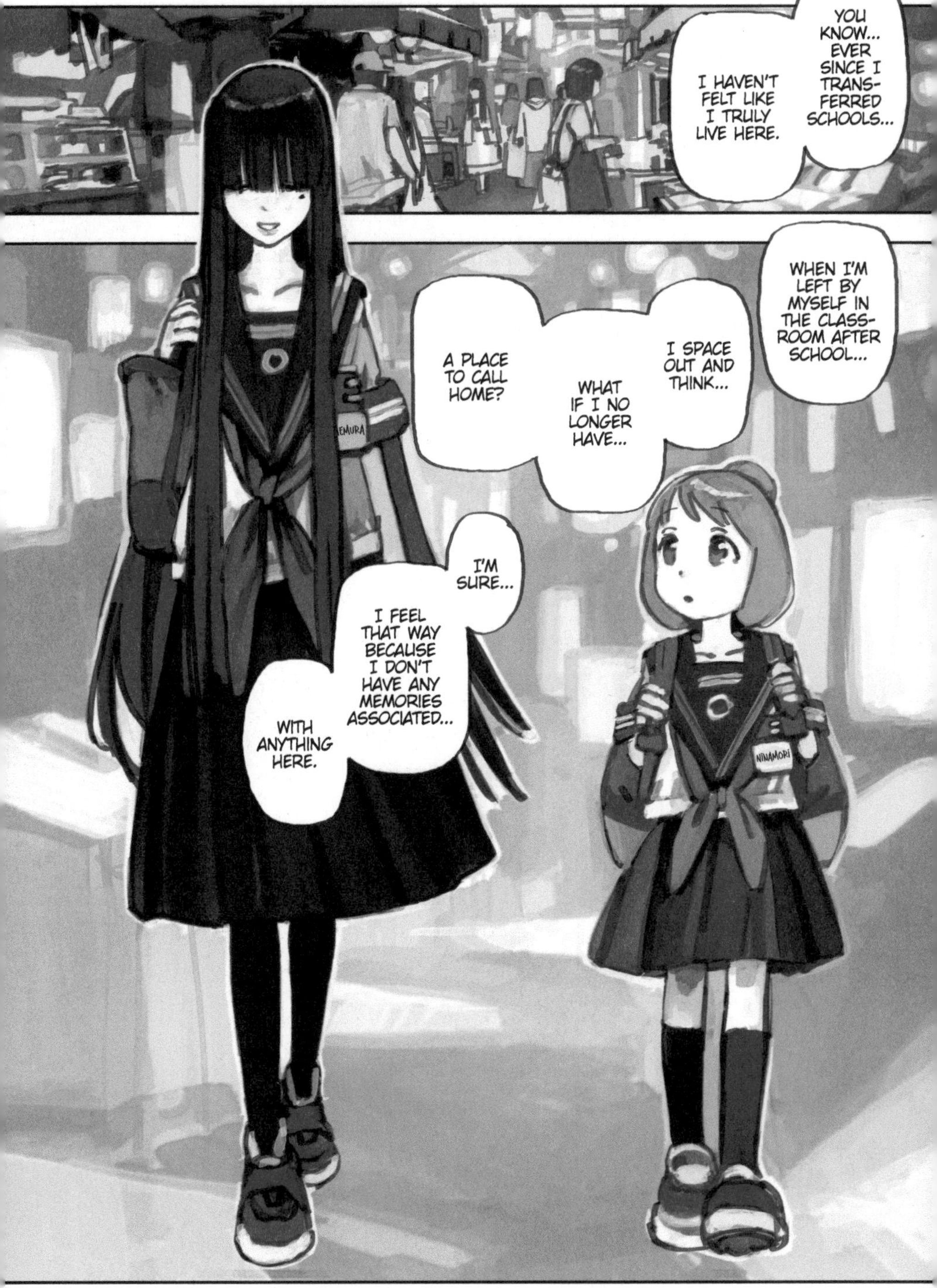
YOU KNOW... EVER SINCE I TRANSFERRED SCHOOLS...
I HAVEN'T FELT LIKE I TRULY LIVE HERE.
WHEN I'M LEFT BY MYSELF IN THE CLASSROOM AFTER SCHOOL...
I SPACE OUT AND THINK...
WHAT IF I NO LONGER HAVE...
A PLACE TO CALL HOME?
I'M SURE...
I FEEL THAT WAY BECAUSE I DON'T HAVE ANY MEMORIES ASSOCIATED...
WITH ANYTHING HERE.
NINAMORI

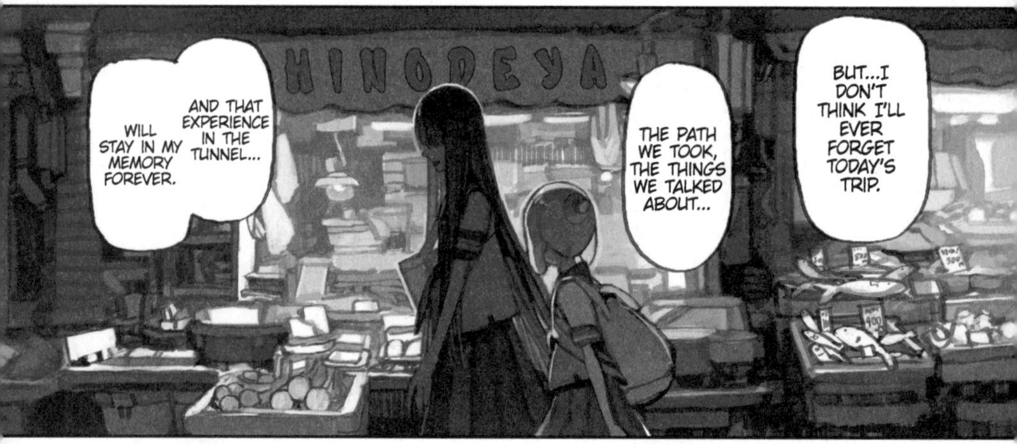
HINODEYA
BUT...I DON'T THINK I'LL EVER FORGET TODAY'S TRIP.
THE PATH WE TOOK, THE THINGS WE TALKED ABOUT...
AND THAT EXPERIENCE IN THE TUNNEL...
WILL STAY IN MY MEMORY FOREVER.

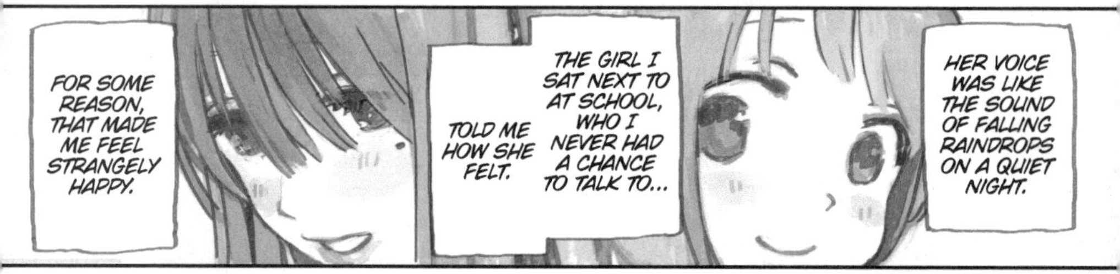
HER VOICE WAS LIKE THE SOUND OF FALLING RAINDROPS ON A QUIET NIGHT.
THE GIRL I SAT NEXT TO AT SCHOOL, WHO I NEVER HAD A CHANCE TO TALK TO...
TOLD ME HOW SHE FELT.
FOR SOME REASON, THAT MADE ME FEEL STRANGELY HAPPY.

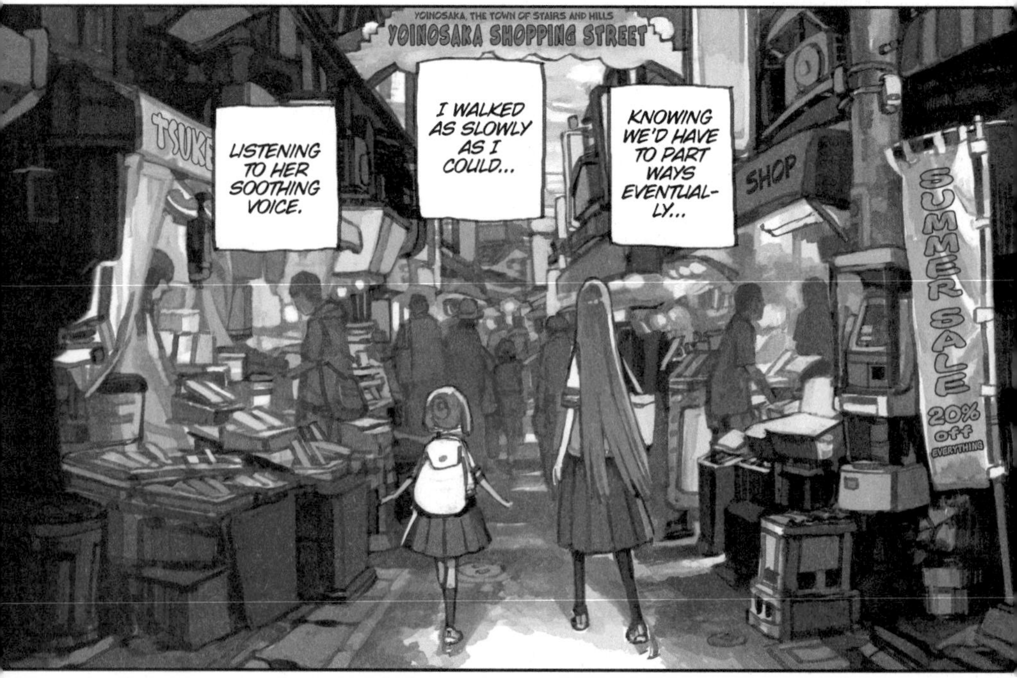
YOINOSAKA, THE TOWN OF STAIRS AND HILLS
YOINOSAKA SHOPPING STREET
KNOWING WE'D HAVE TO PART WAYS EVENTUAL-LY...
I WALKED AS SLOWLY AS I COULD...
LISTENING TO HER SOOTHING VOICE.
SHOP
SUMMER SALE
20% off
EVERYTHING

NIGHTFALL
TRAVELERS
LEAVE ONLY FOOTPRINTS

NIGHTFALL
TRAVELERS
LEAVE ONLY FOOTPRINTS

Intermission: Good Night Akane-chan @ Coming Home After Chapter 1

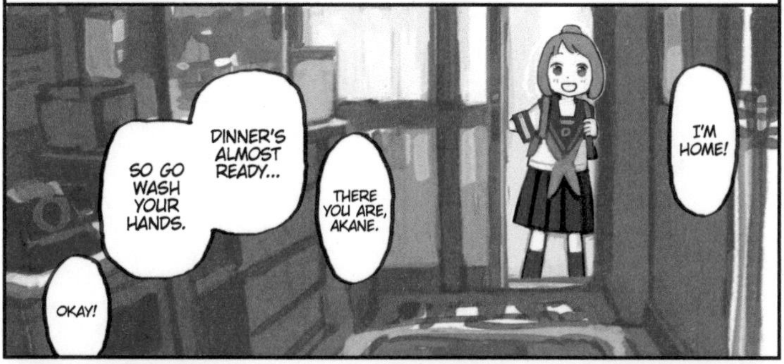
I'M HOME!
THERE YOU ARE, AKANE.
DINNER'S ALMOST READY...
SO GO WASH YOUR HANDS.
OKAY!

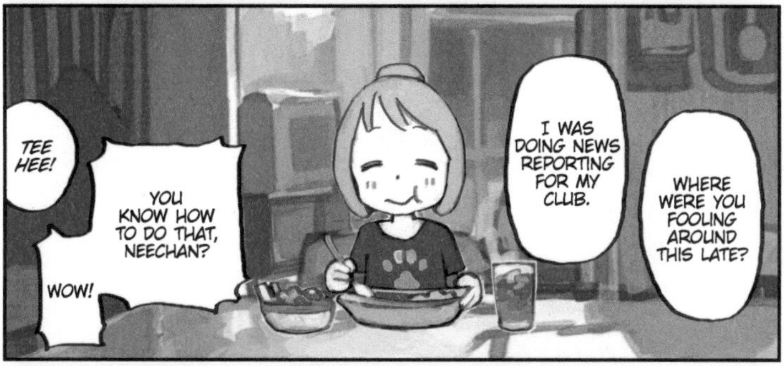
WHERE WERE YOU FOOLING AROUND THIS LATE?
I WAS DOING NEWS REPORTING FOR MY CLUB.
YOU KNOW HOW TO DO THAT, NEECHAN?
TEE HEE!
WOW!

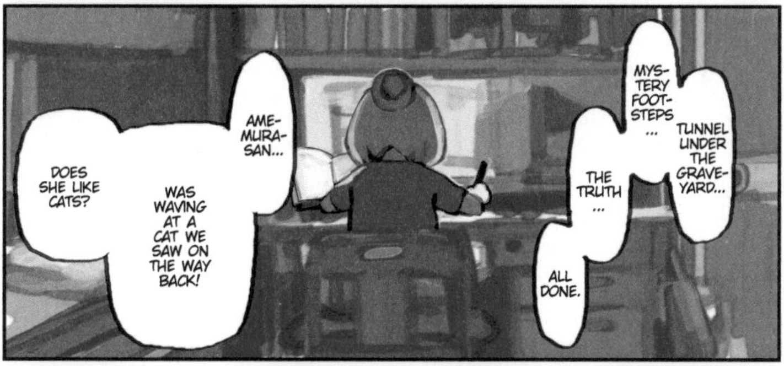
MYS-TERY FOOT-STEPS ...
TUNNEL UNDER THE GRAVE-YARD...
THE TRUTH ...
ALL DONE.
AME-MURA-SAN...
WAS WAVING AT A CAT WE SAW ON THE WAY BACK!
DOES SHE LIKE CATS?

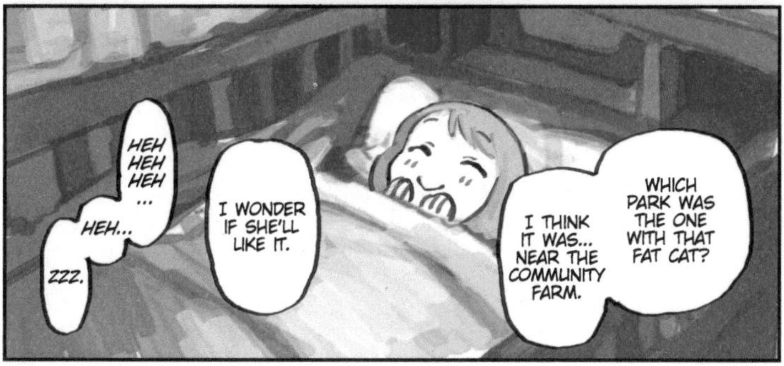
WHICH PARK WAS THE ONE WITH THAT FAT CAT?
I THINK IT WAS... NEAR THE COMMUNITY FARM.
I WONDER IF SHE'LL LIKE IT.
HEH HEH HEH ...
HEH...
ZZZ.

NIGHTFALL TRAVELERS

LEAVE ONLY FOOTPRINTS

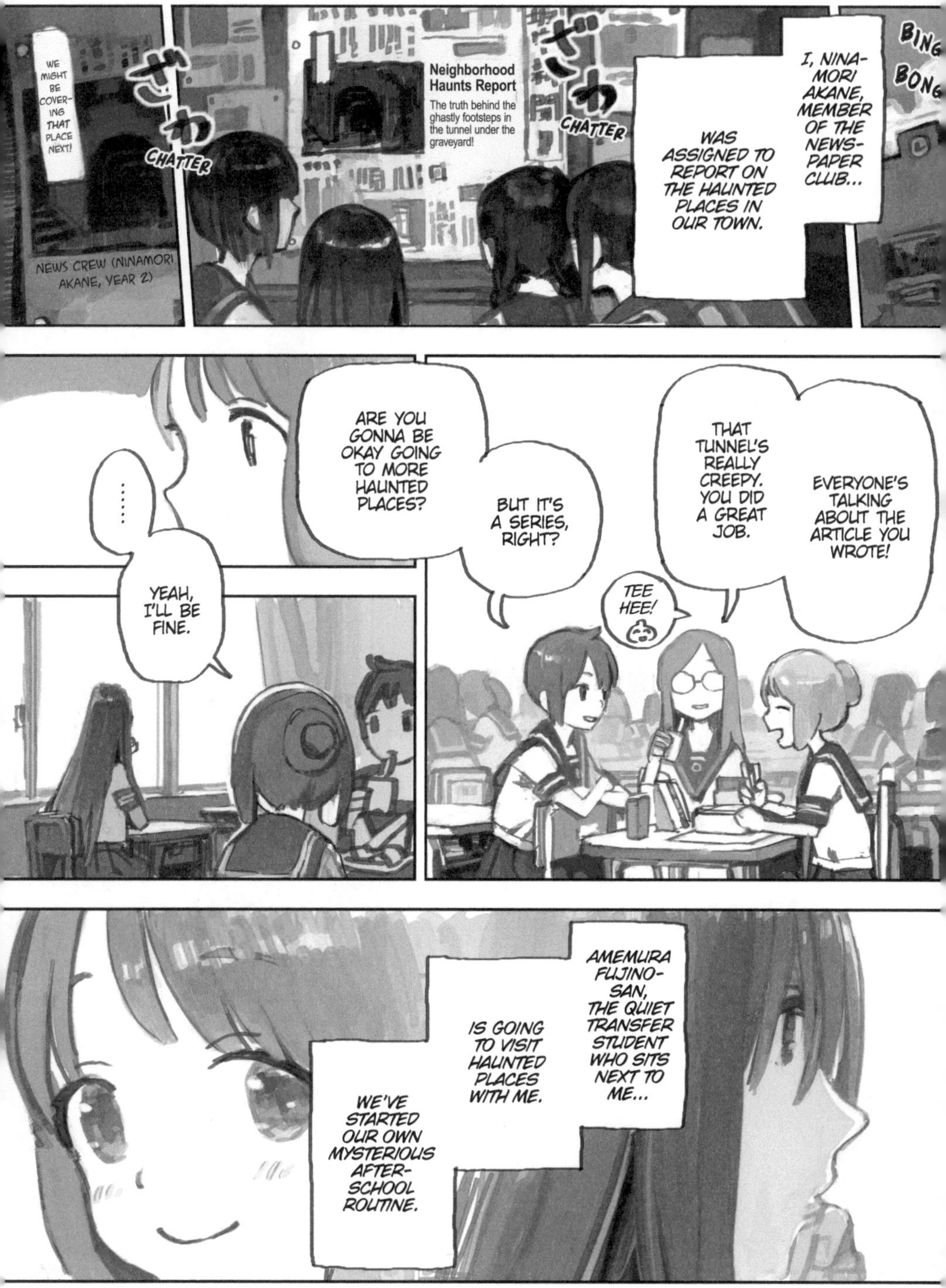
BING BONG
I, NINAMORI AKANE, MEMBER OF THE NEWSPAPER CLUB...
WAS ASSIGNED TO REPORT ON THE HAUNTED PLACES IN OUR TOWN.
ざわ CHATTER
Neighborhood Haunts Report
The truth behind the ghastly footsteps in the tunnel under the graveyard!
WE MIGHT BE COVERING THAT PLACE NEXT!
ざわ CHATTER
NEWS CREW (NINAMORI AKANE, YEAR 2)
EVERYONE'S TALKING ABOUT THE ARTICLE YOU WROTE!
THAT TUNNEL'S REALLY CREEPY. YOU DID A GREAT JOB.
TEE HEE!
BUT IT'S A SERIES, RIGHT?
ARE YOU GONNA BE OKAY GOING TO MORE HAUNTED PLACES?
......
YEAH, I'LL BE FINE.
AMEMURA FUJINO-SAN, THE QUIET TRANSFER STUDENT WHO SITS NEXT TO ME...
IS GOING TO VISIT HAUNTED PLACES WITH ME.
WE'VE STARTED OUR OWN MYSTERIOUS AFTER-SCHOOL ROUTINE.

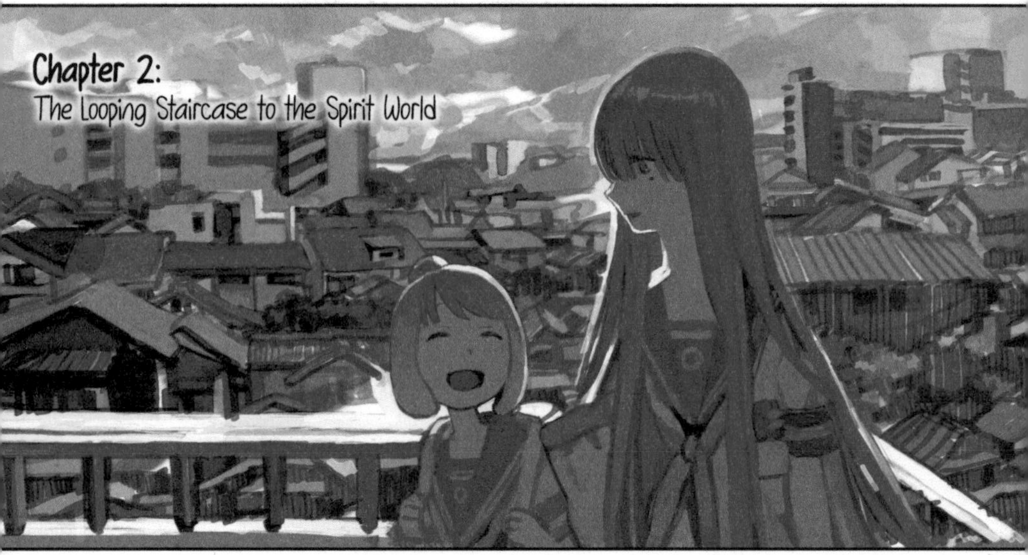
Chapter 2:
The Looping Staircase to the Spirit World

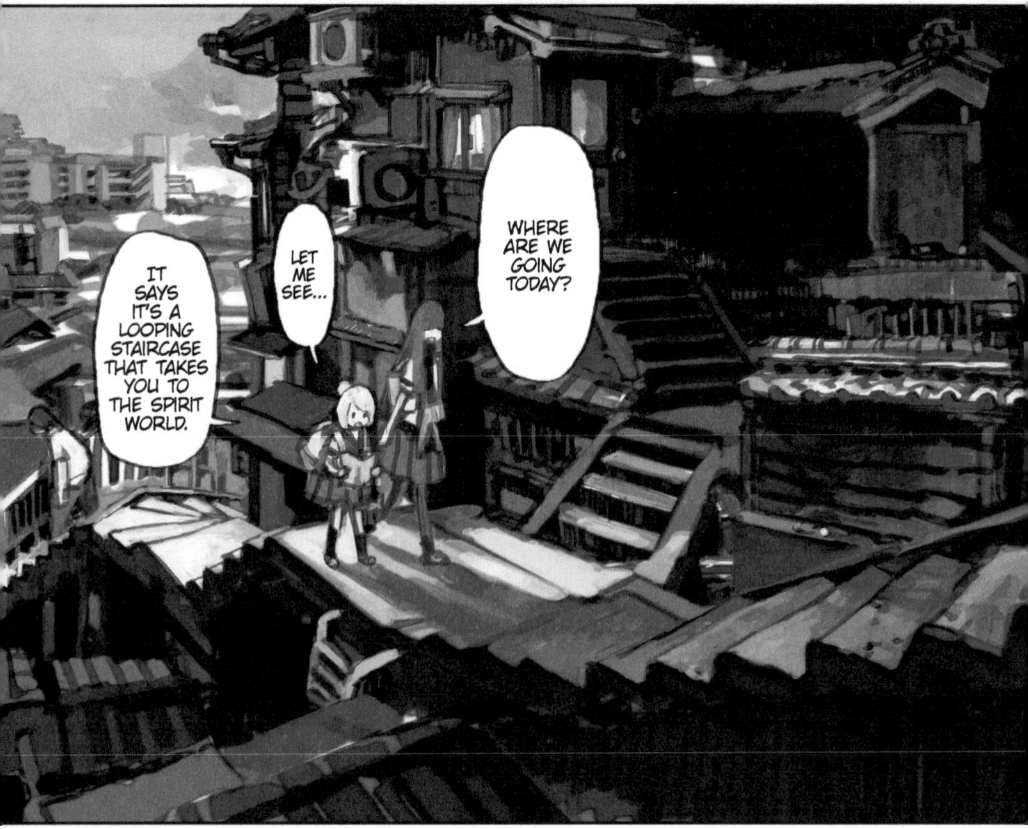
WHERE ARE WE GOING TODAY?
LET ME SEE...
IT SAYS IT'S A LOOPING STAIRCASE THAT TAKES YOU TO THE SPIRIT WORLD.

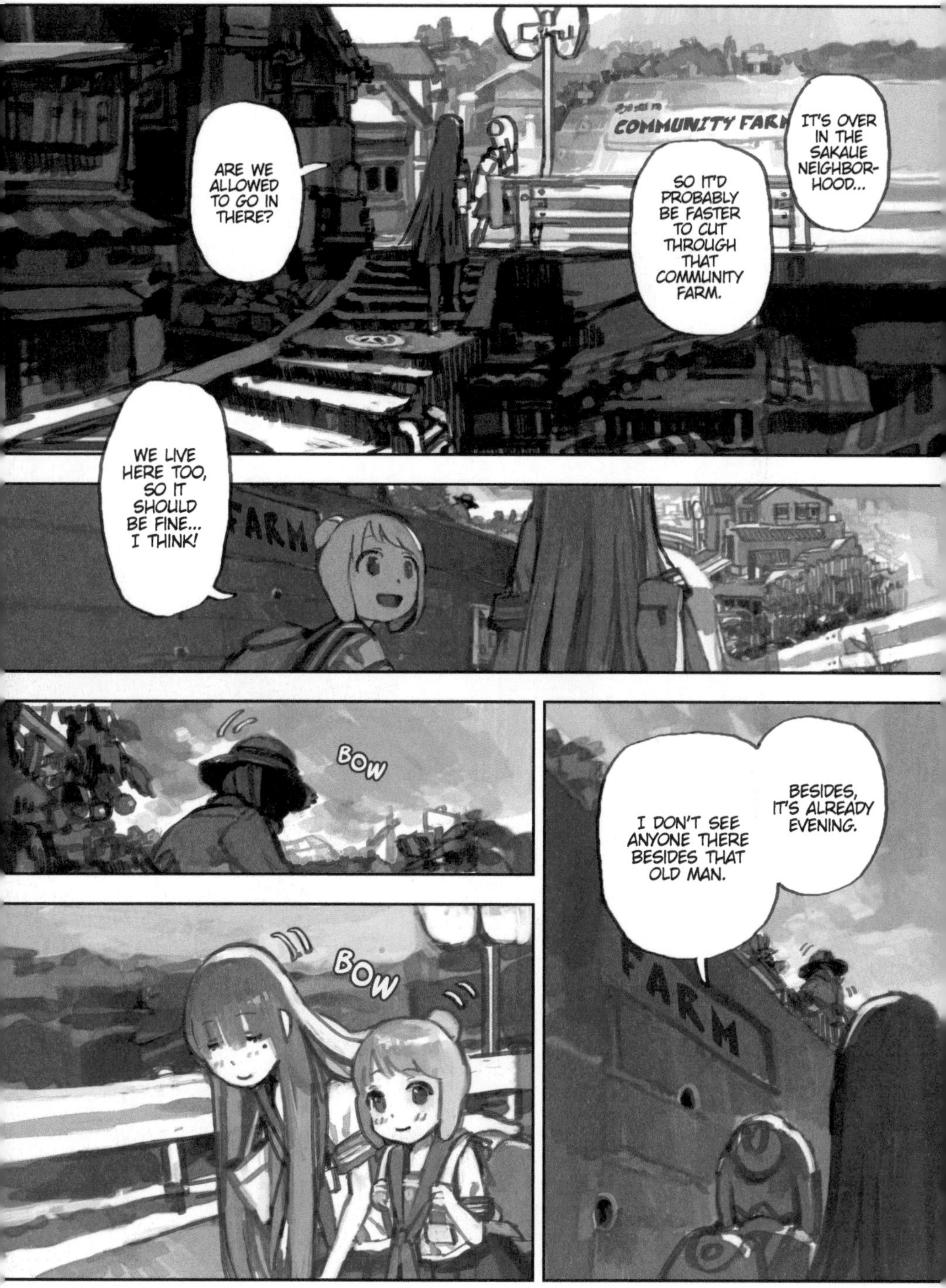
COMMUNITY FARM
IT'S OVER IN THE SAKAUE NEIGHBOR-HOOD...
SO IT'D PROBABLY BE FASTER TO CUT THROUGH THAT COMMUNITY FARM.
ARE WE ALLOWED TO GO IN THERE?
WE LIVE HERE TOO, SO IT SHOULD BE FINE... I THINK!
FARM
BESIDES, IT'S ALREADY EVENING.
I DON'T SEE ANYONE THERE BESIDES THAT OLD MAN.
FARM
BOW
BOW

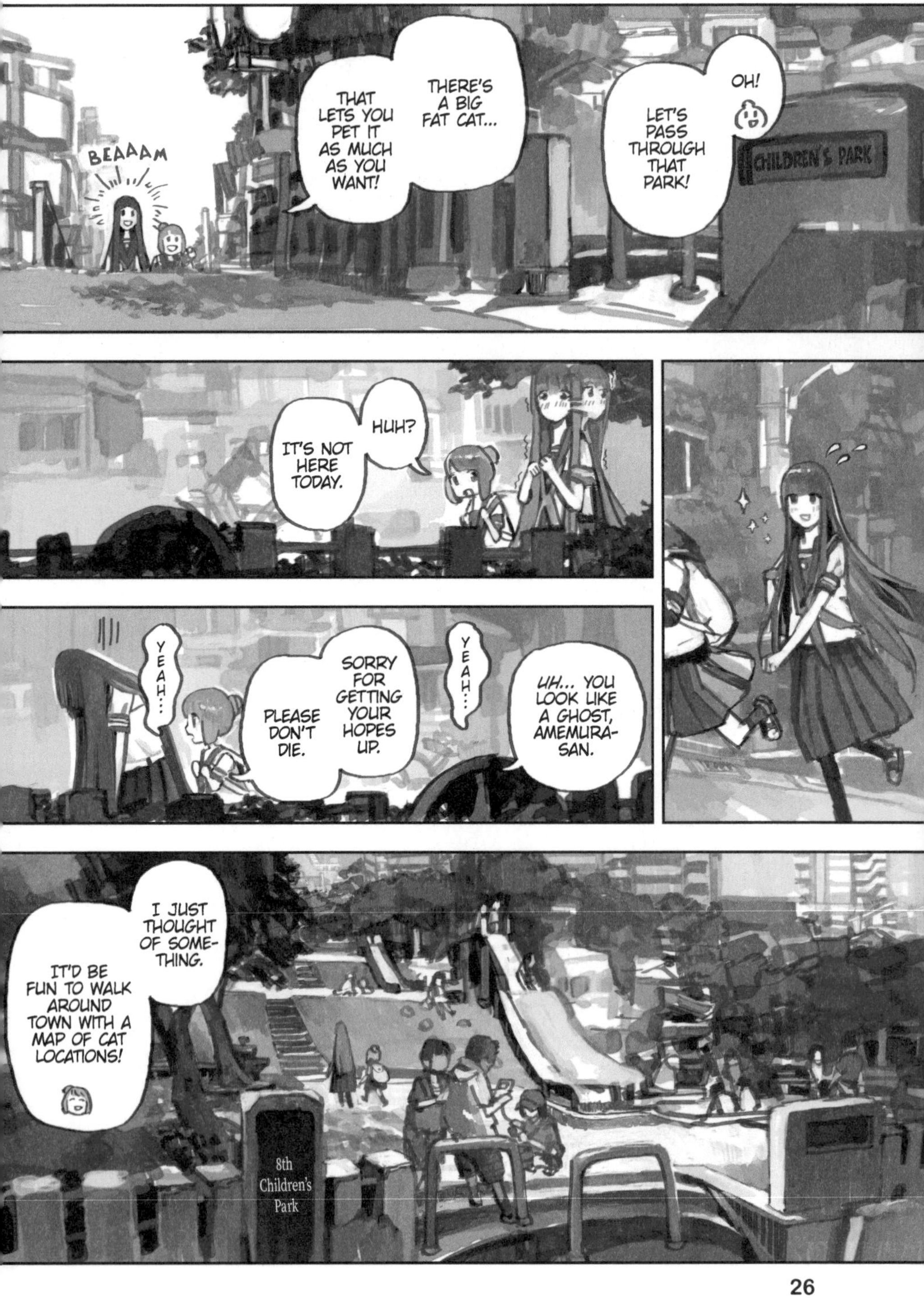
OH!
LET'S PASS THROUGH THAT PARK!
CHILDREN'S PARK
THERE'S A BIG FAT CAT...
THAT LETS YOU PET IT AS MUCH AS YOU WANT!
BEAAAM
HUH?
IT'S NOT HERE TODAY.
UH... YOU LOOK LIKE A GHOST, AMEMURA-SAN.
YEAH...
SORRY FOR GETTING YOUR HOPES UP.
PLEASE DON'T DIE.
YEAH...
I JUST THOUGHT OF SOME-THING.
IT'D BE FUN TO WALK AROUND TOWN WITH A MAP OF CAT LOCATIONS!
8th Children's Park

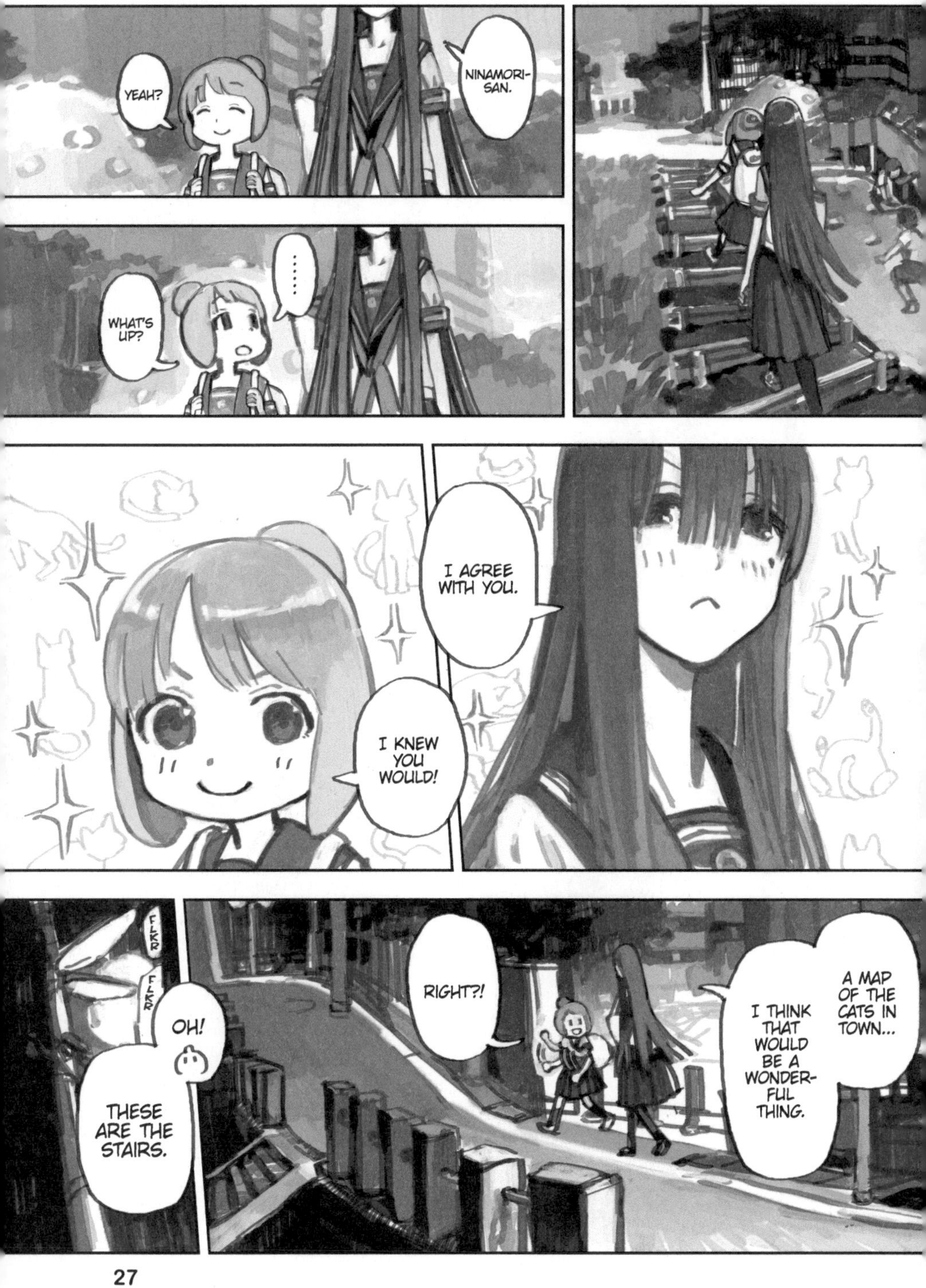
NINAMORI-SAN.
YEAH?
......
WHAT'S UP?
I AGREE WITH YOU.
I KNEW YOU WOULD!
A MAP OF THE CATS IN TOWN...
I THINK THAT WOULD BE A WONDERFUL THING.
RIGHT?!
FLKR
FLKR
OH!
THESE ARE THE STAIRS.

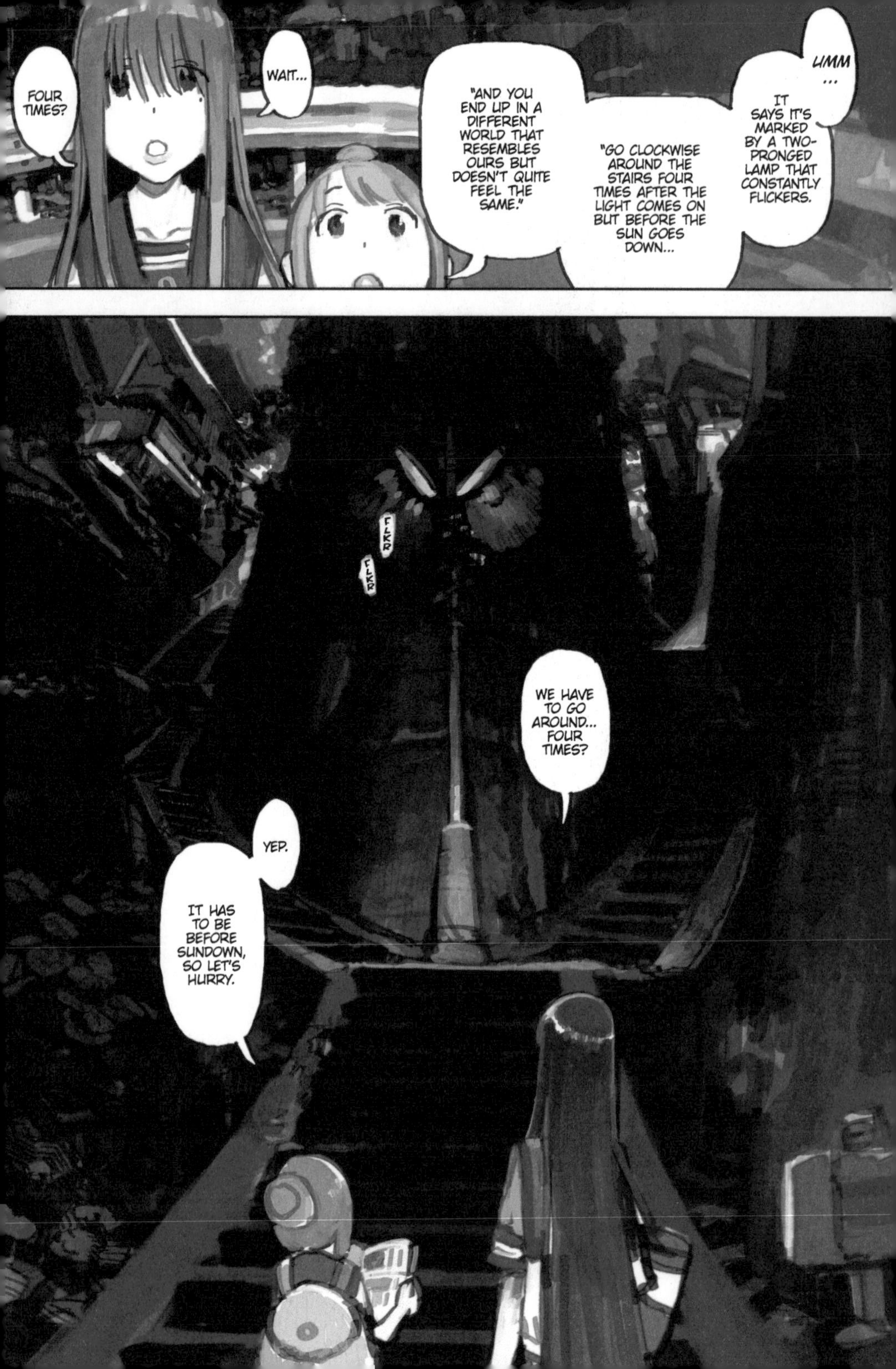
UMM...
IT SAYS IT'S MARKED BY A TWO-PRONGED LAMP THAT CONSTANTLY FLICKERS.
"GO CLOCKWISE AROUND THE STAIRS FOUR TIMES AFTER THE LIGHT COMES ON BUT BEFORE THE SUN GOES DOWN...
"AND YOU END UP IN A DIFFERENT WORLD THAT RESEMBLES OURS BUT DOESN'T QUITE FEEL THE SAME."
WAIT...
FOUR TIMES?
FLKR
FLKR
WE HAVE TO GO AROUND... FOUR TIMES?
YEP.
IT HAS TO BE BEFORE SUNDOWN, SO LET'S HURRY.

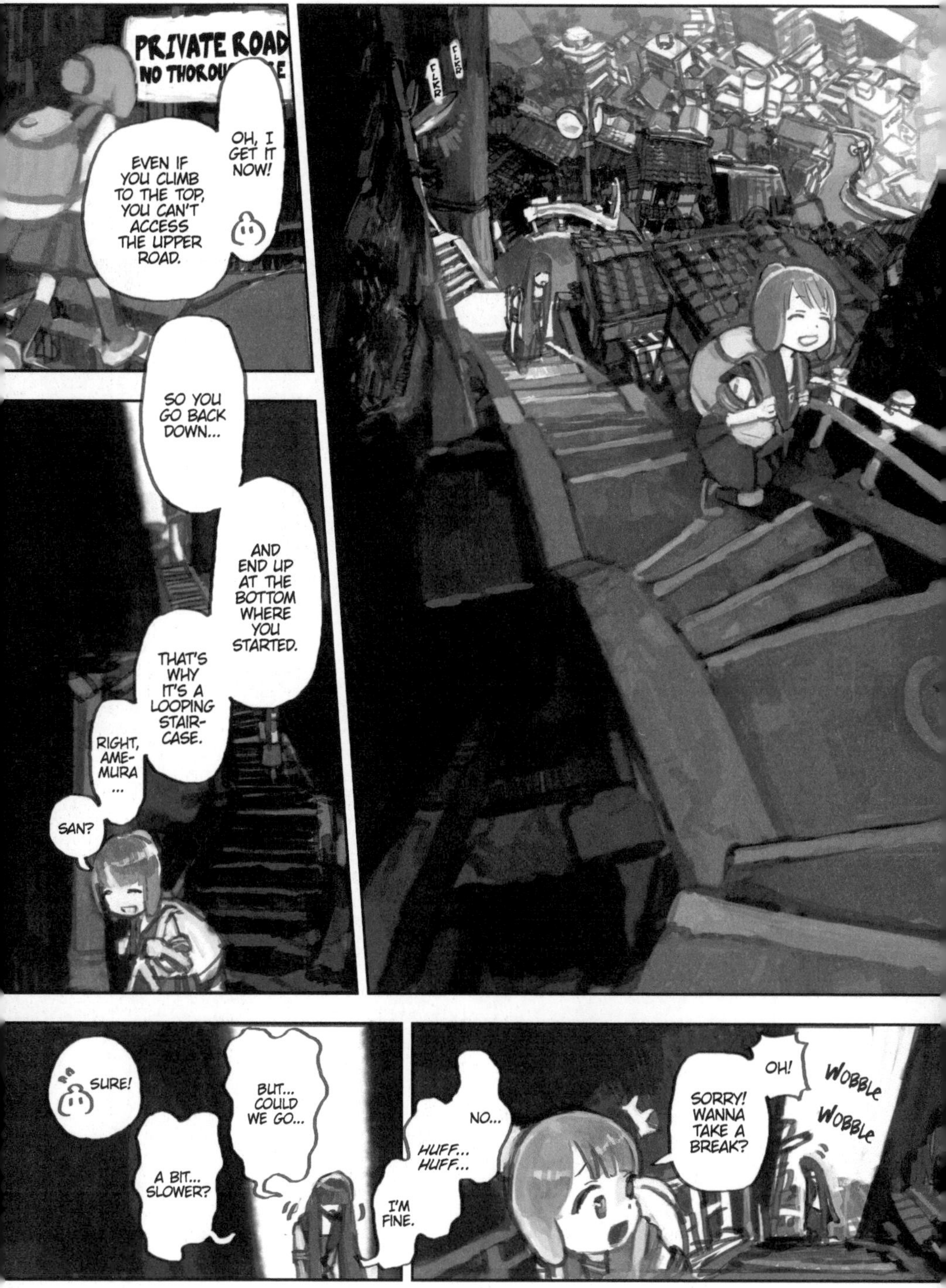
FLKR
FLKR
PRIVATE ROAD
OH, I GET IT NOW!
EVEN IF YOU CLIMB TO THE TOP, YOU CAN'T ACCESS THE UPPER ROAD.
SO YOU GO BACK DOWN...
AND END UP AT THE BOTTOM WHERE YOU STARTED.
THAT'S WHY IT'S A LOOPING STAIR-CASE.
RIGHT, AME-MURA...
SAN?
OH!
SORRY! WANNA TAKE A BREAK?
WOBBLE
WOBBLE
NO...
HUFF... HUFF...
I'M FINE.
BUT... COULD WE GO...
A BIT... SLOWER?
SURE!

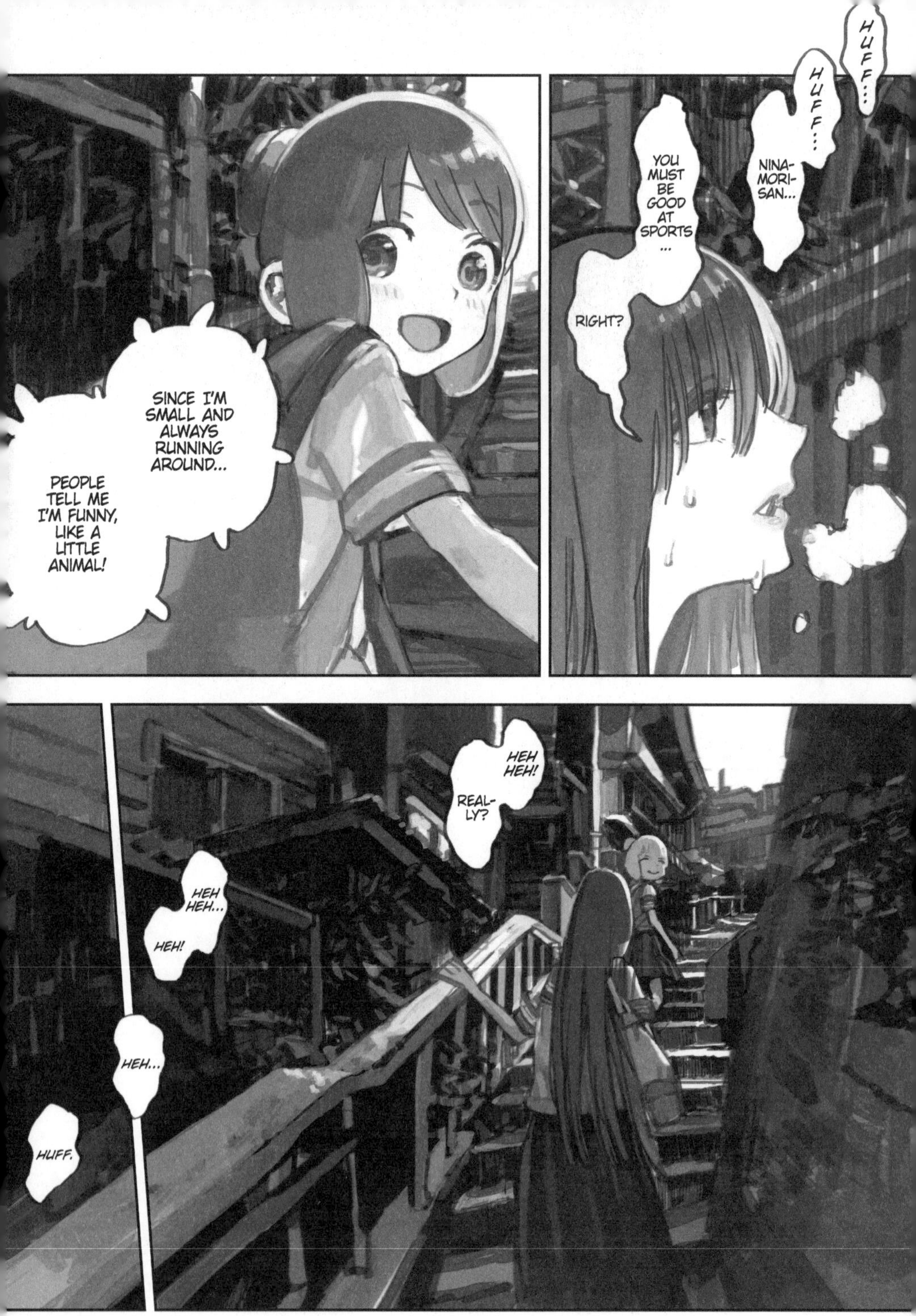
HUFF...
HUFF...
NINA-MORI-SAN...
YOU MUST BE GOOD AT SPORTS...
RIGHT?
SINCE I'M SMALL AND ALWAYS RUNNING AROUND...
PEOPLE TELL ME I'M FUNNY, LIKE A LITTLE ANIMAL!
HEH HEH!
REAL-LY?
HEH HEH...
HEH!
HEH...
HUFF.

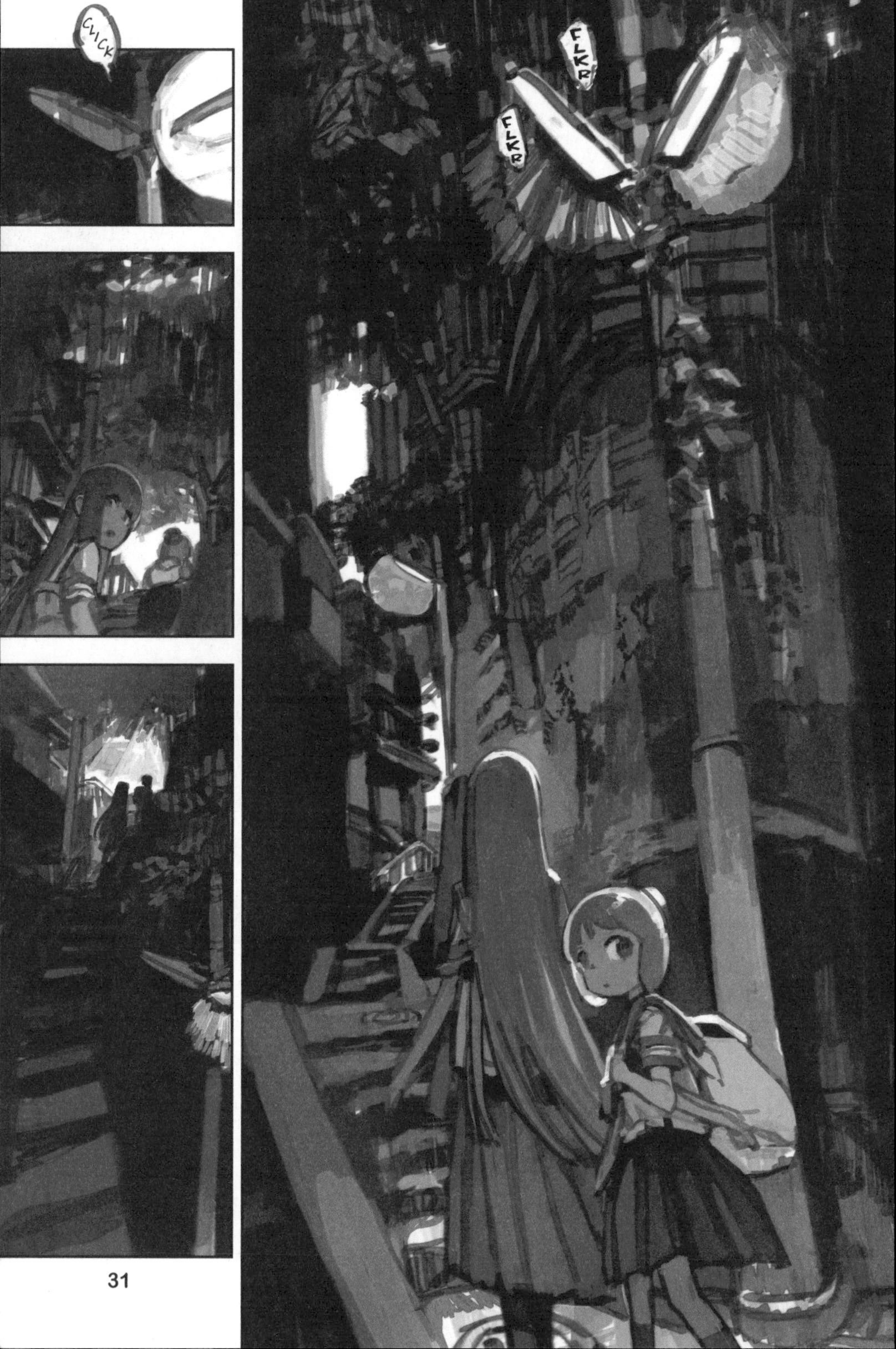
FLKR
FLKR
CLICK

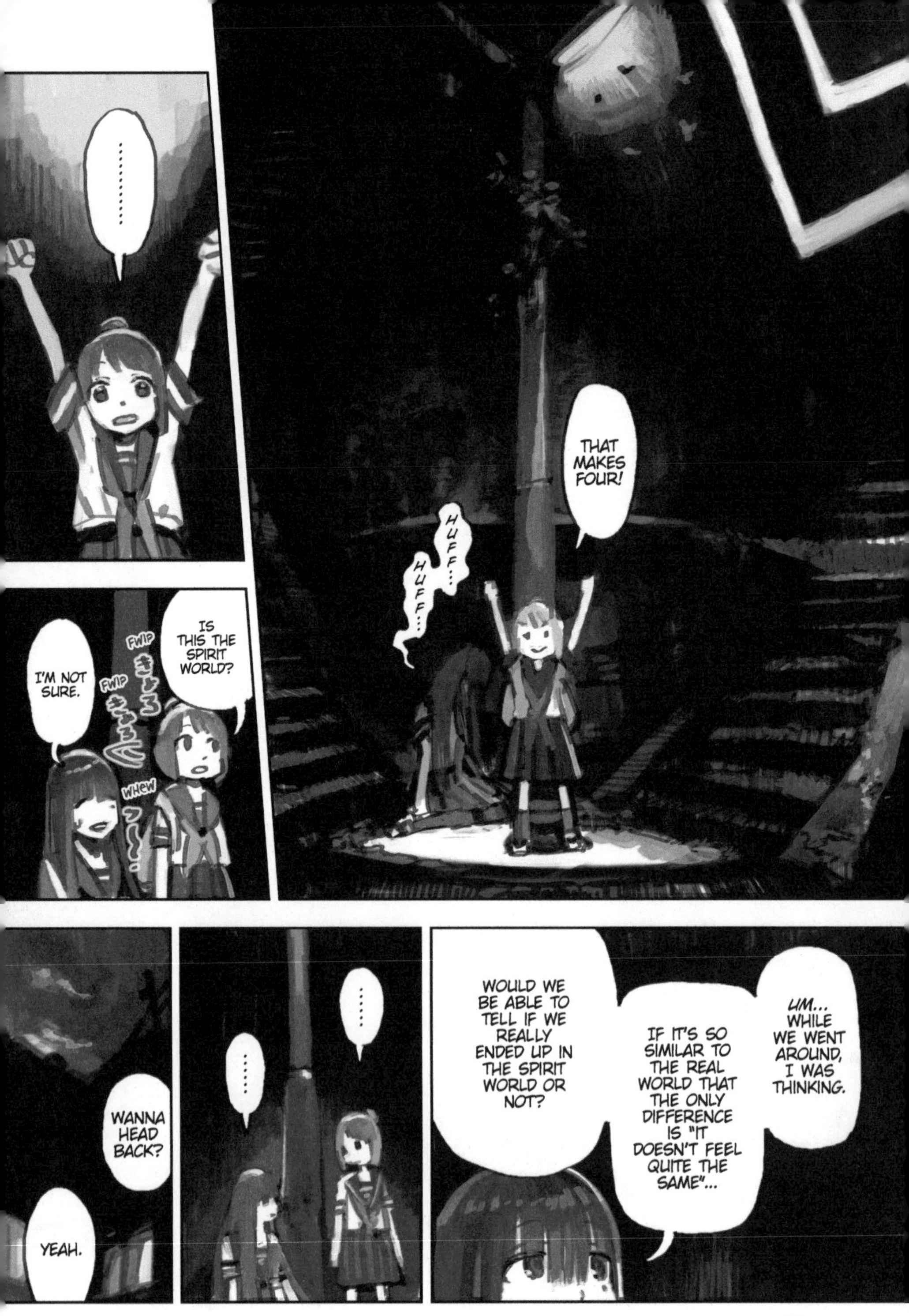

HUFF... HUFF...
THAT MAKES FOUR!
......
IS THIS THE SPIRIT WORLD?
FWIP きょろ
FWIP きょろ
I'M NOT SURE.
WHEW ふ〜
UM... WHILE WE WENT AROUND, I WAS THINKING.
IF IT'S SO SIMILAR TO THE REAL WORLD THAT THE ONLY DIFFERENCE IS "IT DOESN'T FEEL QUITE THE SAME"...
WOULD WE BE ABLE TO TELL IF WE REALLY ENDED UP IN THE SPIRIT WORLD OR NOT?
......
......
WANNA HEAD BACK?
YEAH.

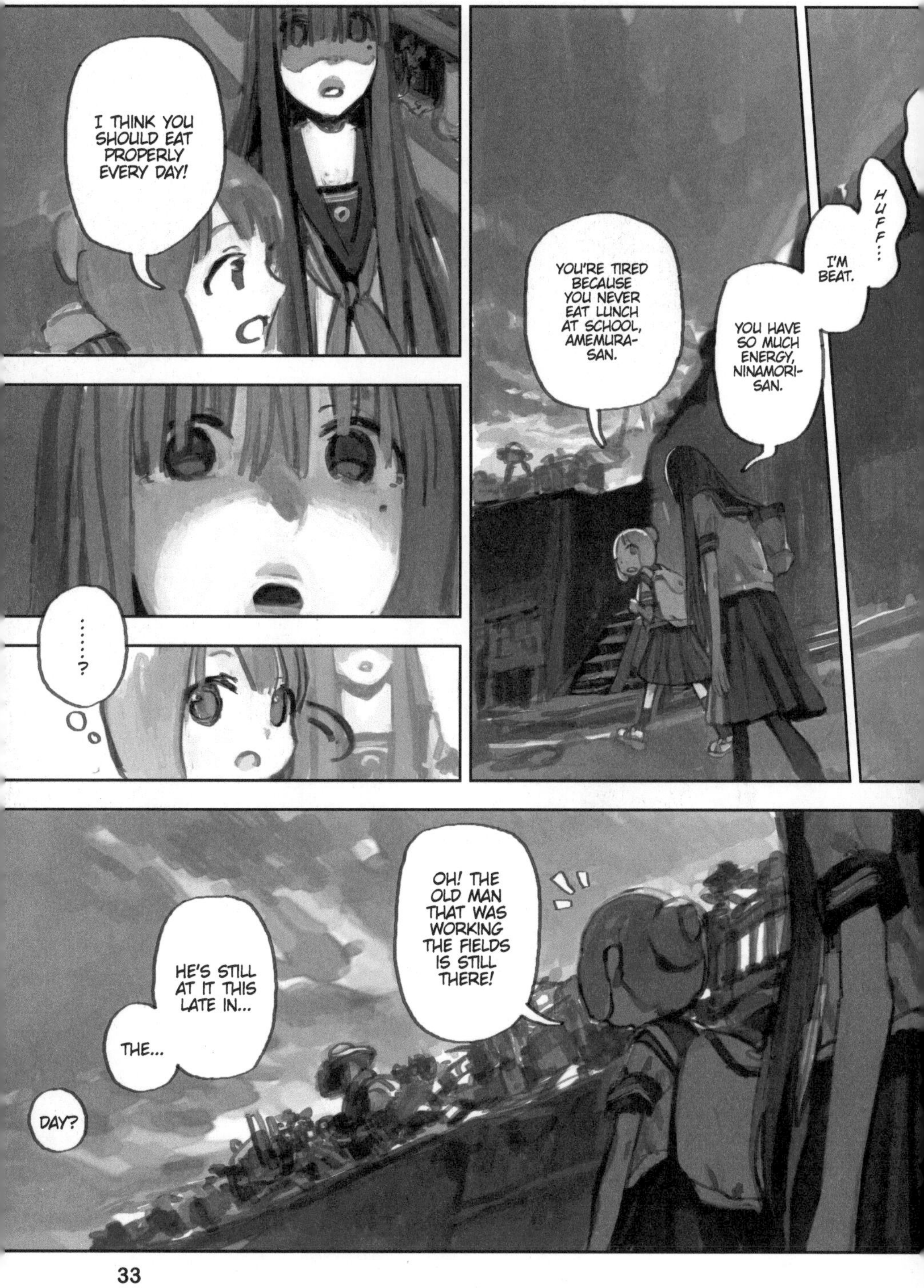
HUFF...
I'M BEAT.
YOU HAVE SO MUCH ENERGY, NINAMORI-SAN.
YOU'RE TIRED BECAUSE YOU NEVER EAT LUNCH AT SCHOOL, AMEMURA-SAN.
I THINK YOU SHOULD EAT PROPERLY EVERY DAY!
......?
OH! THE OLD MAN THAT WAS WORKING THE FIELDS IS STILL THERE!
HE'S STILL AT IT THIS LATE IN...
THE...
DAY?

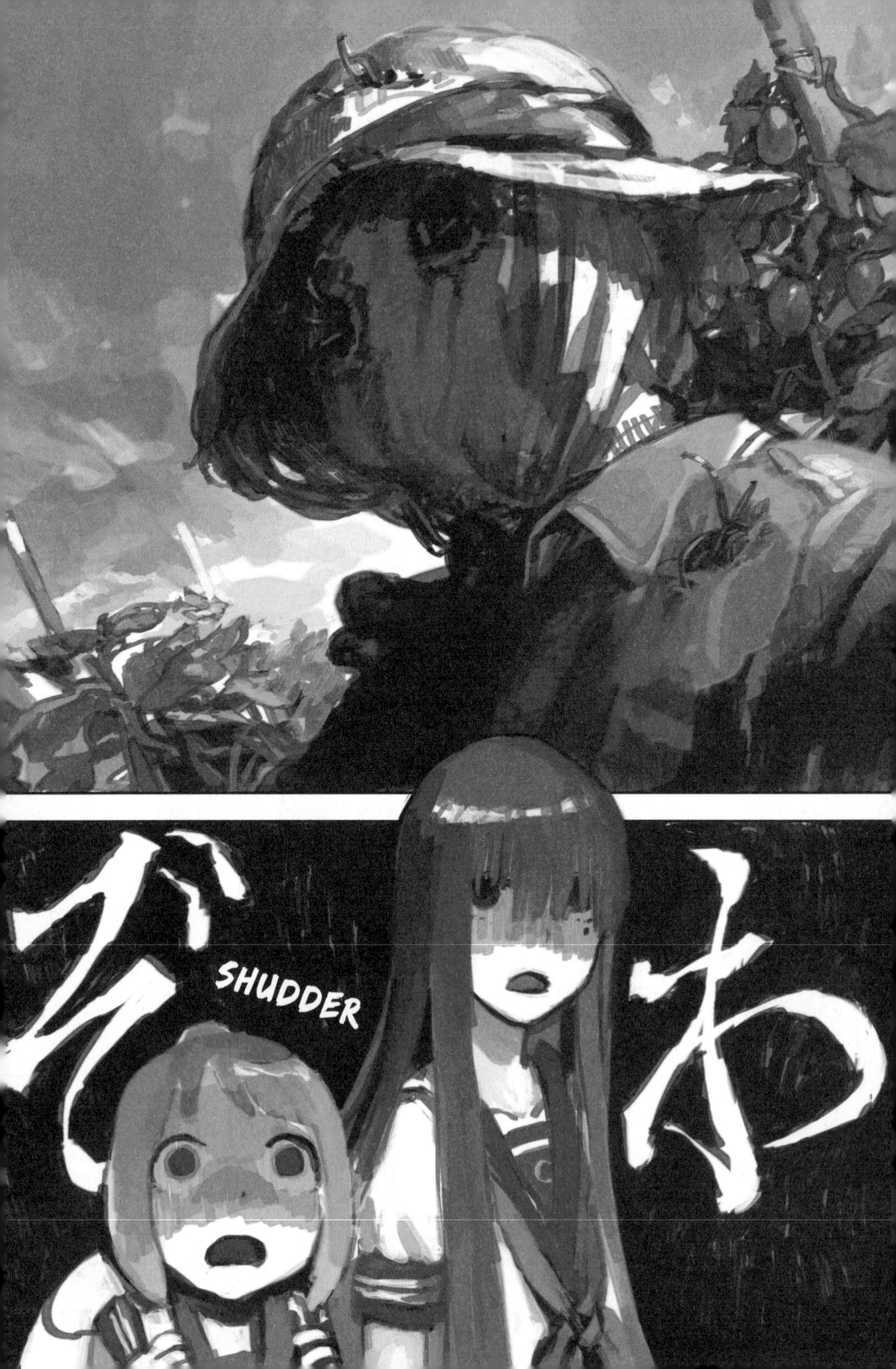
SHUDDER

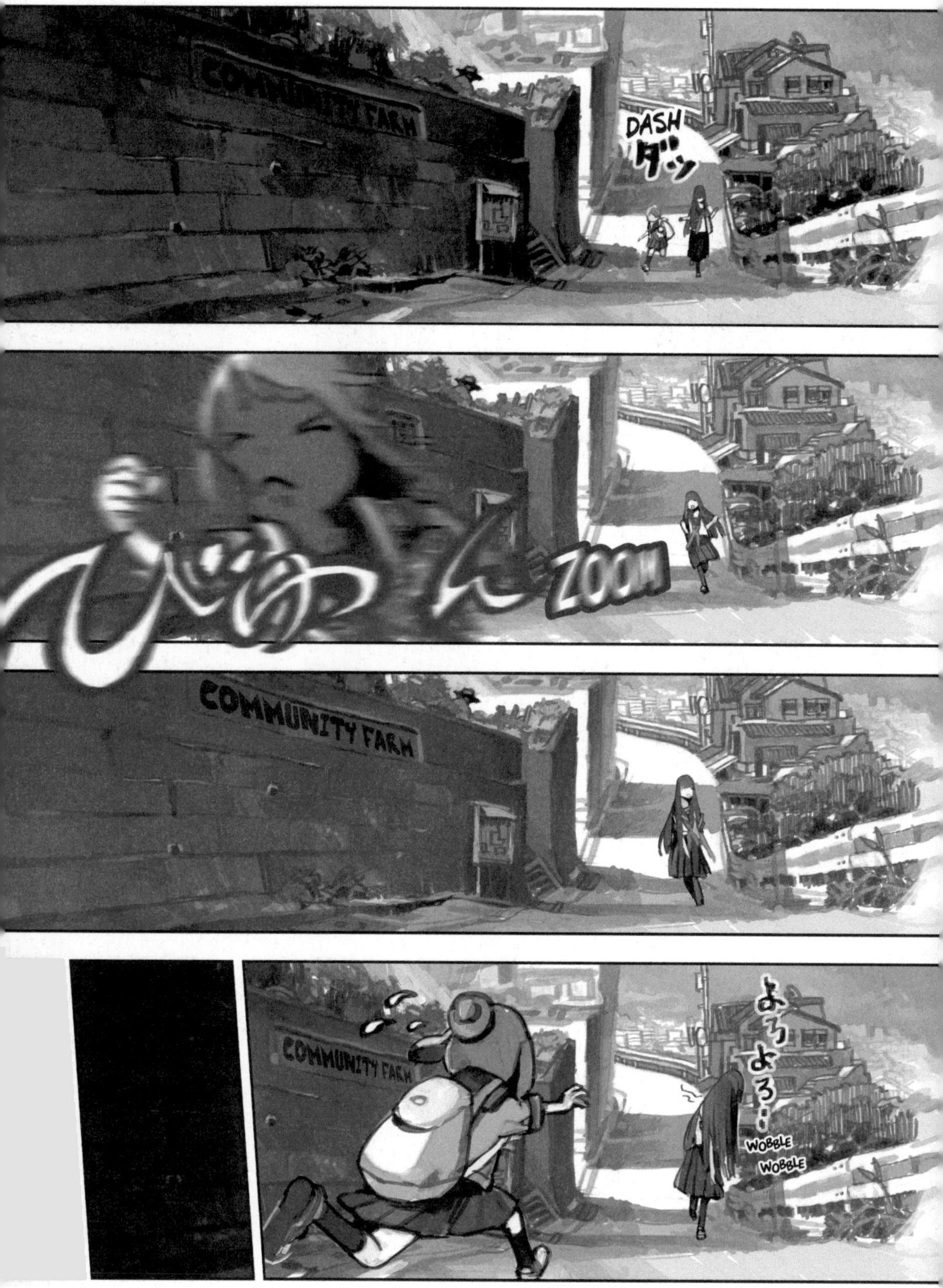
COMMUNITY FARM
DASH
ダッ
ZOOM
COMMUNITY FARM
COMMUNITY FARM
よろよろ‥
WOBBLE
WOBBLE

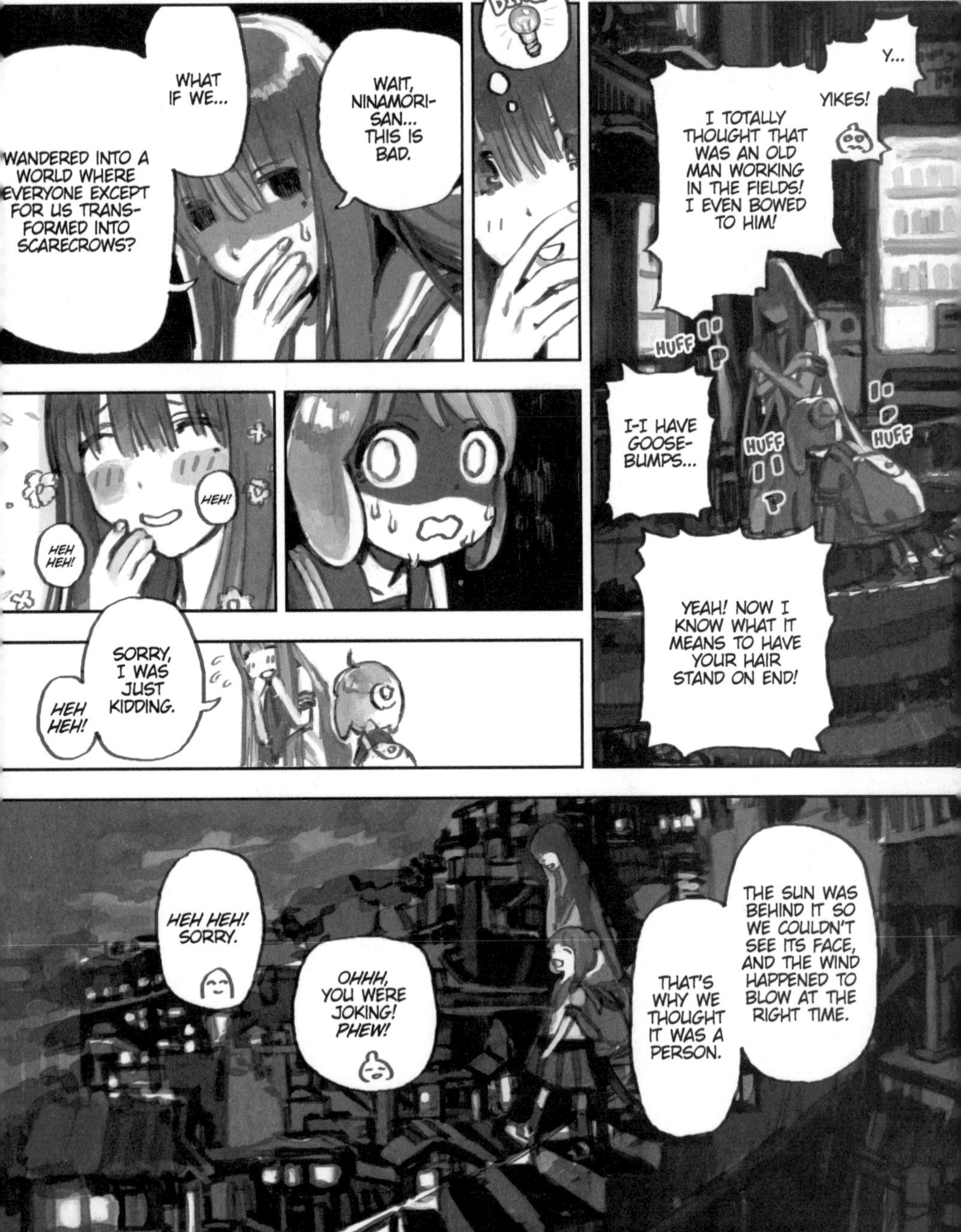
Y...
YIKES!
I TOTALLY THOUGHT THAT WAS AN OLD MAN WORKING IN THE FIELDS! I EVEN BOWED TO HIM!
HUFF
I-I HAVE GOOSE-BUMPS...
HUFF
HUFF
YEAH! NOW I KNOW WHAT IT MEANS TO HAVE YOUR HAIR STAND ON END!
DING
WAIT, NINAMORI-SAN... THIS IS BAD.
WHAT IF WE...
WANDERED INTO A WORLD WHERE EVERYONE EXCEPT FOR US TRANS-FORMED INTO SCARECROWS?
HEH!
HEH HEH!
SORRY, I WAS JUST KIDDING.
HEH HEH!
THE SUN WAS BEHIND IT SO WE COULDN'T SEE ITS FACE, AND THE WIND HAPPENED TO BLOW AT THE RIGHT TIME.
THAT'S WHY WE THOUGHT IT WAS A PERSON.
OHHH, YOU WERE JOKING! PHEW!
HEH HEH! SORRY.

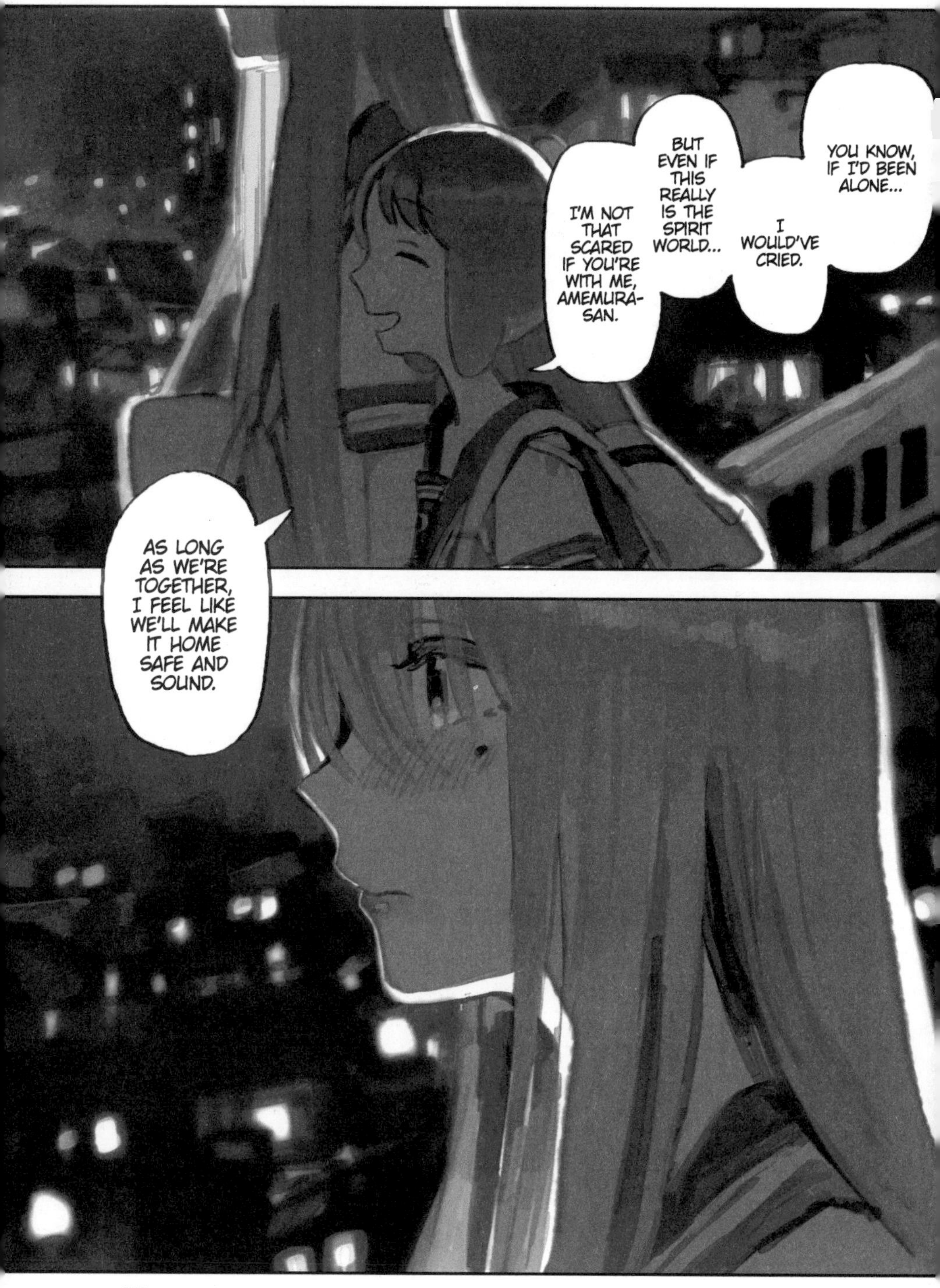
YOU KNOW, IF I'D BEEN ALONE...
I WOULD'VE CRIED.
BUT EVEN IF THIS REALLY IS THE SPIRIT WORLD...
I'M NOT THAT SCARED IF YOU'RE WITH ME, AMEMURA-SAN.
AS LONG AS WE'RE TOGETHER, I FEEL LIKE WE'LL MAKE IT HOME SAFE AND SOUND.

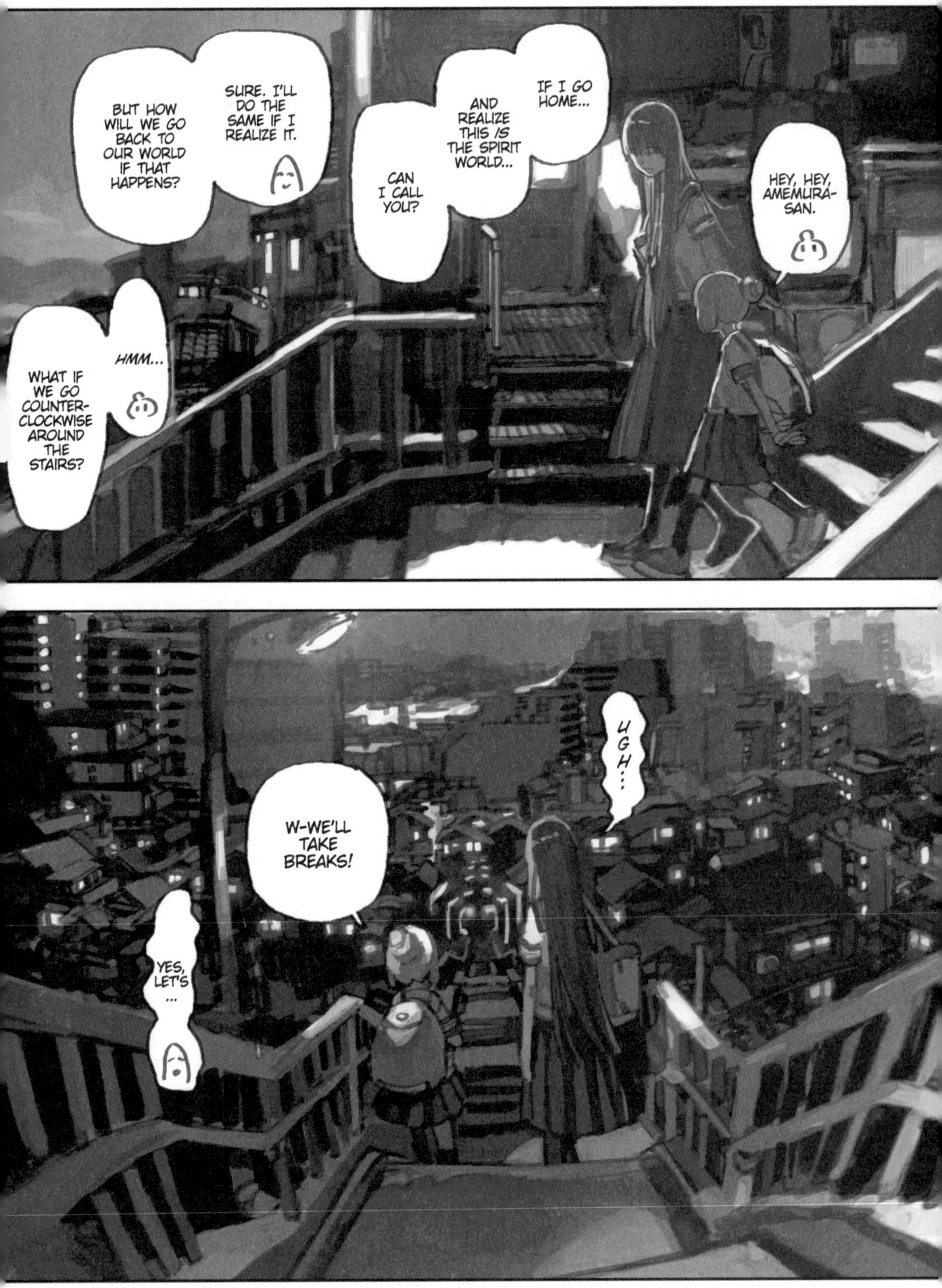
HEY, HEY, AMEMURA-SAN.
IF I GO HOME...
AND REALIZE THIS *IS* THE SPIRIT WORLD...
CAN I CALL YOU?
SURE. I'LL DO THE SAME IF I REALIZE IT.
BUT HOW WILL WE GO BACK TO OUR WORLD IF THAT HAPPENS?
HMM...
WHAT IF WE GO COUNTER-CLOCKWISE AROUND THE STAIRS?
UGH...
W-WE'LL TAKE BREAKS!
YES, LET'S...

NIGHTFALL
TRAVELERS

LEAVE ONLY FOOTPRINTS

NIGHTFALL TRAVELERS

LEAVE ONLY FOOTPRINTS

Intermission: Good Night Akane-chan @ Coming Home After Chapter 2

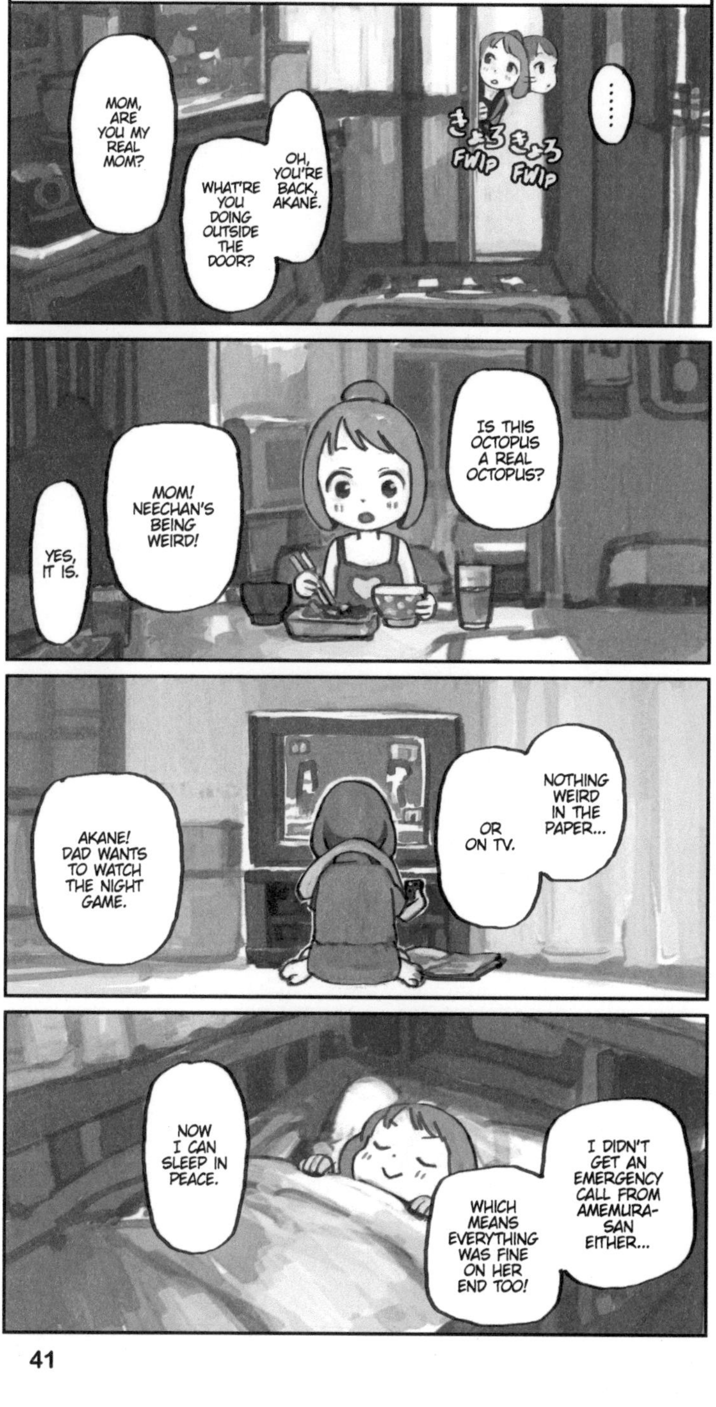
......
きょろきょろ
FWIP FWIP
OH, YOU'RE BACK, AKANE.
WHAT'RE YOU DOING OUTSIDE THE DOOR?
MOM, ARE YOU MY REAL MOM?
IS THIS OCTOPUS A REAL OCTOPUS?
MOM! NEECHAN'S BEING WEIRD!
YES, IT IS.
NOTHING WEIRD IN THE PAPER...
OR ON TV.
AKANE! DAD WANTS TO WATCH THE NIGHT GAME.
I DIDN'T GET AN EMERGENCY CALL FROM AMEMURA-SAN EITHER...
WHICH MEANS EVERYTHING WAS FINE ON HER END TOO!
NOW I CAN SLEEP IN PEACE.

NIGHTFALL TRAVELERS
LEAVE ONLY FOOTPRINTS

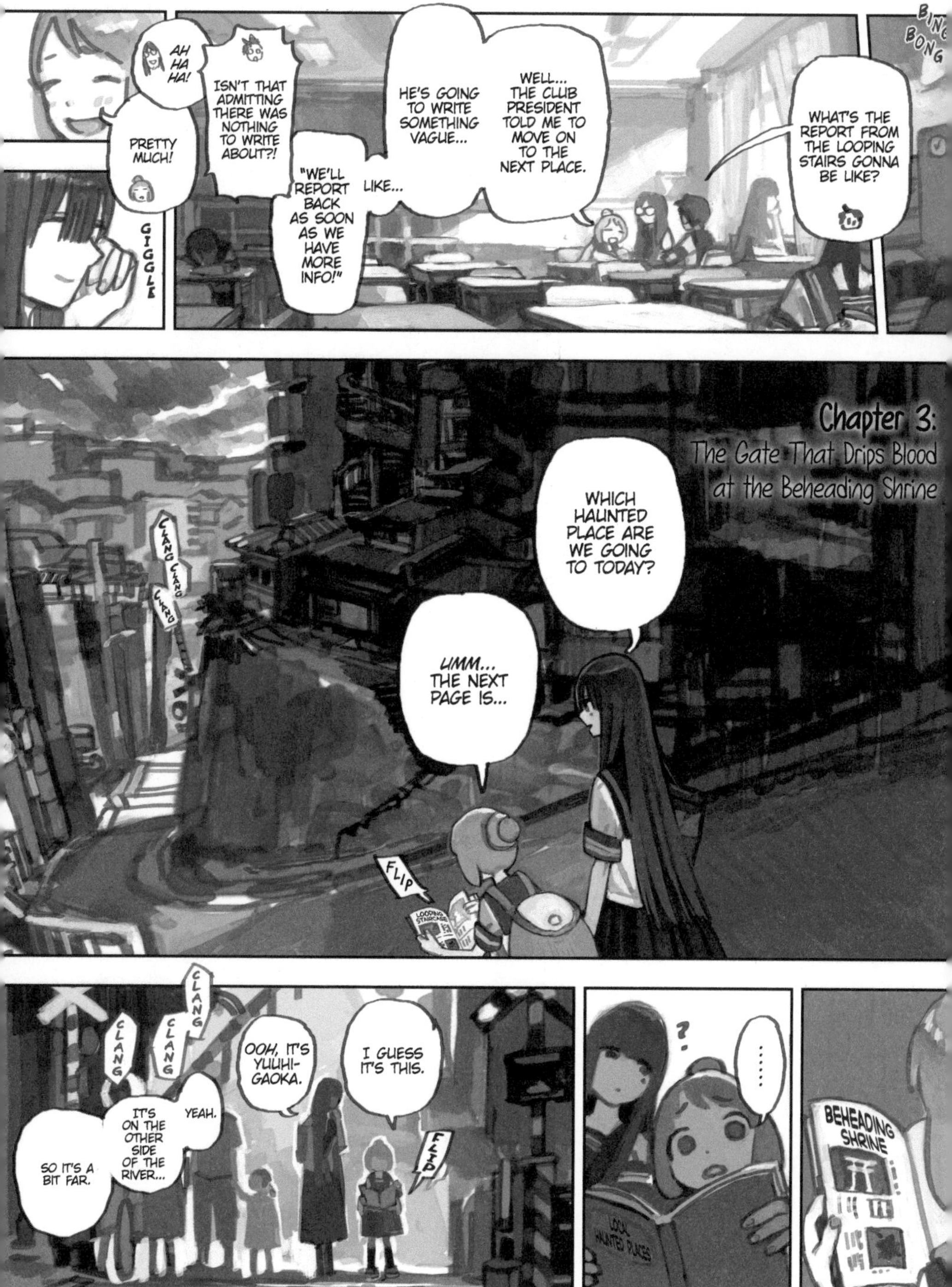
BING BONG
WHAT'S THE REPORT FROM THE LOOPING STAIRS GONNA BE LIKE?
WELL... THE CLUB PRESIDENT TOLD ME TO MOVE ON TO THE NEXT PLACE.
HE'S GOING TO WRITE SOMETHING VAGUE...
LIKE...
"WE'LL REPORT BACK AS SOON AS WE HAVE MORE INFO!"
ISN'T THAT ADMITTING THERE WAS NOTHING TO WRITE ABOUT?!
AH HA HA!
PRETTY MUCH!
GIGGLE
Chapter 3:
The Gate That Drips Blood at the Beheading Shrine
WHICH HAUNTED PLACE ARE WE GOING TO TODAY?
UMM... THE NEXT PAGE IS...
CLANG CLANG CLANG
FLIP
LOOPING STAIRCASE
BEHEADING SHRINE
?
......
LOCAL HAUNTED PLACES
I GUESS IT'S THIS.
FLIP
OOH, IT'S YUUHI-GAOKA.
YEAH.
IT'S ON THE OTHER SIDE OF THE RIVER...
SO IT'S A BIT FAR.
CLANG
CLANG
CLANG

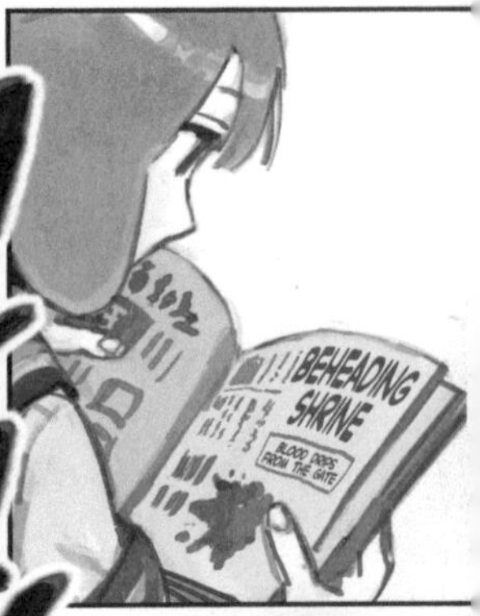
BEHEADING SHRINE
BLOOD DRIPS FROM THE GATE
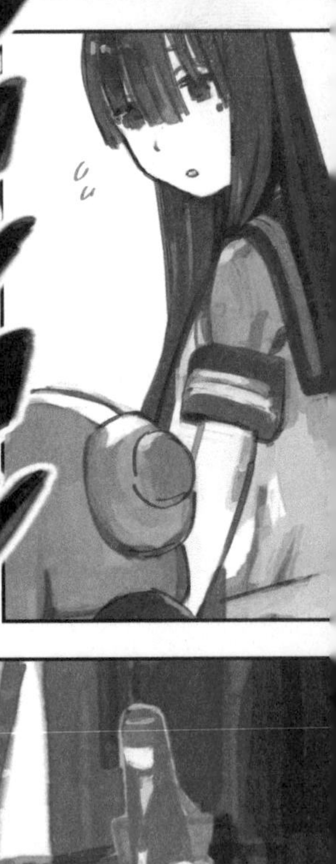
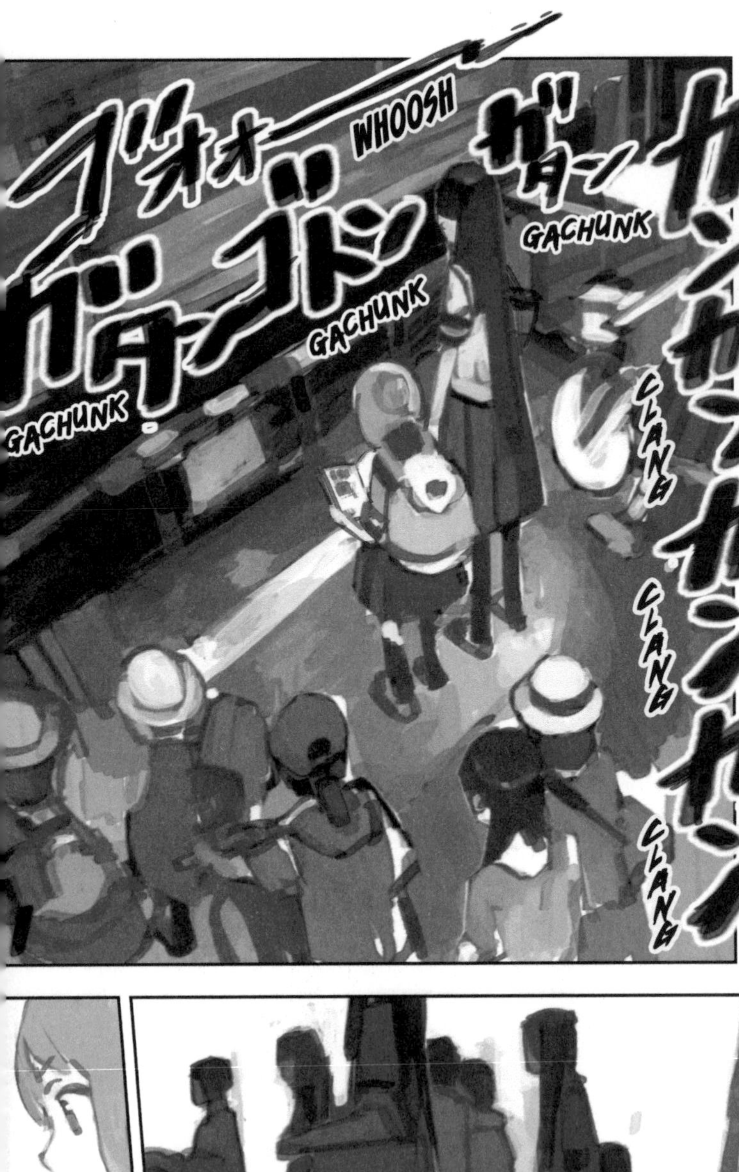
カンカンカンカン
CLANG CLANG CLANG
ガタン
GACHUNK
ブォオー
WHOOSH
ガタンゴトン
GACHUNK
GACHUNK
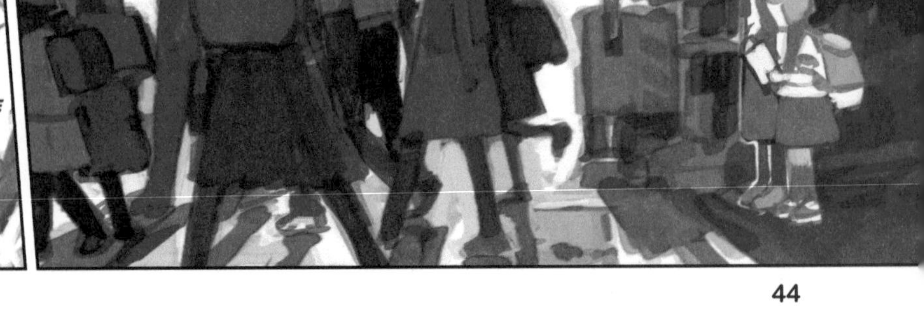
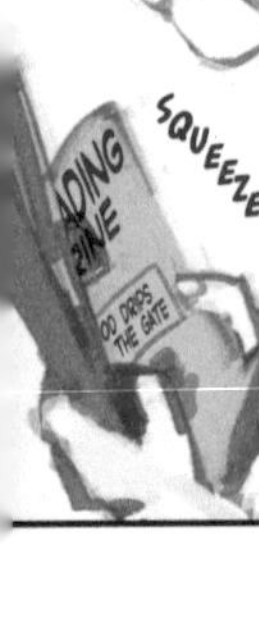
SQUEEZE
ADING
ZINE
OOD DRIPS
THE GATE

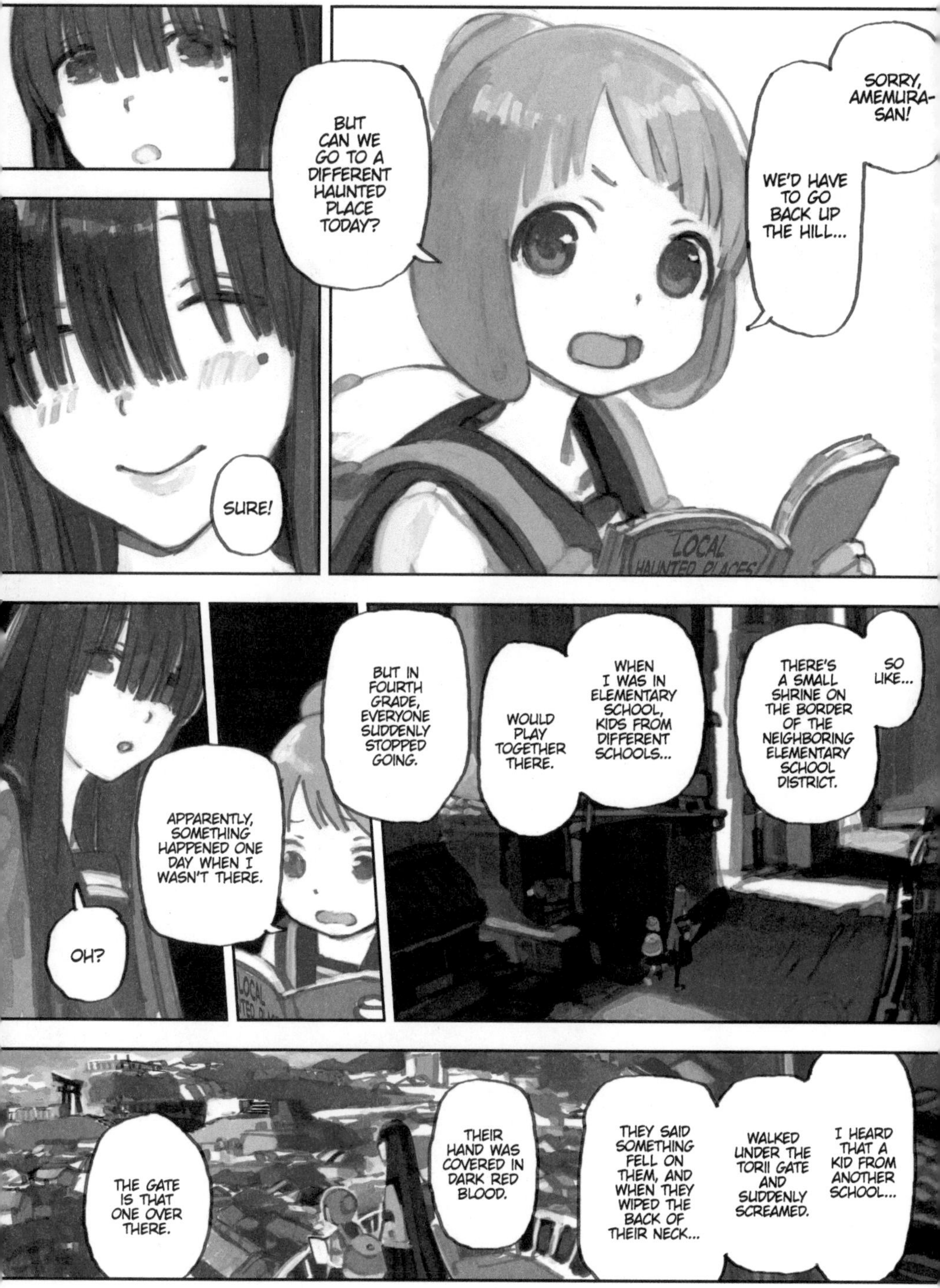

SORRY, AMEMURA-SAN!
WE'D HAVE TO GO BACK UP THE HILL...
BUT CAN WE GO TO A DIFFERENT HAUNTED PLACE TODAY?
SURE!
SO LIKE...
THERE'S A SMALL SHRINE ON THE BORDER OF THE NEIGHBORING ELEMENTARY SCHOOL DISTRICT.
WHEN I WAS IN ELEMENTARY SCHOOL, KIDS FROM DIFFERENT SCHOOLS...
WOULD PLAY TOGETHER THERE.
BUT IN FOURTH GRADE, EVERYONE SUDDENLY STOPPED GOING.
APPARENTLY, SOMETHING HAPPENED ONE DAY WHEN I WASN'T THERE.
OH?
I HEARD THAT A KID FROM ANOTHER SCHOOL...
WALKED UNDER THE TORII GATE AND SUDDENLY SCREAMED.
THEY SAID SOMETHING FELL ON THEM, AND WHEN THEY WIPED THE BACK OF THEIR NECK...
THEIR HAND WAS COVERED IN DARK RED BLOOD.
THE GATE IS THAT ONE OVER THERE.

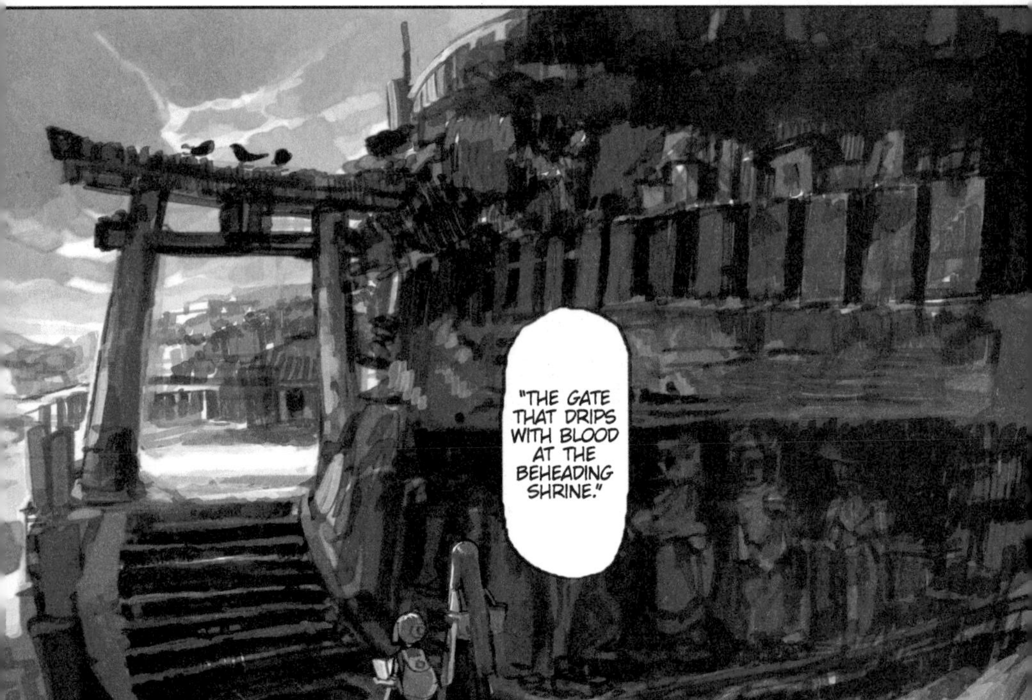
"THE GATE THAT DRIPS WITH BLOOD AT THE BEHEADING SHRINE."

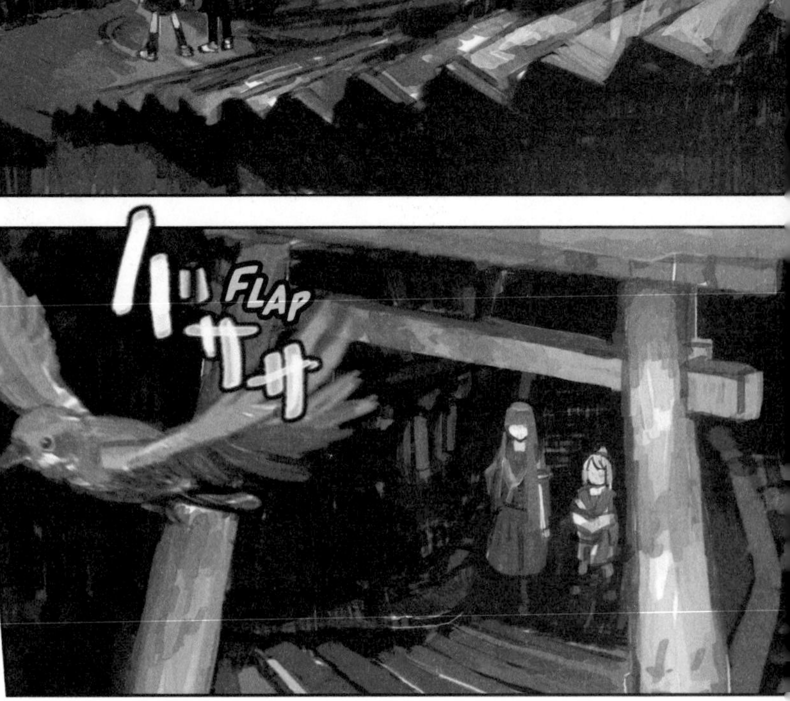
FLAP

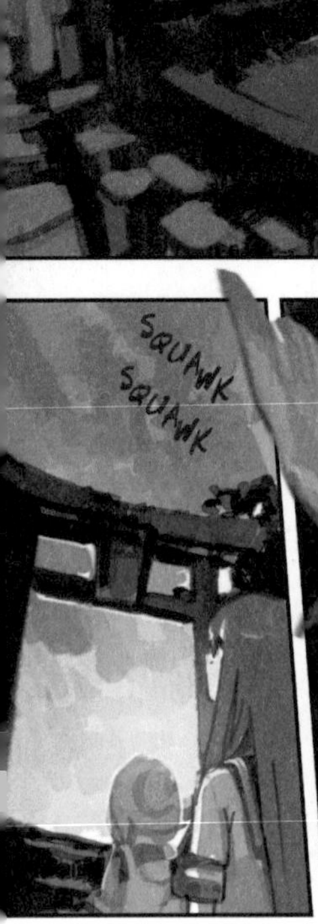
SQUAWK
SQUAWK

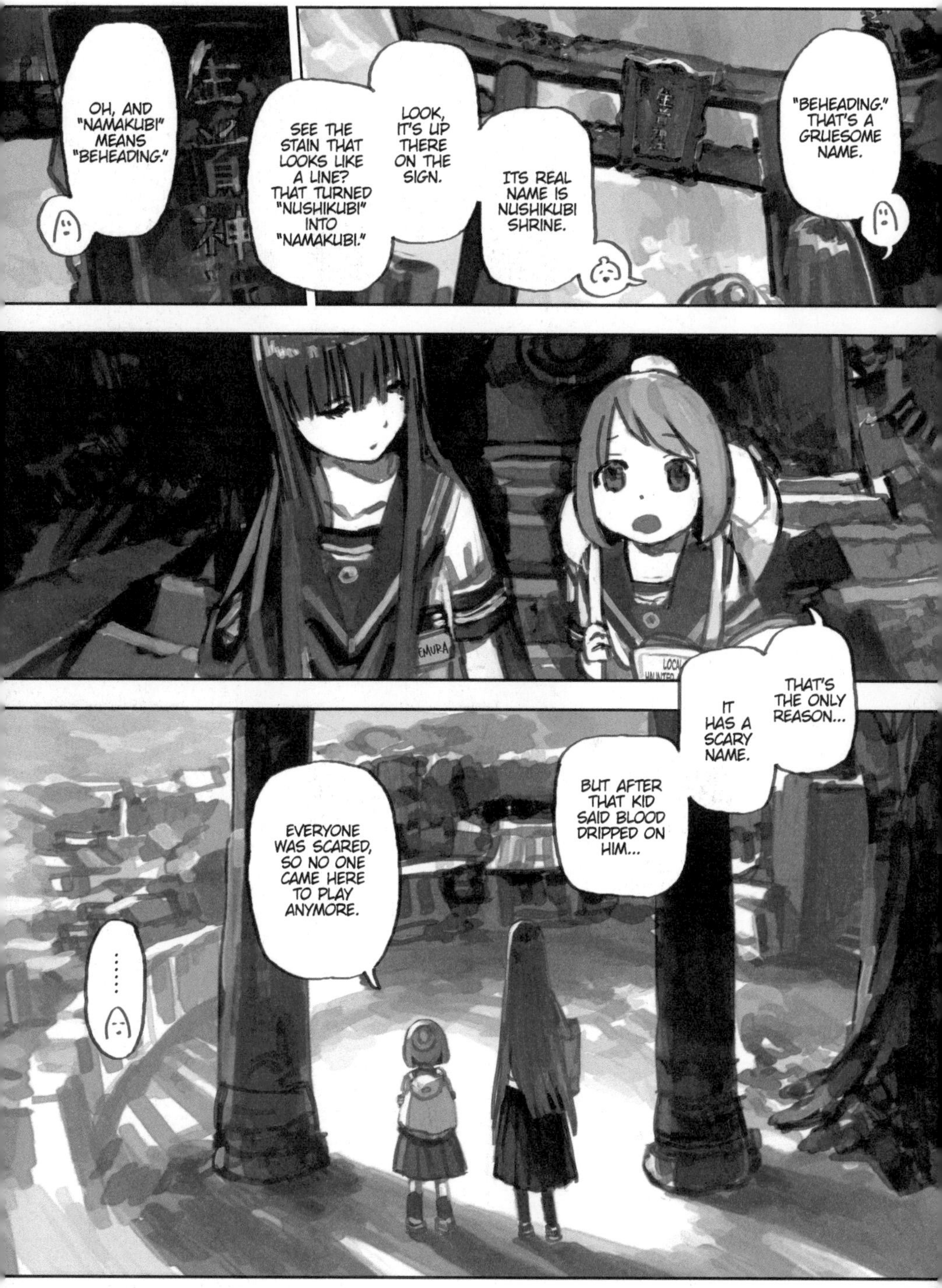
"BEHEADING." THAT'S A GRUESOME NAME.
ITS REAL NAME IS NUSHIKUBI SHRINE.
LOOK, IT'S UP THERE ON THE SIGN.
SEE THE STAIN THAT LOOKS LIKE A LINE? THAT TURNED "NUSHIKUBI" INTO "NAMAKUBI."
OH, AND "NAMAKUBI" MEANS "BEHEADING."
THAT'S THE ONLY REASON...
IT HAS A SCARY NAME.
BUT AFTER THAT KID SAID BLOOD DRIPPED ON HIM...
EVERYONE WAS SCARED, SO NO ONE CAME HERE TO PLAY ANYMORE.
......

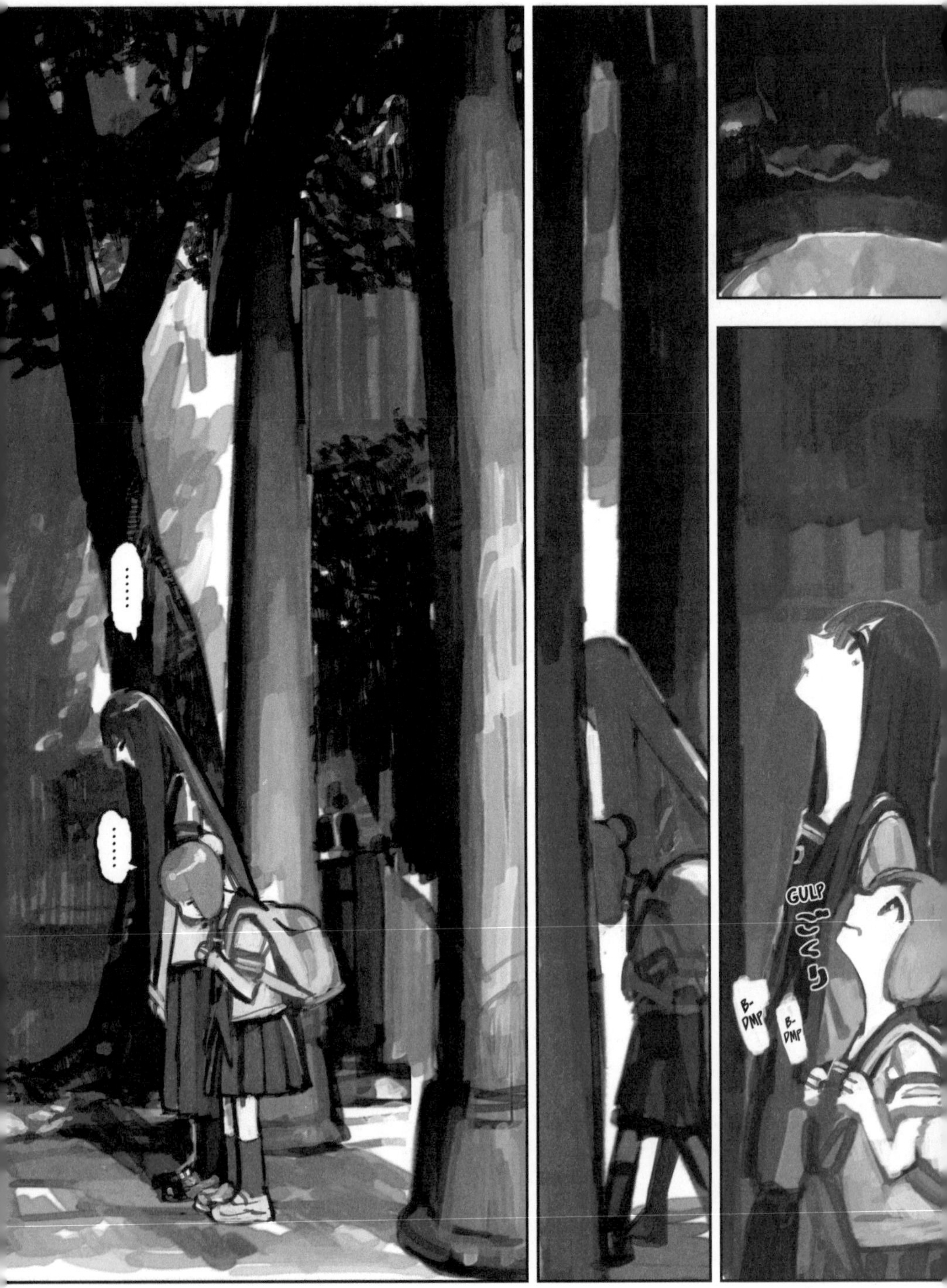
GULP
ごくり
B-DMP
B-DMP
......
......

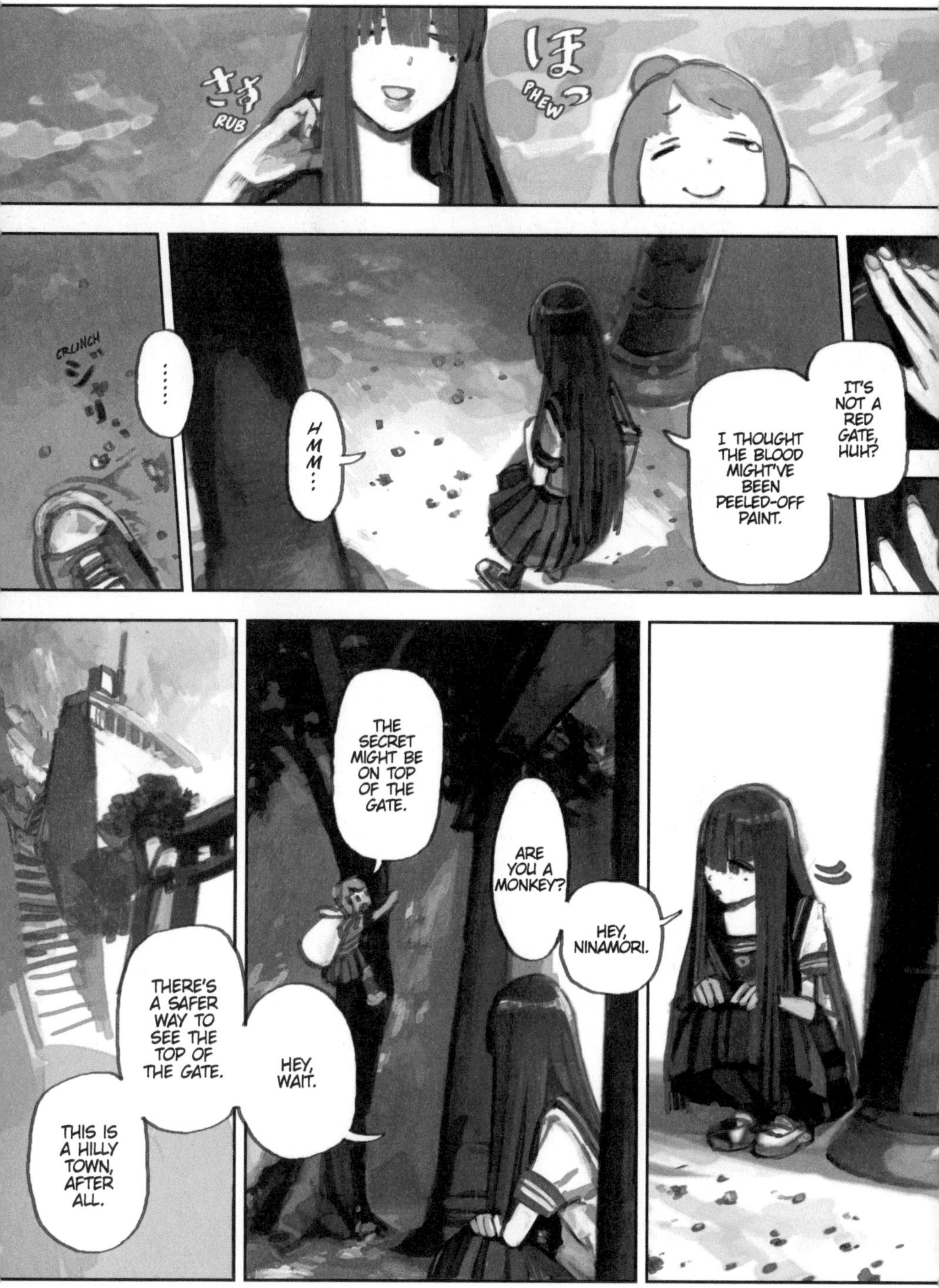
ほっ
PHEW
さす
RUB
IT'S NOT A RED GATE, HUH?
I THOUGHT THE BLOOD MIGHT'VE BEEN PEELED-OFF PAINT.
HMM...
......
CRUNCH
HEY, NINAMORI.
THE SECRET MIGHT BE ON TOP OF THE GATE.
ARE YOU A MONKEY?
HEY, WAIT.
THERE'S A SAFER WAY TO SEE THE TOP OF THE GATE.
THIS IS A HILLY TOWN, AFTER ALL.

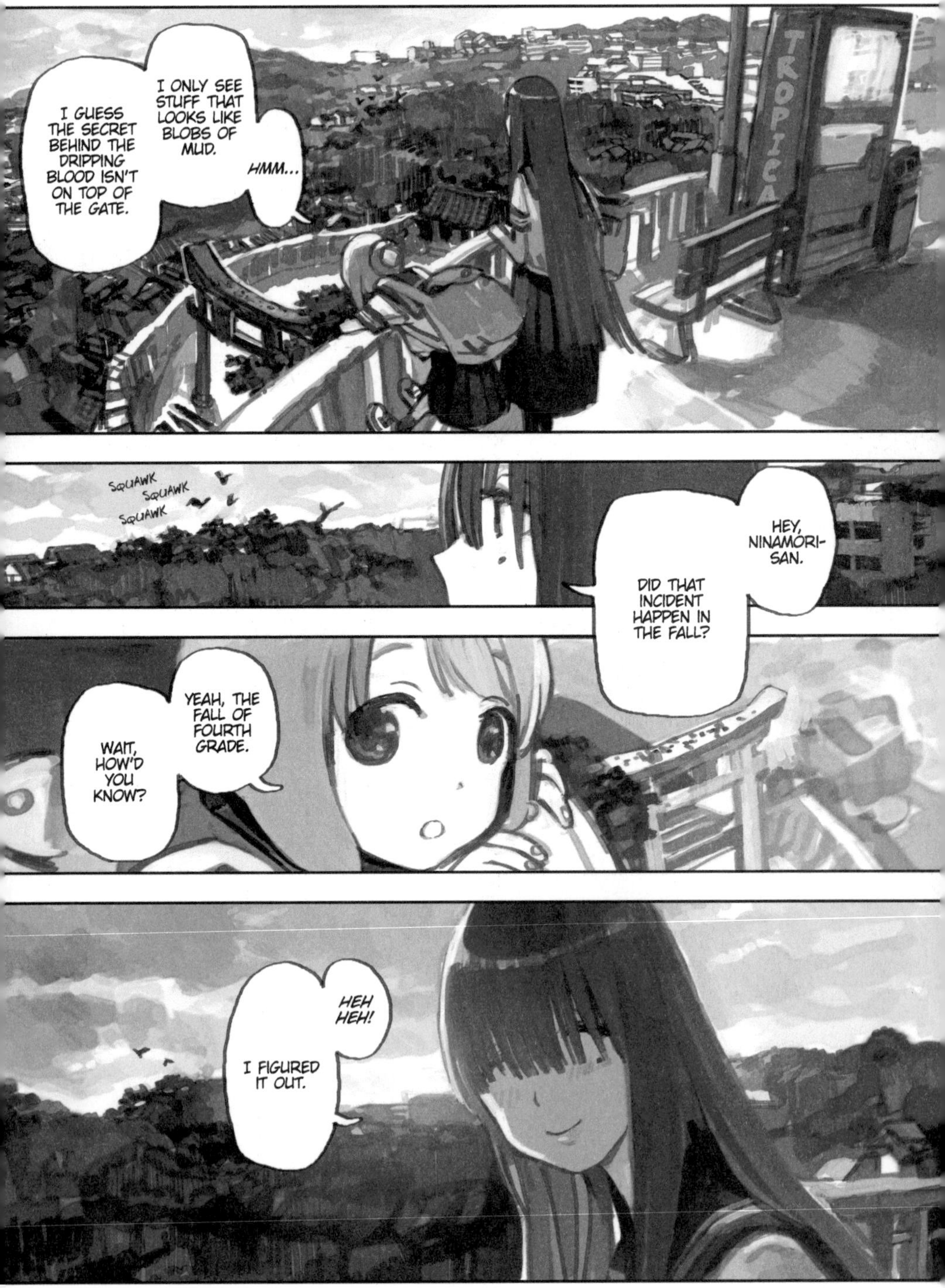
TROPICA
HMM...
I ONLY SEE STUFF THAT LOOKS LIKE BLOBS OF MUD.
I GUESS THE SECRET BEHIND THE DRIPPING BLOOD ISN'T ON TOP OF THE GATE.
HEY, NINAMORI-SAN.
DID THAT INCIDENT HAPPEN IN THE FALL?
SQUAWK SQUAWK SQUAWK
YEAH, THE FALL OF FOURTH GRADE.
WAIT, HOW'D YOU KNOW?
HEH HEH!
I FIGURED IT OUT.

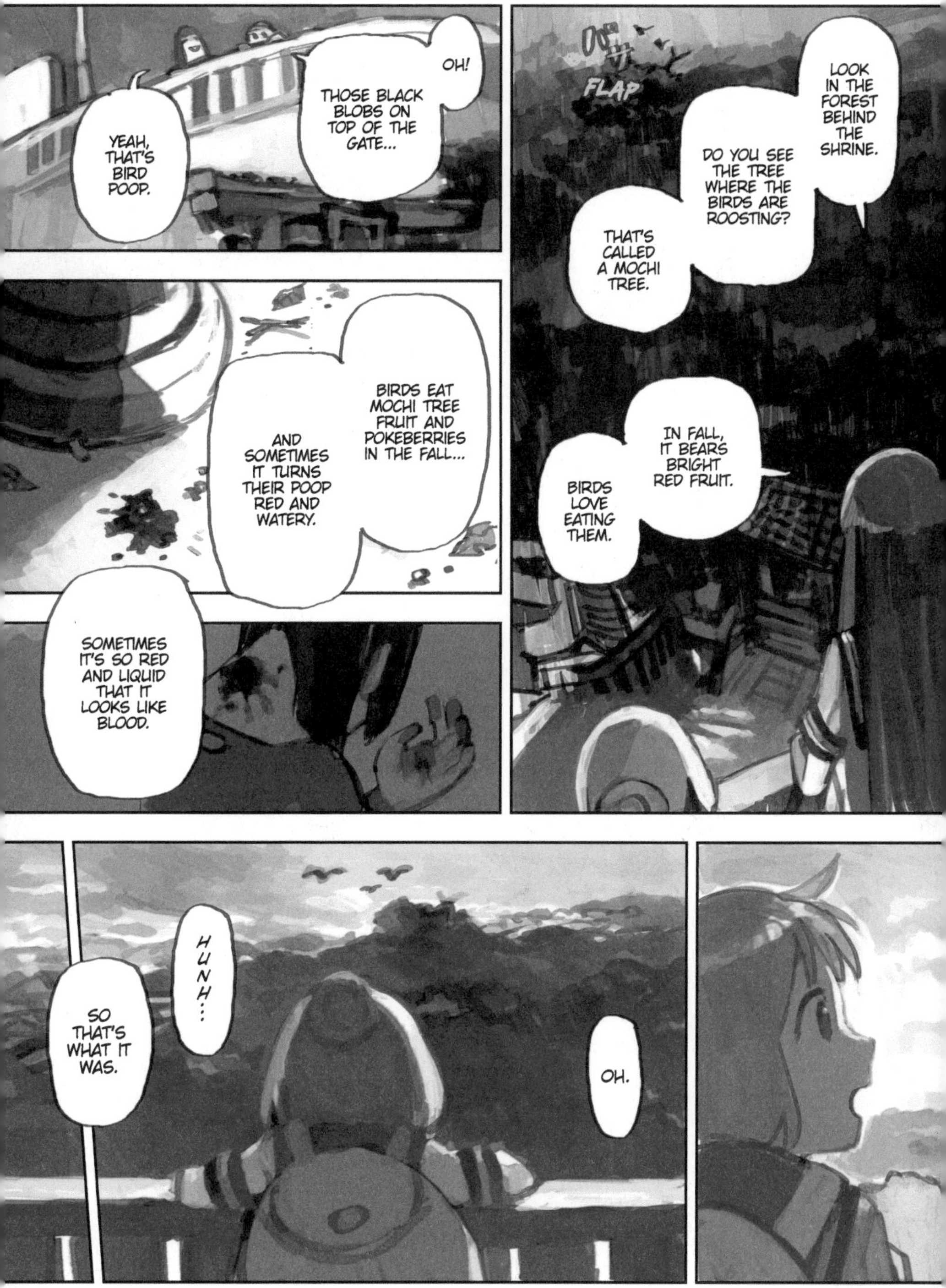
LOOK IN THE FOREST BEHIND THE SHRINE.
FLAP
DO YOU SEE THE TREE WHERE THE BIRDS ARE ROOSTING?
THAT'S CALLED A MOCHI TREE.
IN FALL, IT BEARS BRIGHT RED FRUIT.
BIRDS LOVE EATING THEM.
OH!
THOSE BLACK BLOBS ON TOP OF THE GATE...
YEAH, THAT'S BIRD POOP.
BIRDS EAT MOCHI TREE FRUIT AND POKEBERRIES IN THE FALL...
AND SOMETIMES IT TURNS THEIR POOP RED AND WATERY.
SOMETIMES IT'S SO RED AND LIQUID THAT IT LOOKS LIKE BLOOD.
OH.
HUNH...
SO THAT'S WHAT IT WAS.

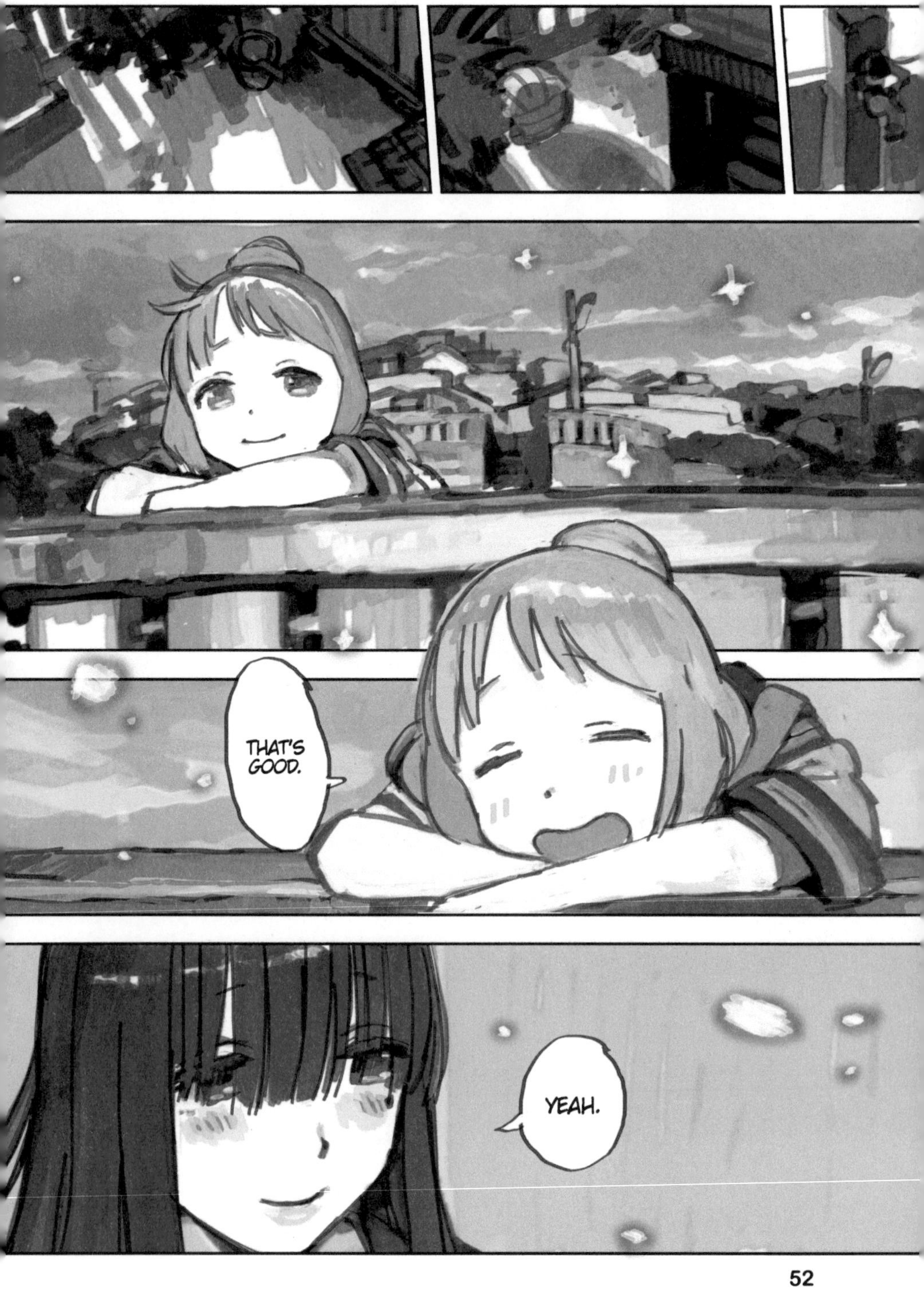
THAT'S GOOD.
YEAH.

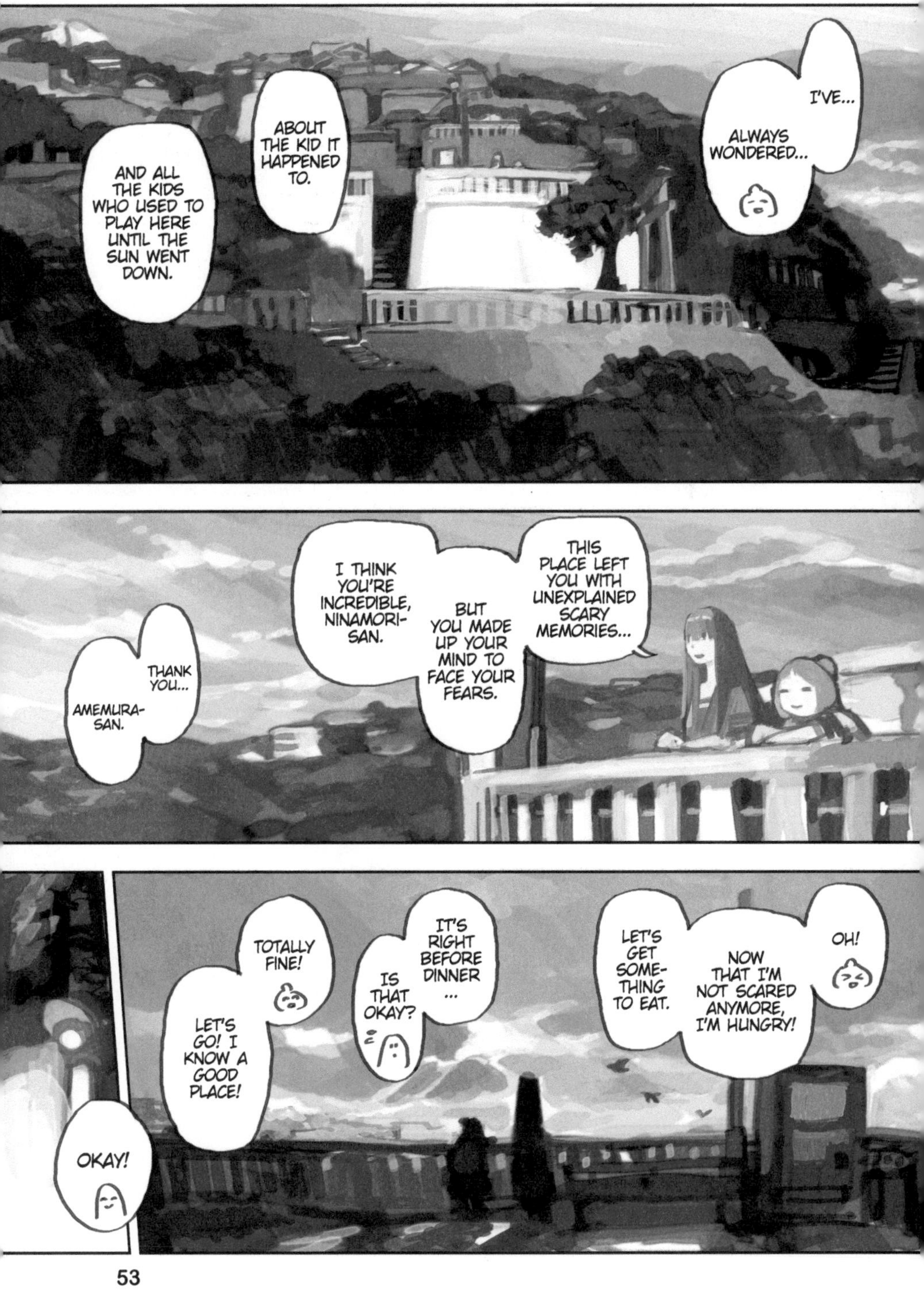
I'VE... ALWAYS WONDERED...
ABOUT THE KID IT HAPPENED TO.
AND ALL THE KIDS WHO USED TO PLAY HERE UNTIL THE SUN WENT DOWN.
THIS PLACE LEFT YOU WITH UNEXPLAINED SCARY MEMORIES...
BUT YOU MADE UP YOUR MIND TO FACE YOUR FEARS.
I THINK YOU'RE INCREDIBLE, NINAMORI-SAN.
THANK YOU... AMEMURA-SAN.
OH!
NOW THAT I'M NOT SCARED ANYMORE, I'M HUNGRY!
LET'S GET SOME-THING TO EAT.
IT'S RIGHT BEFORE DINNER...
IS THAT OKAY?
TOTALLY FINE!
LET'S GO! I KNOW A GOOD PLACE!
OKAY!

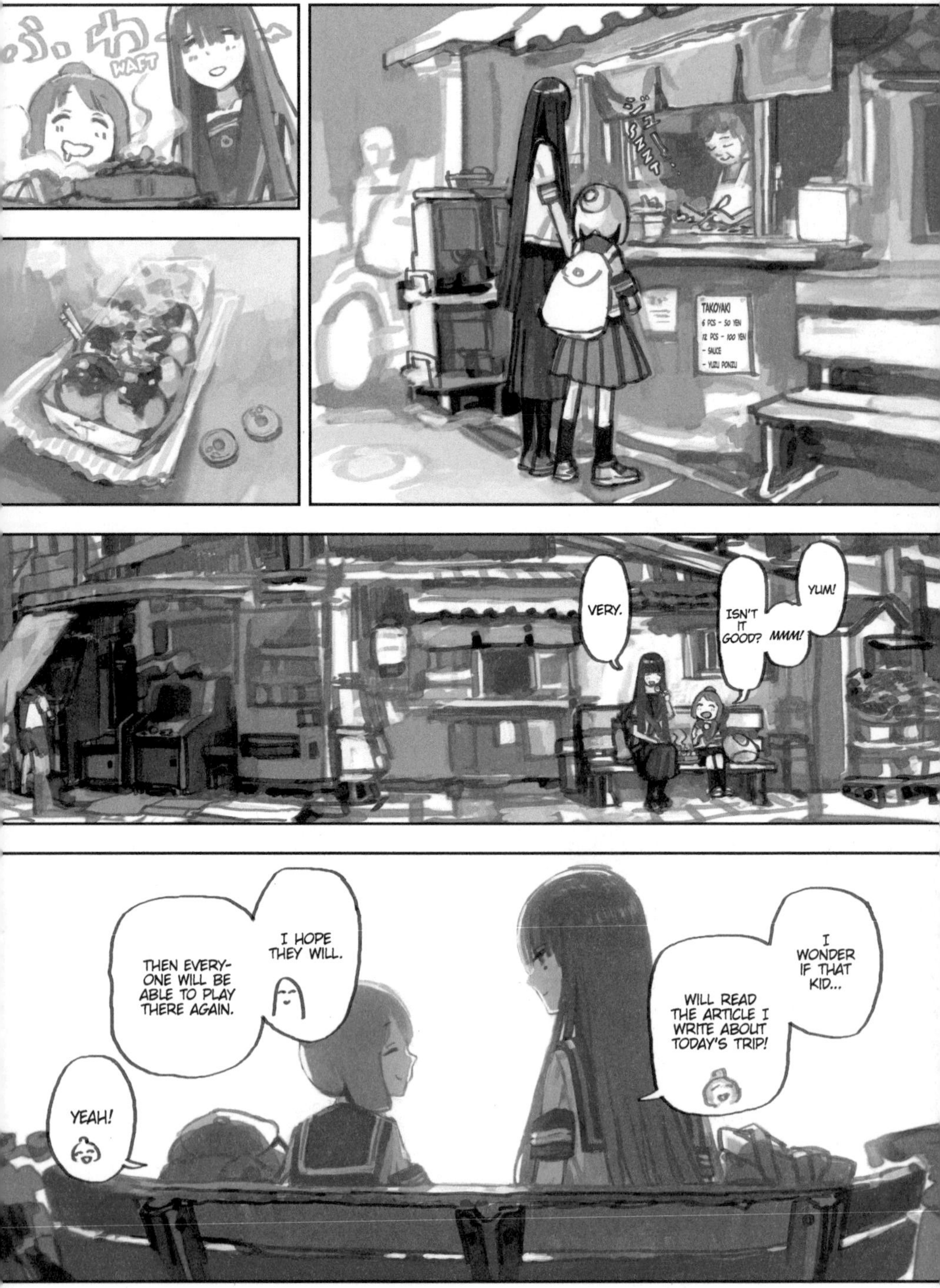
ジュー…
SNNNT
TAKOYAKI
6 PCS - 50 YEN
12 PCS - 100 YEN
- SAUCE
- YUZU PONZU
ふわ
WAFT
YUM!
MMM!
ISN'T IT GOOD?
VERY.
I WONDER IF THAT KID...
WILL READ THE ARTICLE I WRITE ABOUT TODAY'S TRIP!
I HOPE THEY WILL.
THEN EVERY-ONE WILL BE ABLE TO PLAY THERE AGAIN.
YEAH!

NIGHTFALL TRAVELERS

LEAVE ONLY FOOTPRINTS

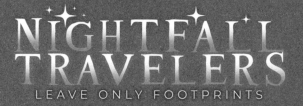

NIGHTFALL TRAVELERS

LEAVE ONLY FOOTPRINTS

Intermission: Good Night Akane-chan @ Coming Home After Chapter 3

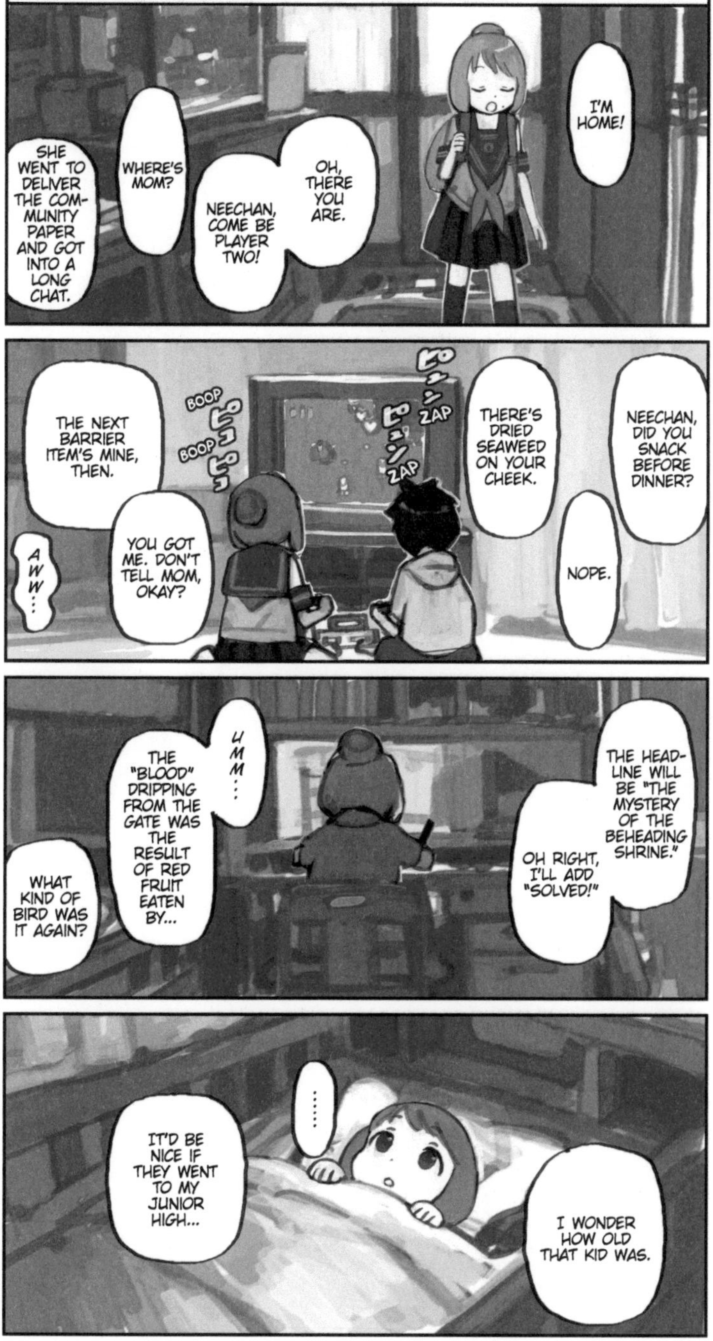

I'M HOME!
OH, THERE YOU ARE.
NEECHAN, COME BE PLAYER TWO!
WHERE'S MOM?
SHE WENT TO DELIVER THE COMMUNITY PAPER AND GOT INTO A LONG CHAT.
NEECHAN, DID YOU SNACK BEFORE DINNER?
NOPE.
THERE'S DRIED SEAWEED ON YOUR CHEEK.
ZAP
ZAP
THE NEXT BARRIER ITEM'S MINE, THEN.
BOOP
BOOP
YOU GOT ME. DON'T TELL MOM, OKAY?
AWW...
THE HEADLINE WILL BE "THE MYSTERY OF THE BEHEADING SHRINE."
OH RIGHT, I'LL ADD "SOLVED!"
UMM...
THE "BLOOD" DRIPPING FROM THE GATE WAS THE RESULT OF RED FRUIT EATEN BY...
WHAT KIND OF BIRD WAS IT AGAIN?
I WONDER HOW OLD THAT KID WAS.
......
IT'D BE NICE IF THEY WENT TO MY JUNIOR HIGH...

NIGHTFALL TRAVELERS

LEAVE ONLY FOOTPRINTS

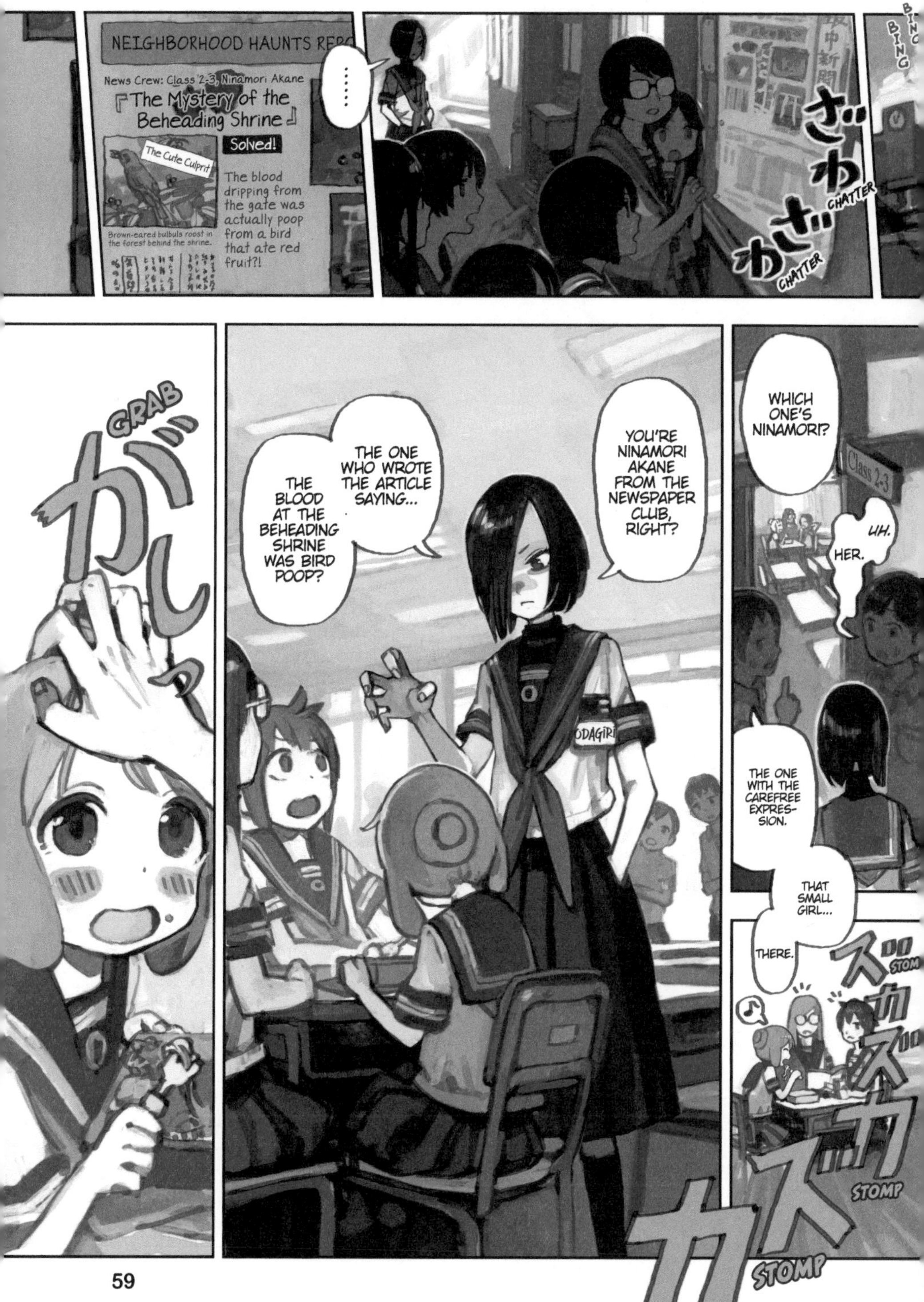
BING
BING
CHATTER
CHATTER
ざわ
ざわ
……
NEIGHBORHOOD HAUNTS REPO
News Crew: Class 2-3, Ninamori Akane
『The Mystery of the Beheading Shrine』
Solved!
The Cute Culprit
Brown-eared bulbuls roost in the forest behind the shrine.
The blood dripping from the gate was actually poop from a bird that ate red fruit?!
WHICH ONE'S NINAMORI?
Class 2-3
UH.
HER.
THE ONE WITH THE CAREFREE EXPRES-SION.
THAT SMALL GIRL...
THERE.
STOM
STOMP
STOMP
カスカスカ
YOU'RE NINAMORI AKANE FROM THE NEWSPAPER CLUB, RIGHT?
THE ONE WHO WROTE THE ARTICLE SAYING...
THE BLOOD AT THE BEHEADING SHRINE WAS BIRD POOP?
ODAGIRI
GRAB
がしっ

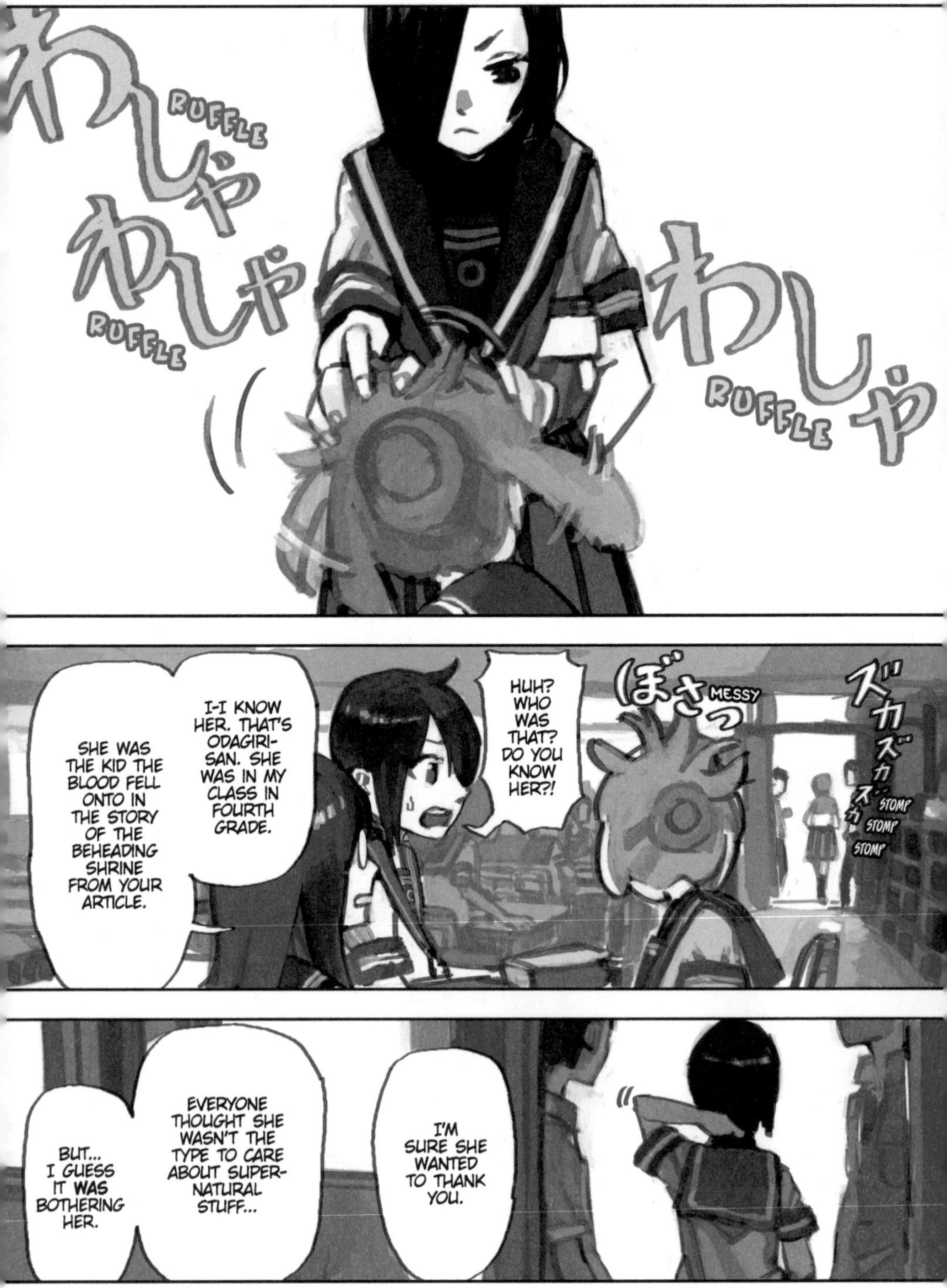
わしゃ
RUFFLE
わしゃ
RUFFLE
わしゃ
RUFFLE
ズカズカズカ
STOMP STOMP STOMP
ぼさっ
MESSY
HUH? WHO WAS THAT? DO YOU KNOW HER?!
I-I KNOW HER. THAT'S ODAGIRI-SAN. SHE WAS IN MY CLASS IN FOURTH GRADE.
SHE WAS THE KID THE BLOOD FELL ONTO IN THE STORY OF THE BEHEADING SHRINE FROM YOUR ARTICLE.
I'M SURE SHE WANTED TO THANK YOU.
EVERYONE THOUGHT SHE WASN'T THE TYPE TO CARE ABOUT SUPER-NATURAL STUFF...
BUT... I GUESS IT WAS BOTHERING HER.

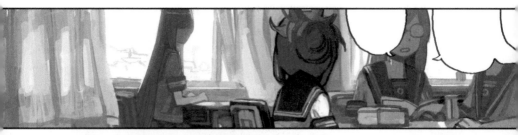

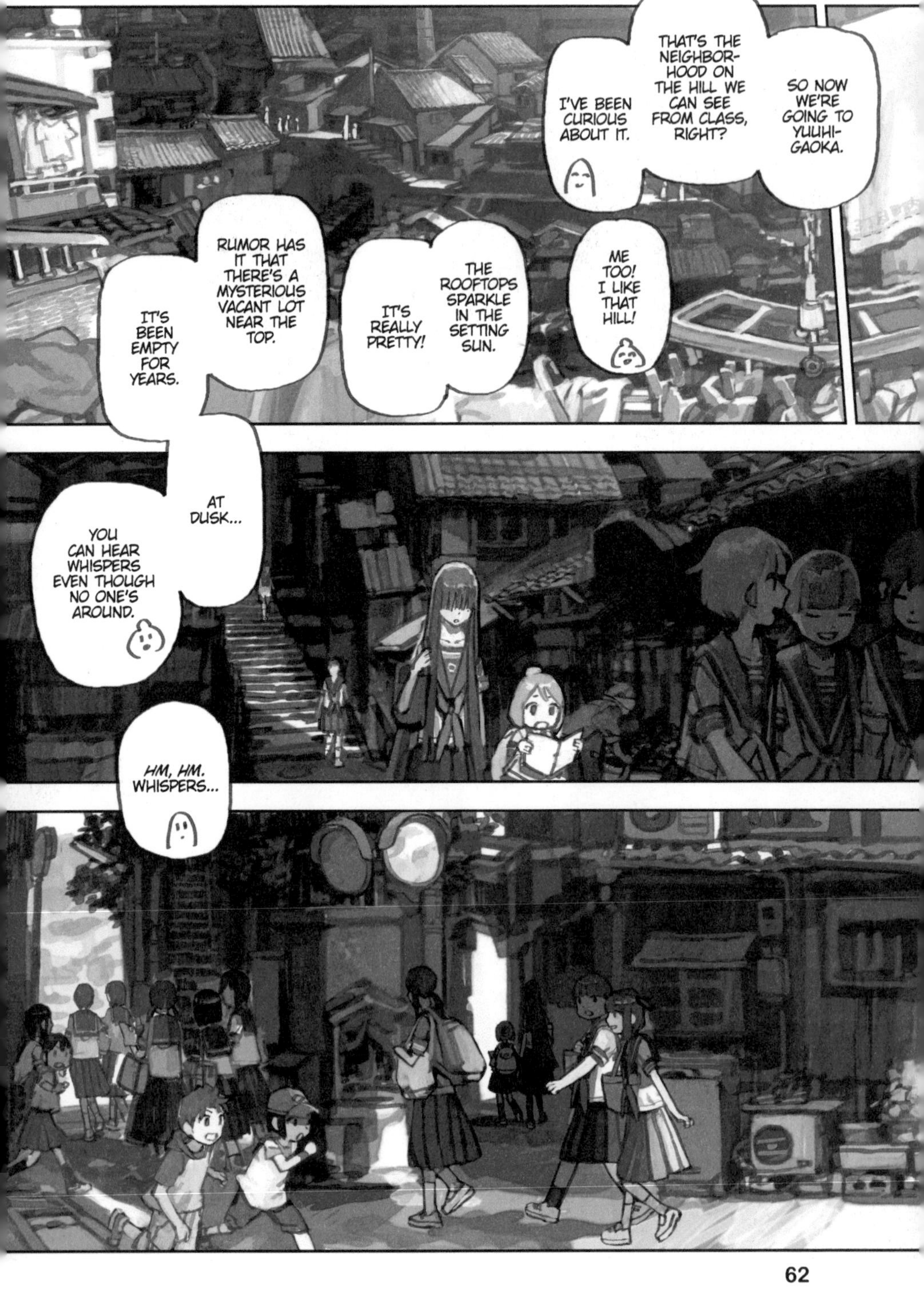
SO NOW WE'RE GOING TO YUUHI-GAOKA.
THAT'S THE NEIGHBOR-HOOD ON THE HILL WE CAN SEE FROM CLASS, RIGHT?
I'VE BEEN CURIOUS ABOUT IT.
ME TOO! I LIKE THAT HILL!
THE ROOFTOPS SPARKLE IN THE SETTING SUN.
IT'S REALLY PRETTY!
RUMOR HAS IT THAT THERE'S A MYSTERIOUS VACANT LOT NEAR THE TOP.
IT'S BEEN EMPTY FOR YEARS.
AT DUSK...
YOU CAN HEAR WHISPERS EVEN THOUGH NO ONE'S AROUND.
HM, HM. WHISPERS...

Chapter 4: The Whispers in the Vacant Lot in Yuuhigaoka

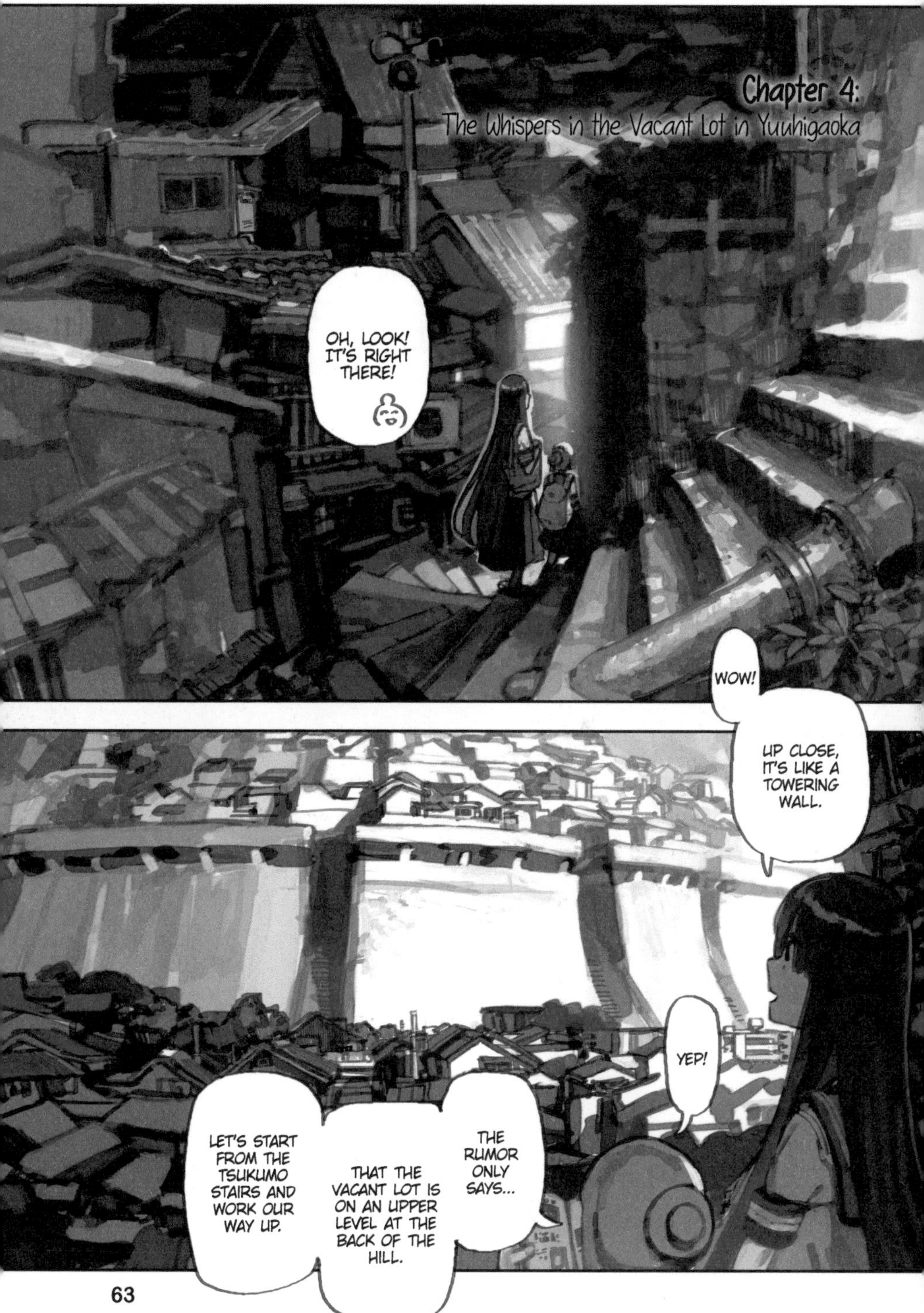
OH, LOOK! IT'S RIGHT THERE!
WOW!
UP CLOSE, IT'S LIKE A TOWERING WALL.
YEP!
THE RUMOR ONLY SAYS...
THAT THE VACANT LOT IS ON AN UPPER LEVEL AT THE BACK OF THE HILL.
LET'S START FROM THE TSUKUMO STAIRS AND WORK OUR WAY UP.

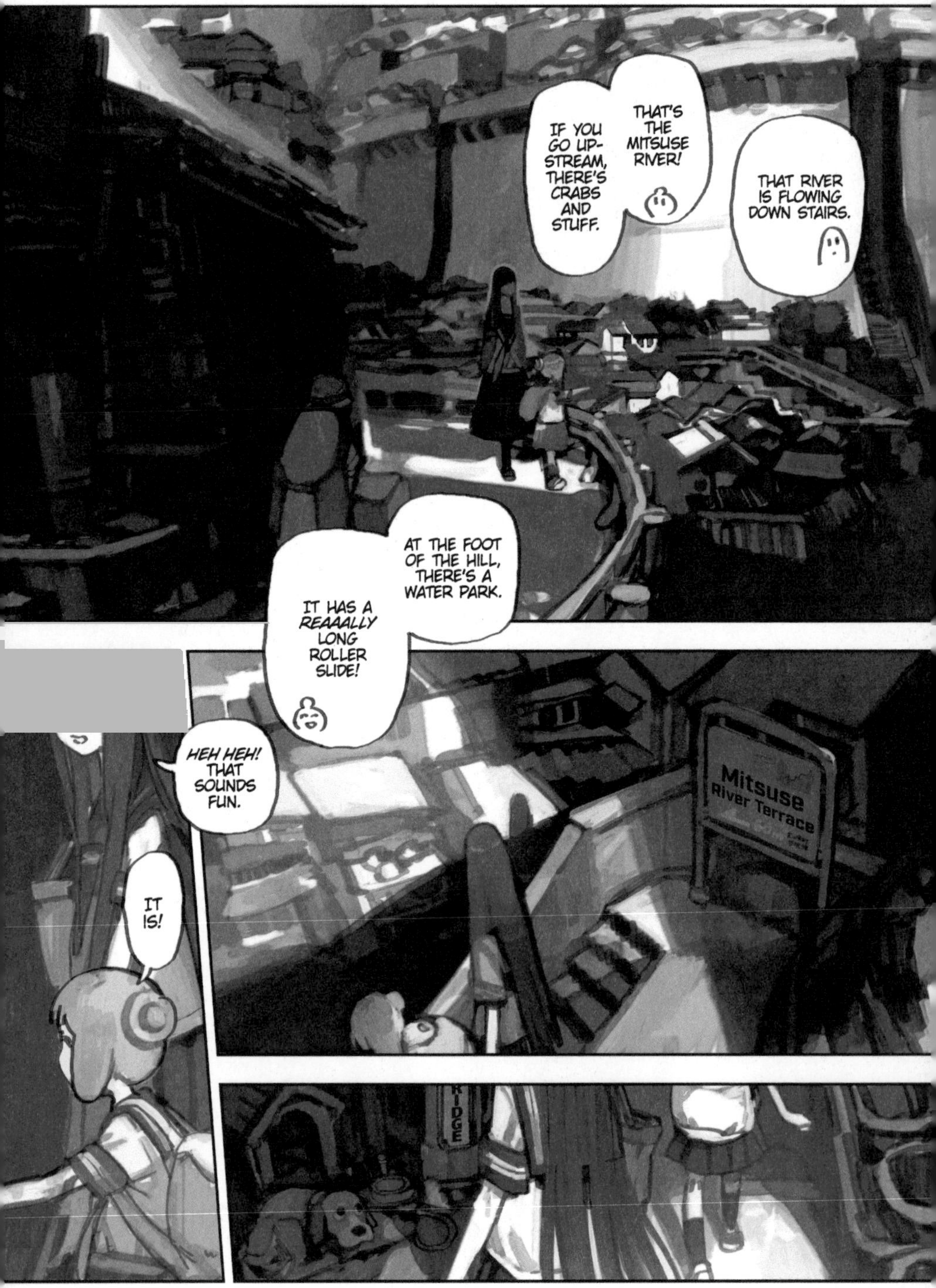
THAT RIVER IS FLOWING DOWN STAIRS.
THAT'S THE MITSUSE RIVER!
IF YOU GO UP-STREAM, THERE'S CRABS AND STUFF.
AT THE FOOT OF THE HILL, THERE'S A WATER PARK.
IT HAS A *REAAALLY* LONG ROLLER SLIDE!
Mitsuse River Terrace
HEH HEH! THAT SOUNDS FUN.
IT IS!

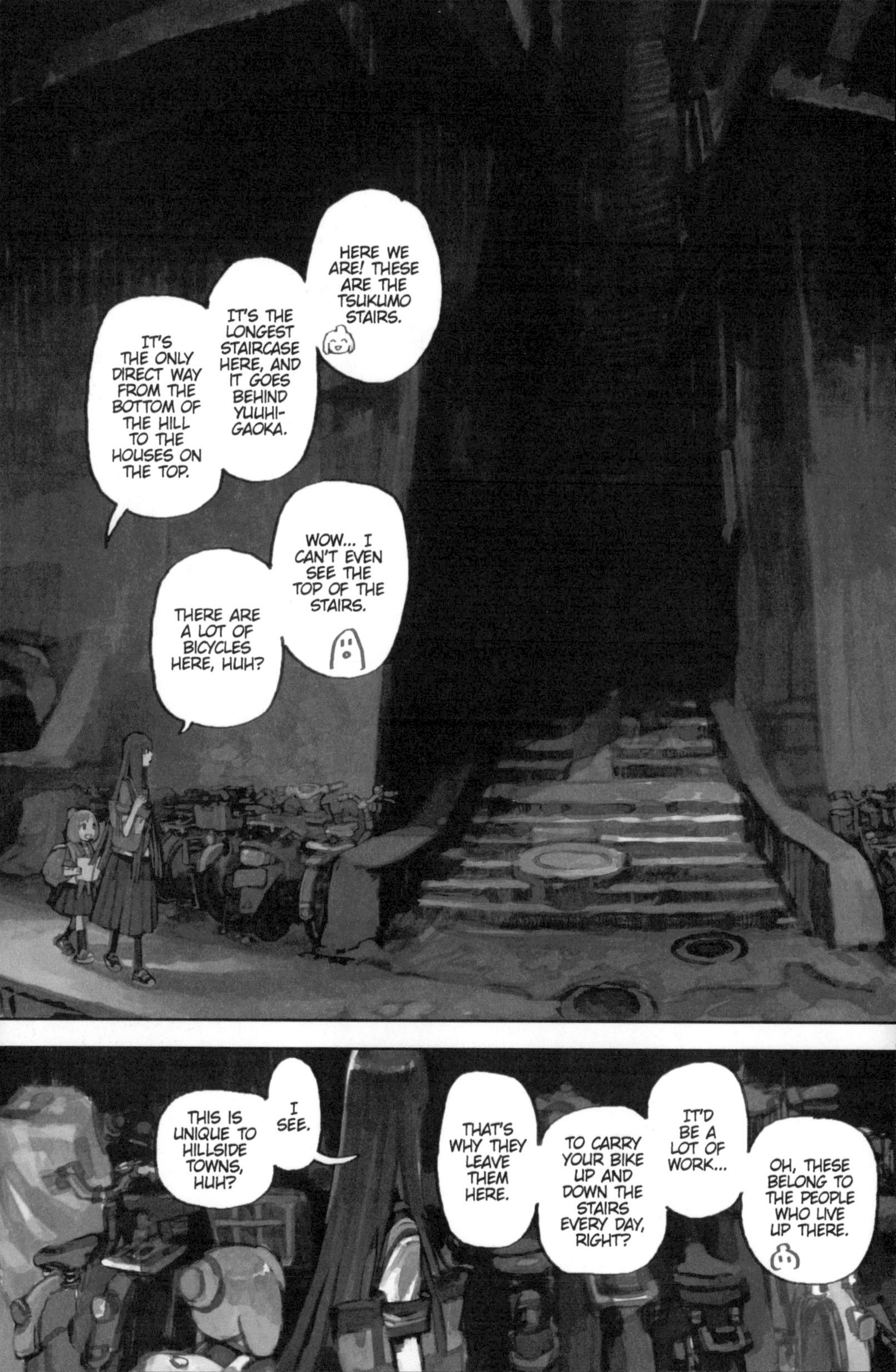
HERE WE ARE! THESE ARE THE TSUKUMO STAIRS.
IT'S THE LONGEST STAIRCASE HERE, AND IT GOES BEHIND YUUHI-GAOKA.
IT'S THE ONLY DIRECT WAY FROM THE BOTTOM OF THE HILL TO THE HOUSES ON THE TOP.
WOW... I CAN'T EVEN SEE THE TOP OF THE STAIRS.
THERE ARE A LOT OF BICYCLES HERE, HUH?
OH, THESE BELONG TO THE PEOPLE WHO LIVE UP THERE.
IT'D BE A LOT OF WORK...
TO CARRY YOUR BIKE UP AND DOWN THE STAIRS EVERY DAY, RIGHT?
THAT'S WHY THEY LEAVE THEM HERE.
I SEE.
THIS IS UNIQUE TO HILLSIDE TOWNS, HUH?

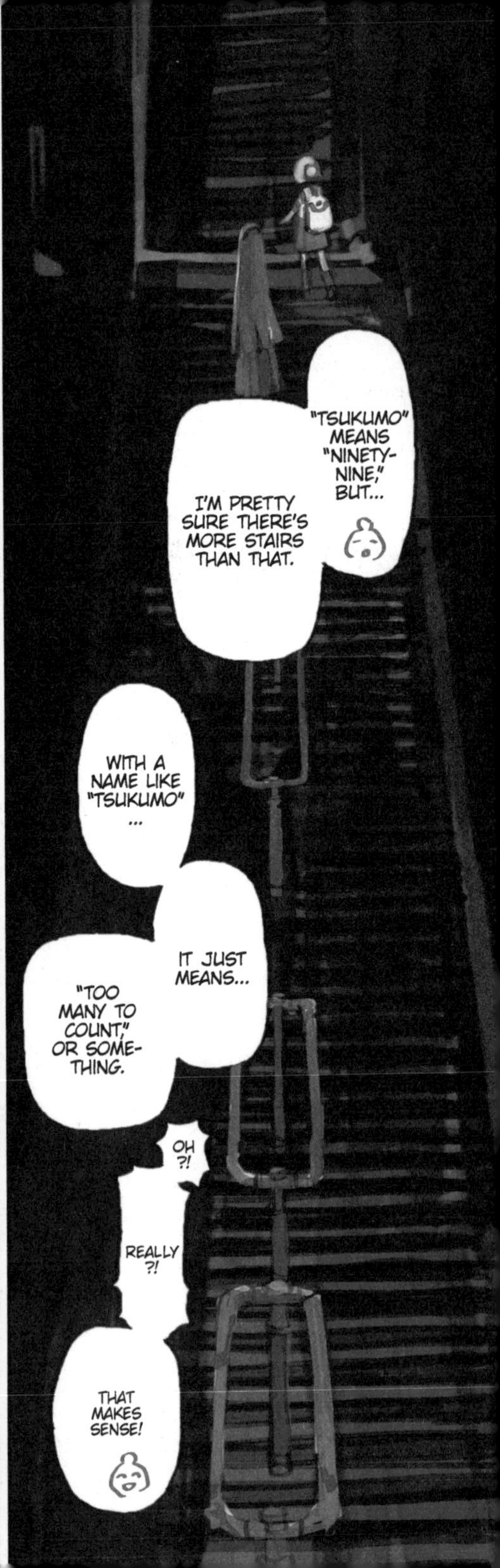
"TSUKUMO" MEANS "NINETY-NINE," BUT...
I'M PRETTY SURE THERE'S MORE STAIRS THAN THAT.
WITH A NAME LIKE "TSUKUMO"...
IT JUST MEANS...
"TOO MANY TO COUNT," OR SOME-THING.
OH?!
REALLY?!
THAT MAKES SENSE!
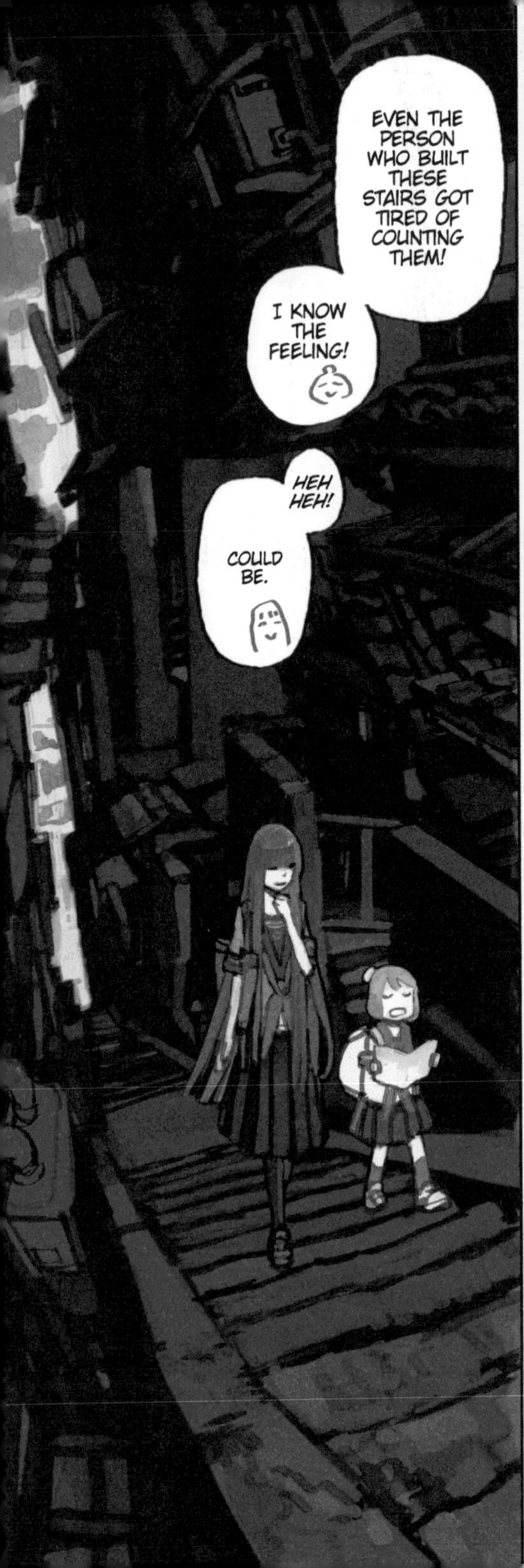
EVEN THE PERSON WHO BUILT THESE STAIRS GOT TIRED OF COUNTING THEM!
I KNOW THE FEELING!
HEH HEH!
COULD BE.

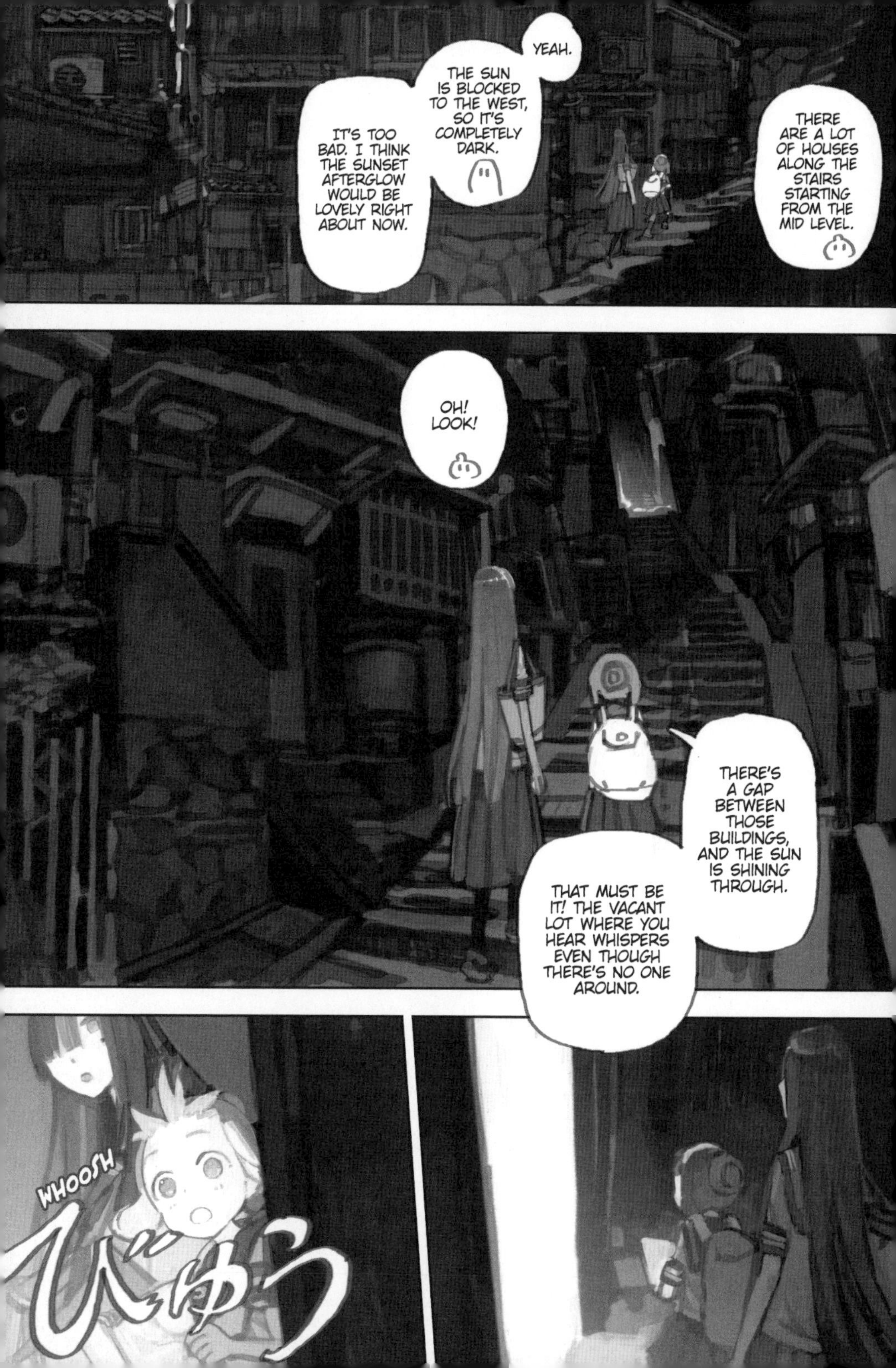
THERE ARE A LOT OF HOUSES ALONG THE STAIRS STARTING FROM THE MID LEVEL.
YEAH.
THE SUN IS BLOCKED TO THE WEST, SO IT'S COMPLETELY DARK.
IT'S TOO BAD. I THINK THE SUNSET AFTERGLOW WOULD BE LOVELY RIGHT ABOUT NOW.
OH! LOOK!
THERE'S A GAP BETWEEN THOSE BUILDINGS, AND THE SUN IS SHINING THROUGH.
THAT MUST BE IT! THE VACANT LOT WHERE YOU HEAR WHISPERS EVEN THOUGH THERE'S NO ONE AROUND.
WHOOSH
びゅう

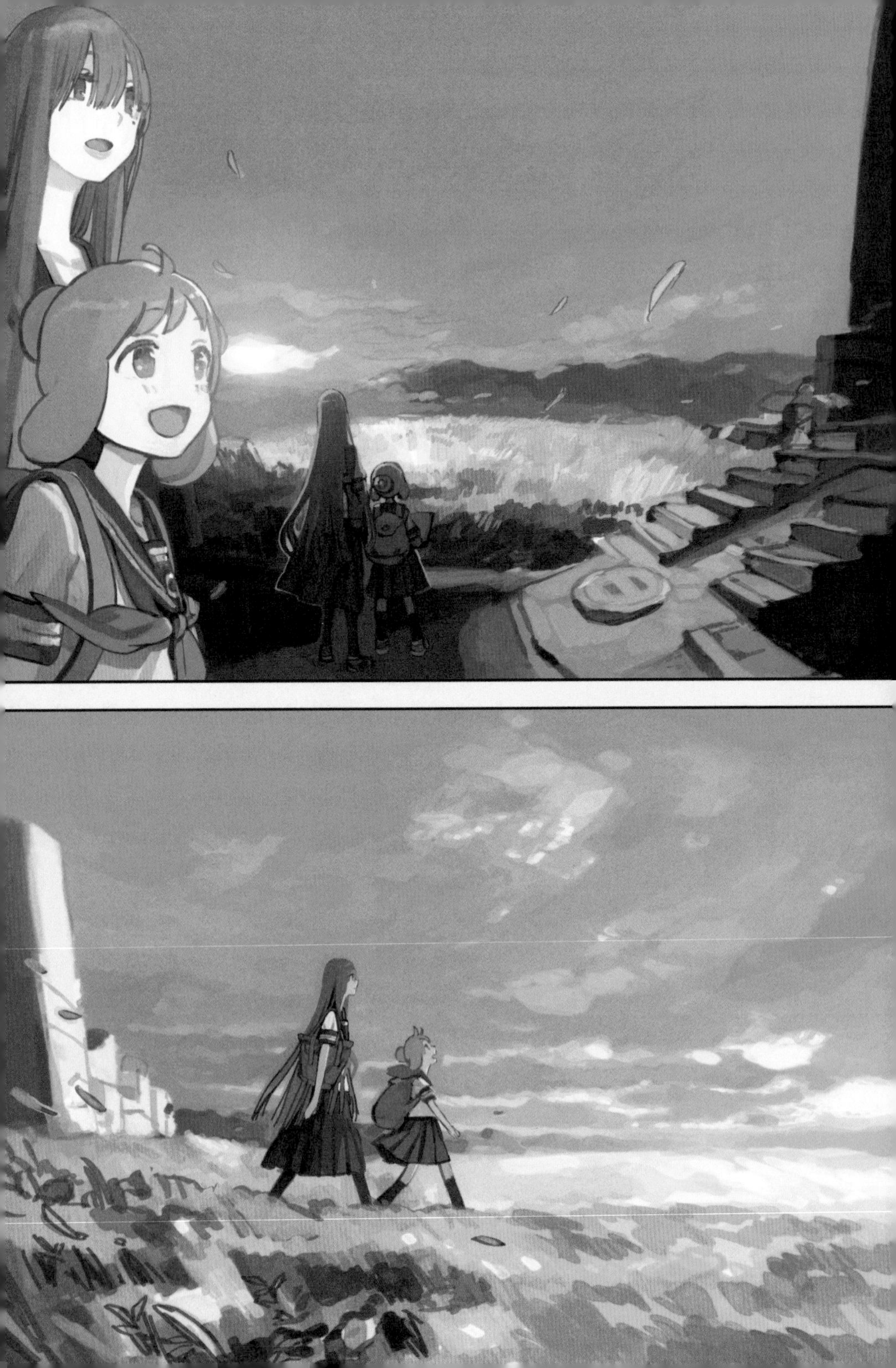

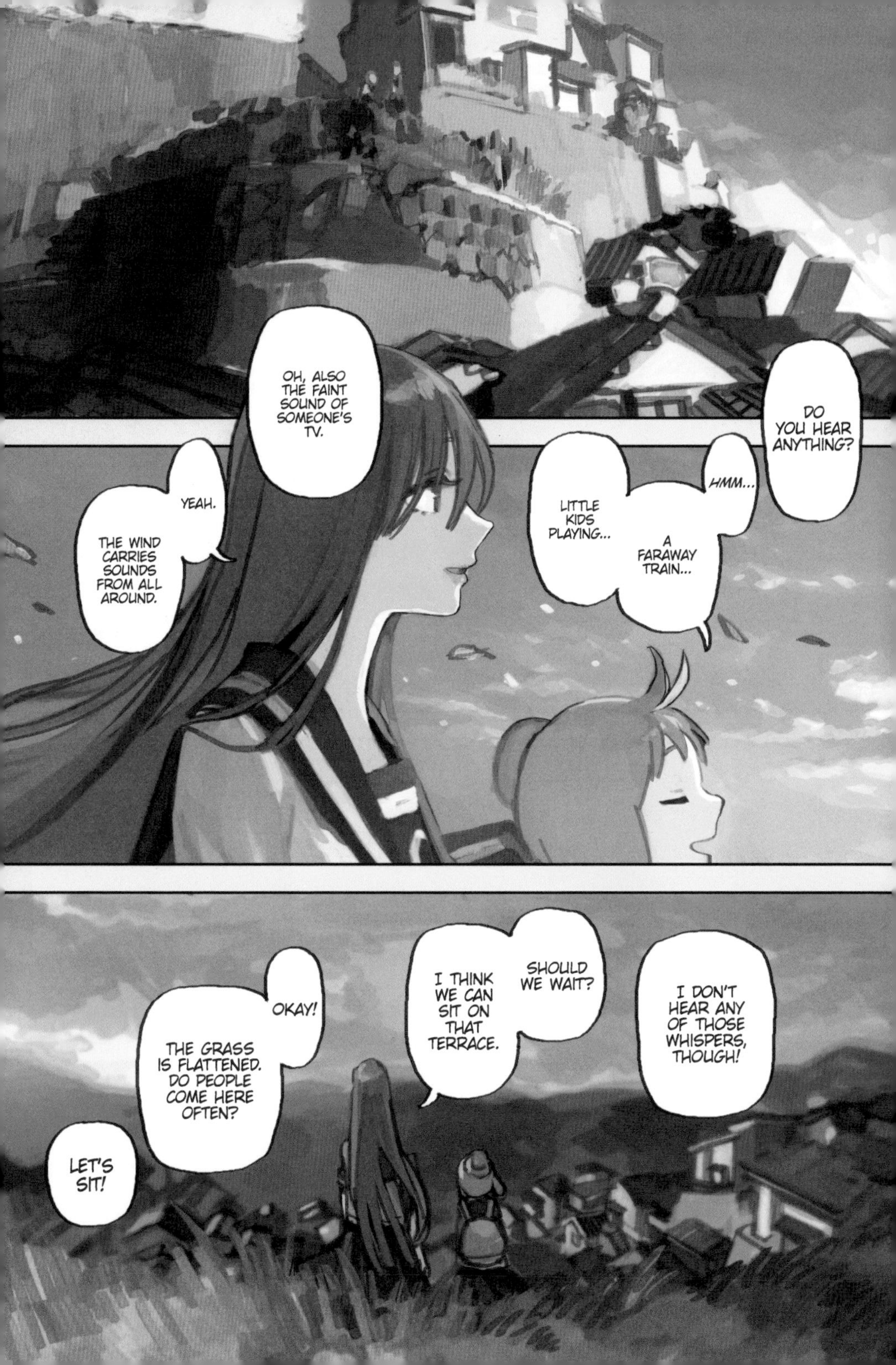
DO YOU HEAR ANYTHING?
HMM... LITTLE KIDS PLAYING... A FARAWAY TRAIN...
OH, ALSO THE FAINT SOUND OF SOMEONE'S TV.
YEAH. THE WIND CARRIES SOUNDS FROM ALL AROUND.
I DON'T HEAR ANY OF THOSE WHISPERS, THOUGH!
SHOULD WE WAIT? I THINK WE CAN SIT ON THAT TERRACE.
OKAY! THE GRASS IS FLATTENED. DO PEOPLE COME HERE OFTEN?
LET'S SIT!

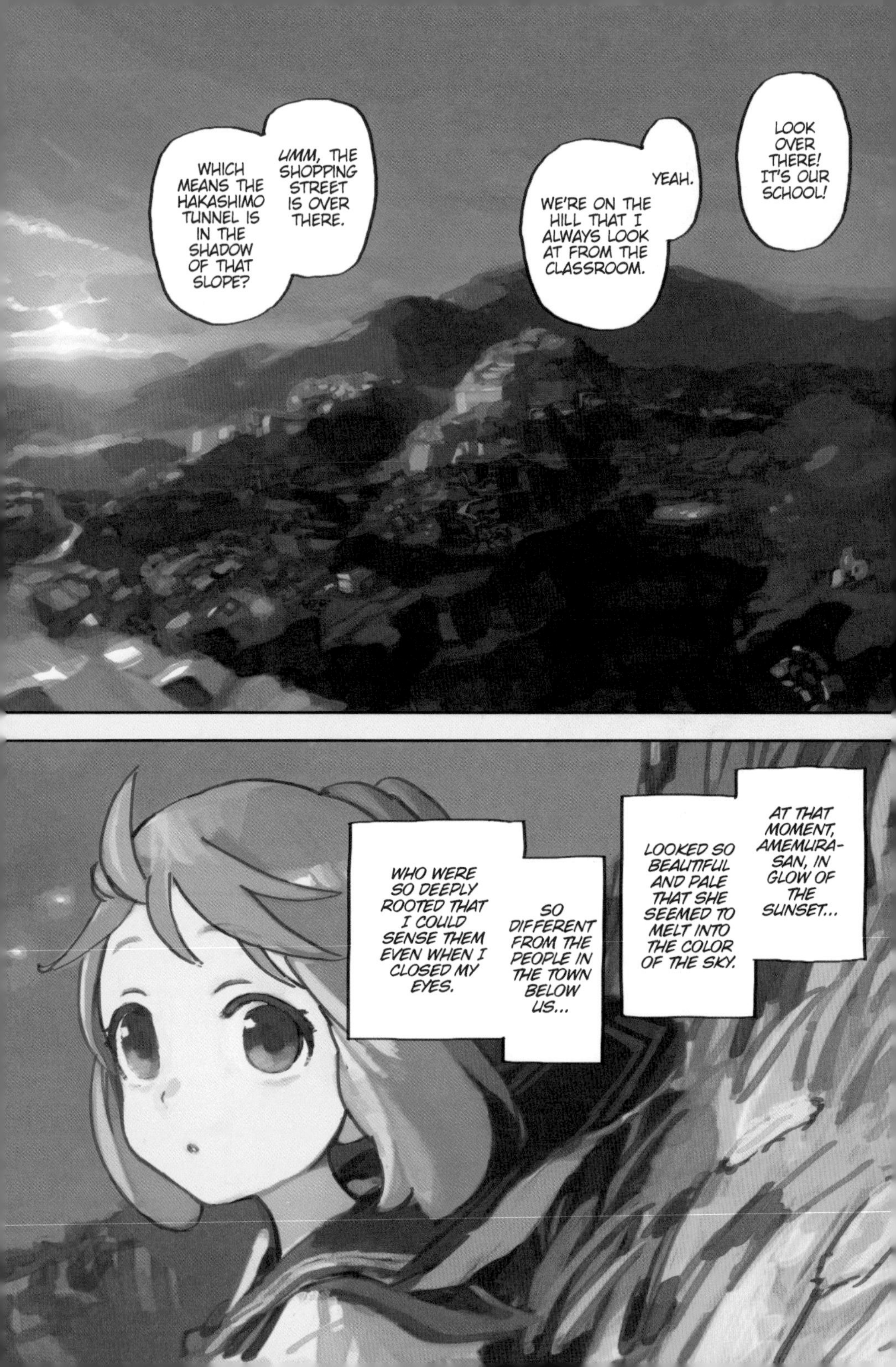
LOOK OVER THERE! IT'S OUR SCHOOL!
YEAH.
WE'RE ON THE HILL THAT I ALWAYS LOOK AT FROM THE CLASSROOM.
UMM, THE SHOPPING STREET IS OVER THERE.
WHICH MEANS THE HAKASHIMO TUNNEL IS IN THE SHADOW OF THAT SLOPE?
AT THAT MOMENT, AMEMURA-SAN, IN GLOW OF THE SUNSET...
LOOKED SO BEAUTIFUL AND PALE THAT SHE SEEMED TO MELT INTO THE COLOR OF THE SKY.
SO DIFFERENT FROM THE PEOPLE IN THE TOWN BELOW US...
WHO WERE SO DEEPLY ROOTED THAT I COULD SENSE THEM EVEN WHEN I CLOSED MY EYES.

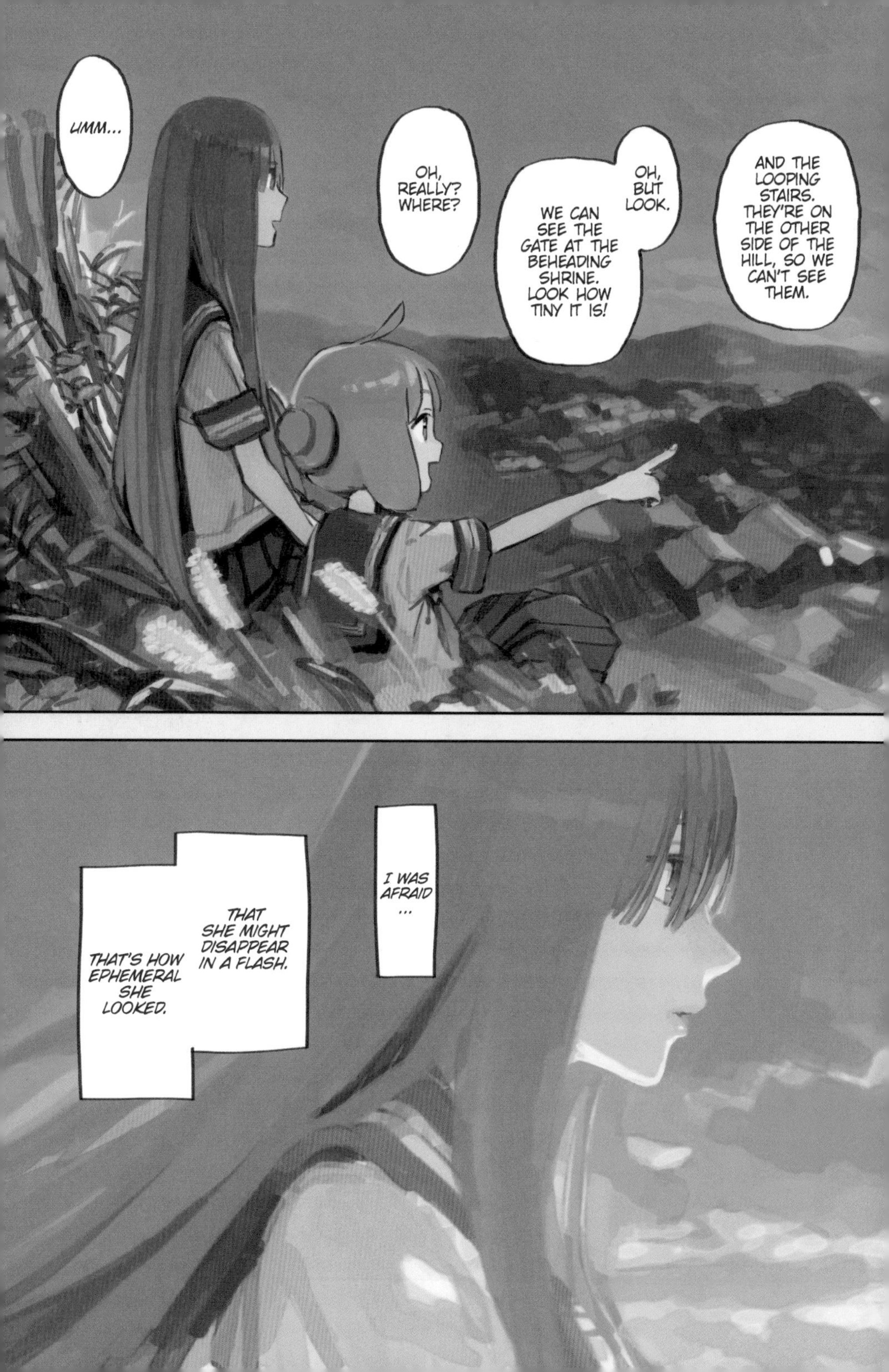
AND THE LOOPING STAIRS. THEY'RE ON THE OTHER SIDE OF THE HILL, SO WE CAN'T SEE THEM.
OH, BUT LOOK.
WE CAN SEE THE GATE AT THE BEHEADING SHRINE. LOOK HOW TINY IT IS!
OH, REALLY? WHERE?
UMM...
I WAS AFRAID ...
THAT SHE MIGHT DISAPPEAR IN A FLASH.
THAT'S HOW EPHEMERAL SHE LOOKED.

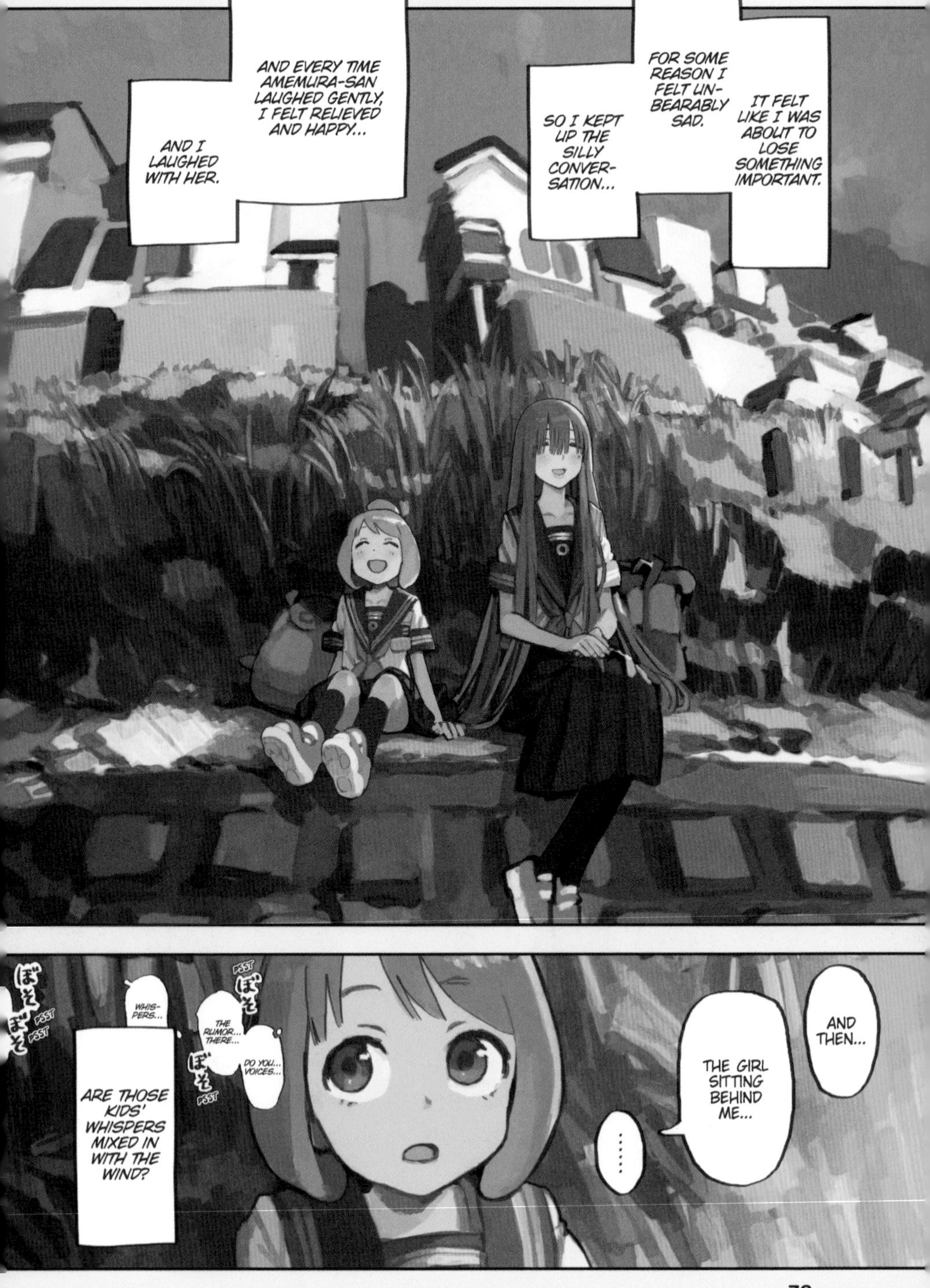
IT FELT LIKE I WAS ABOUT TO LOSE SOMETHING IMPORTANT.
FOR SOME REASON I FELT UN-BEARABLY SAD.
SO I KEPT UP THE SILLY CONVER-SATION...
AND EVERY TIME AMEMURA-SAN LAUGHED GENTLY, I FELT RELIEVED AND HAPPY...
AND I LAUGHED WITH HER.
AND THEN...
THE GIRL SITTING BEHIND ME...
......
ぼそ PSST
ぼそ PSST
DO YOU... VOICES...
THE RUMOR... THERE...
WHISPERS...
ARE THOSE KIDS' WHISPERS MIXED IN WITH THE WIND?
ぼそぼそ PSST PSST

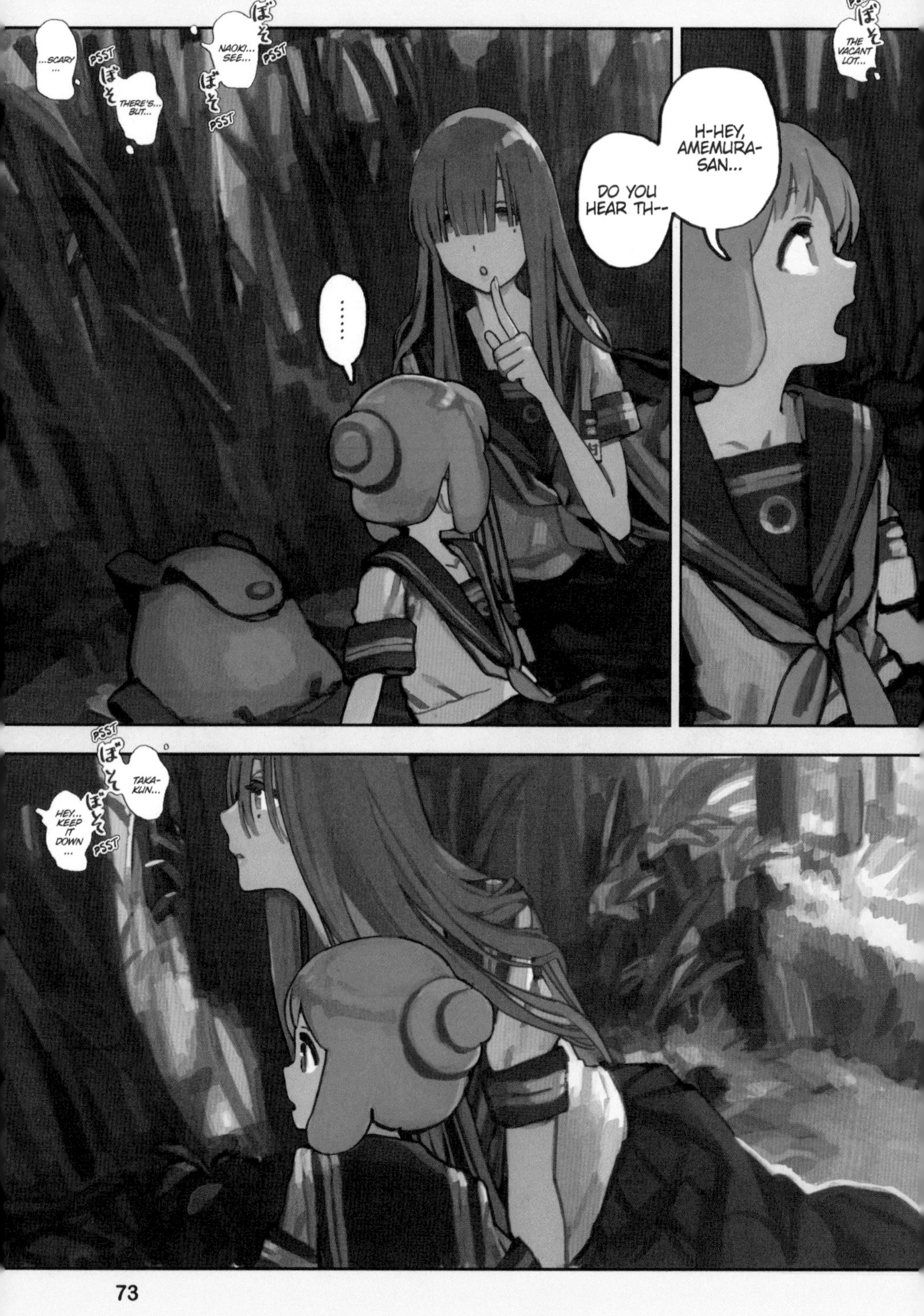
PSST ぼそ
THE VACANT LOT...
H-HEY, AMEMURA-SAN...
DO YOU HEAR TH--
ぼそ PSST
NAOKI... SEE...
ぼそ PSST
THERE'S... BUT...
PSST ぼそ
...SCARY...
......
PSST ぼそ
TAKA-KUN...
ぼそ PSST
HEY... KEEP IT DOWN...

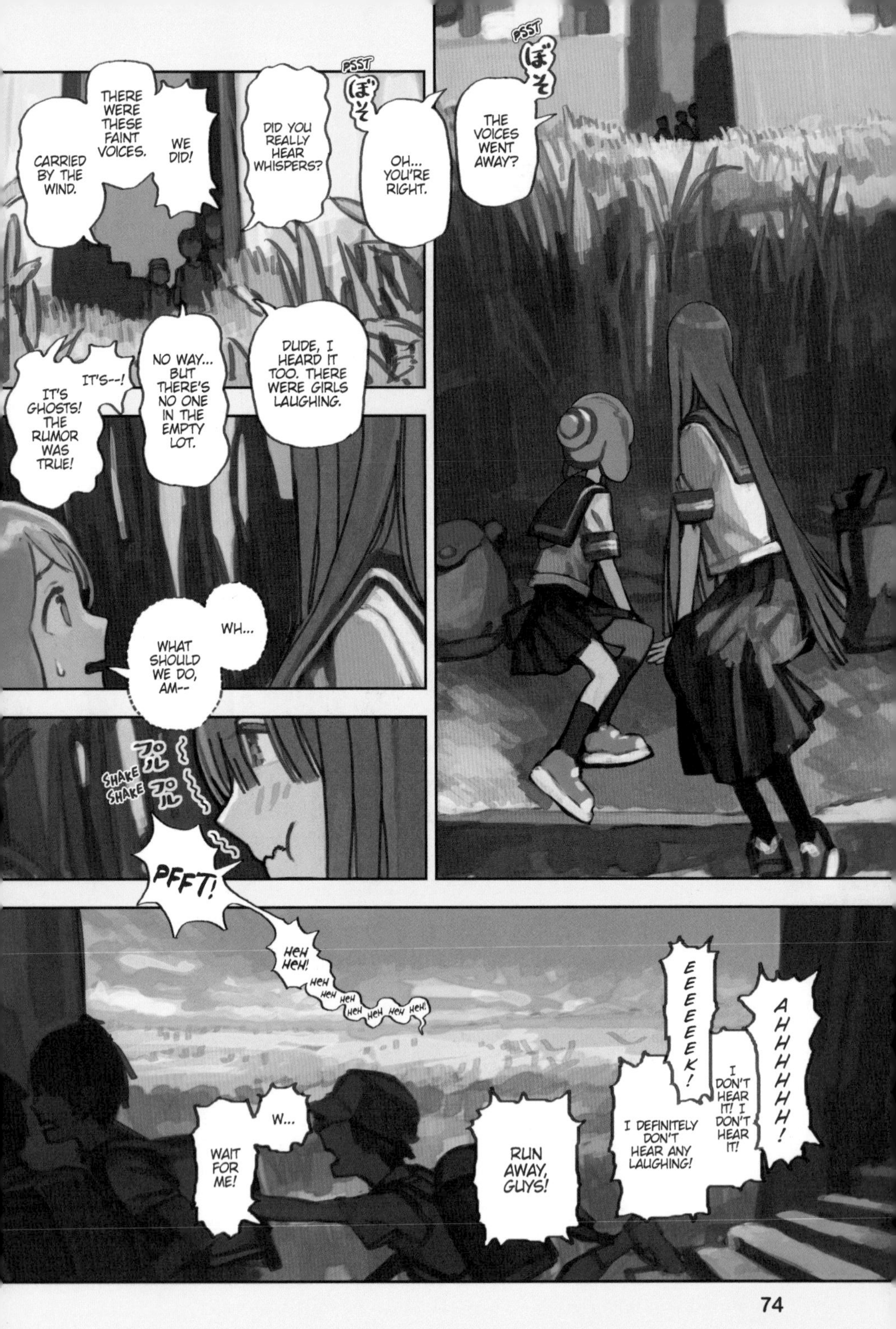
PSST
ぼそ
THE VOICES WENT AWAY?
PSST
ぼそ
OH... YOU'RE RIGHT.
DID YOU REALLY HEAR WHISPERS?
WE DID!
THERE WERE THESE FAINT VOICES.
CARRIED BY THE WIND.
DUDE, I HEARD IT TOO. THERE WERE GIRLS LAUGHING.
NO WAY... BUT THERE'S NO ONE IN THE EMPTY LOT.
IT'S--!
IT'S GHOSTS! THE RUMOR WAS TRUE!
WH...
WHAT SHOULD WE DO, AM--
SHAKE SHAKE
プルプル
PFFT!
HEH HEH! HEH HEH HEH HEH HEH HEH HEH!
AHHHHHH!
I DON'T HEAR IT! I DON'T HEAR IT!
EEEEEEK!
I DEFINITELY DON'T HEAR ANY LAUGHING!
RUN AWAY, GUYS!
W...
WAIT FOR ME!

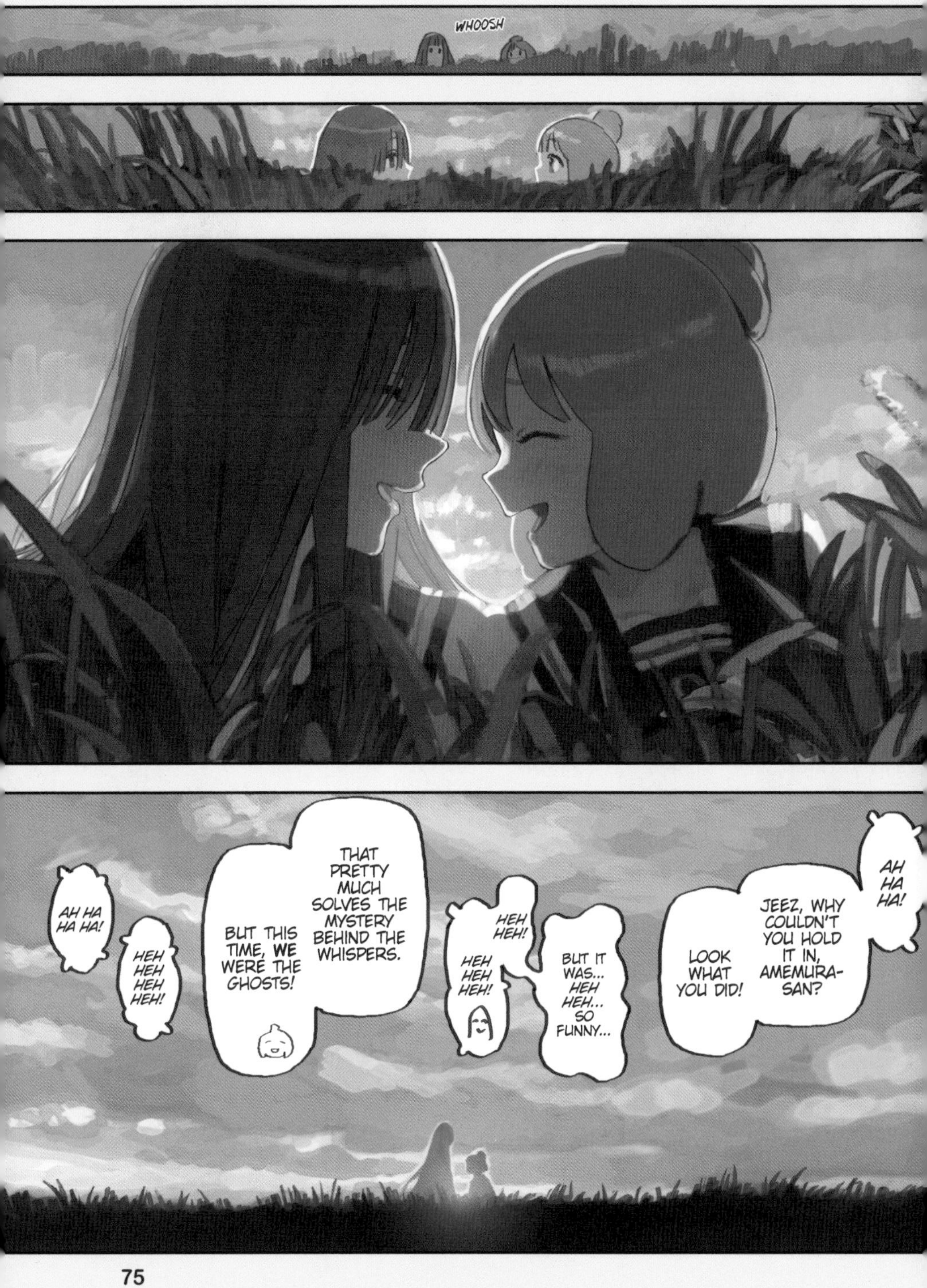
WHOOSH
AH HA HA!
JEEZ, WHY COULDN'T YOU HOLD IT IN, AMEMURA-SAN?
LOOK WHAT YOU DID!
BUT IT WAS... HEH HEH... SO FUNNY...
HEH HEH!
HEH HEH HEH!
THAT PRETTY MUCH SOLVES THE MYSTERY BEHIND THE WHISPERS.
BUT THIS TIME, WE WERE THE GHOSTS!
HEH HEH HEH HEH!
AH HA HA HA!

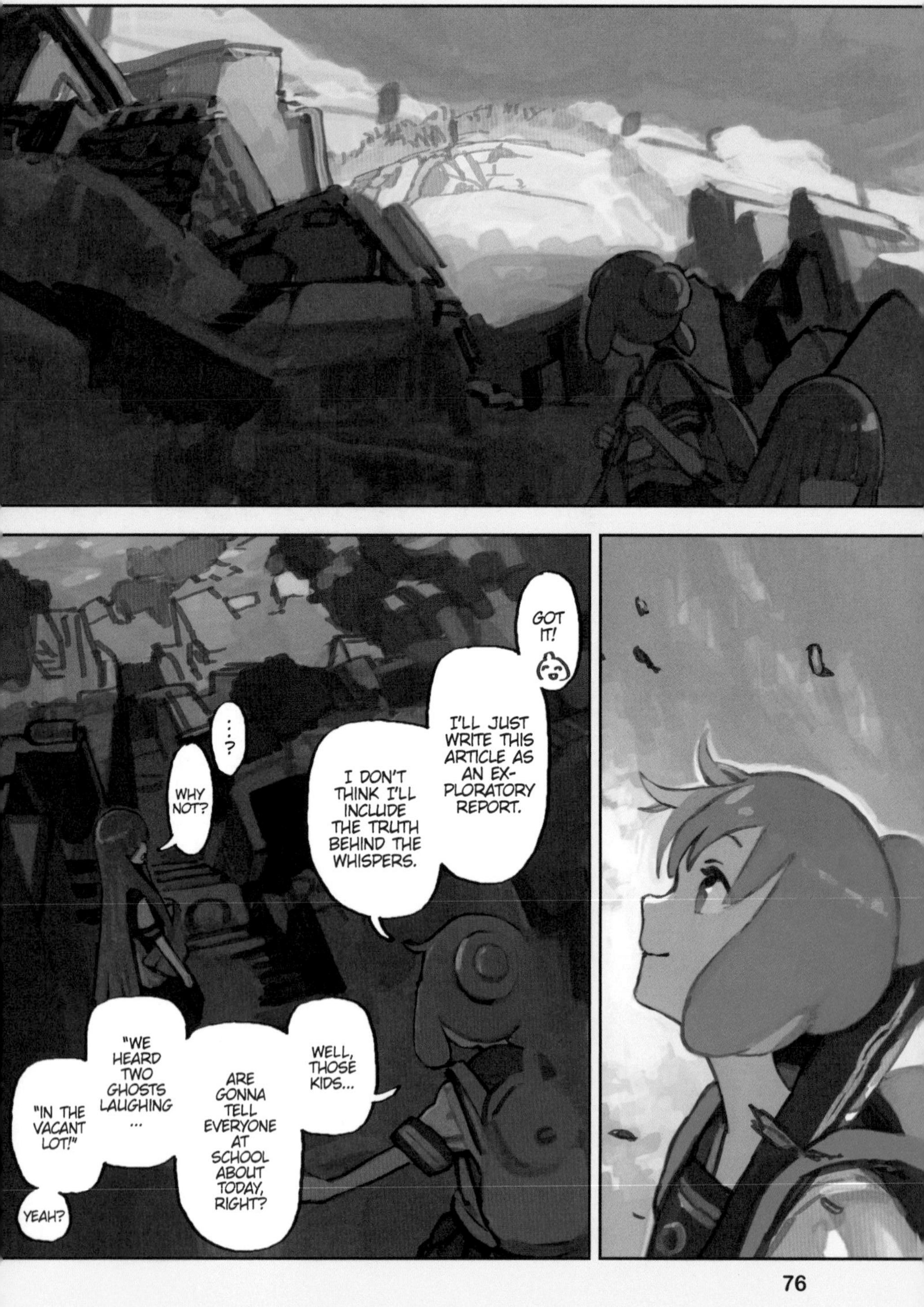
GOT IT!
I'LL JUST WRITE THIS ARTICLE AS AN EX-PLORATORY REPORT.
I DON'T THINK I'LL INCLUDE THE TRUTH BEHIND THE WHISPERS.
...?
WHY NOT?
WELL, THOSE KIDS...
ARE GONNA TELL EVERYONE AT SCHOOL ABOUT TODAY, RIGHT?
"WE HEARD TWO GHOSTS LAUGHING ...
"IN THE VACANT LOT!"
YEAH?

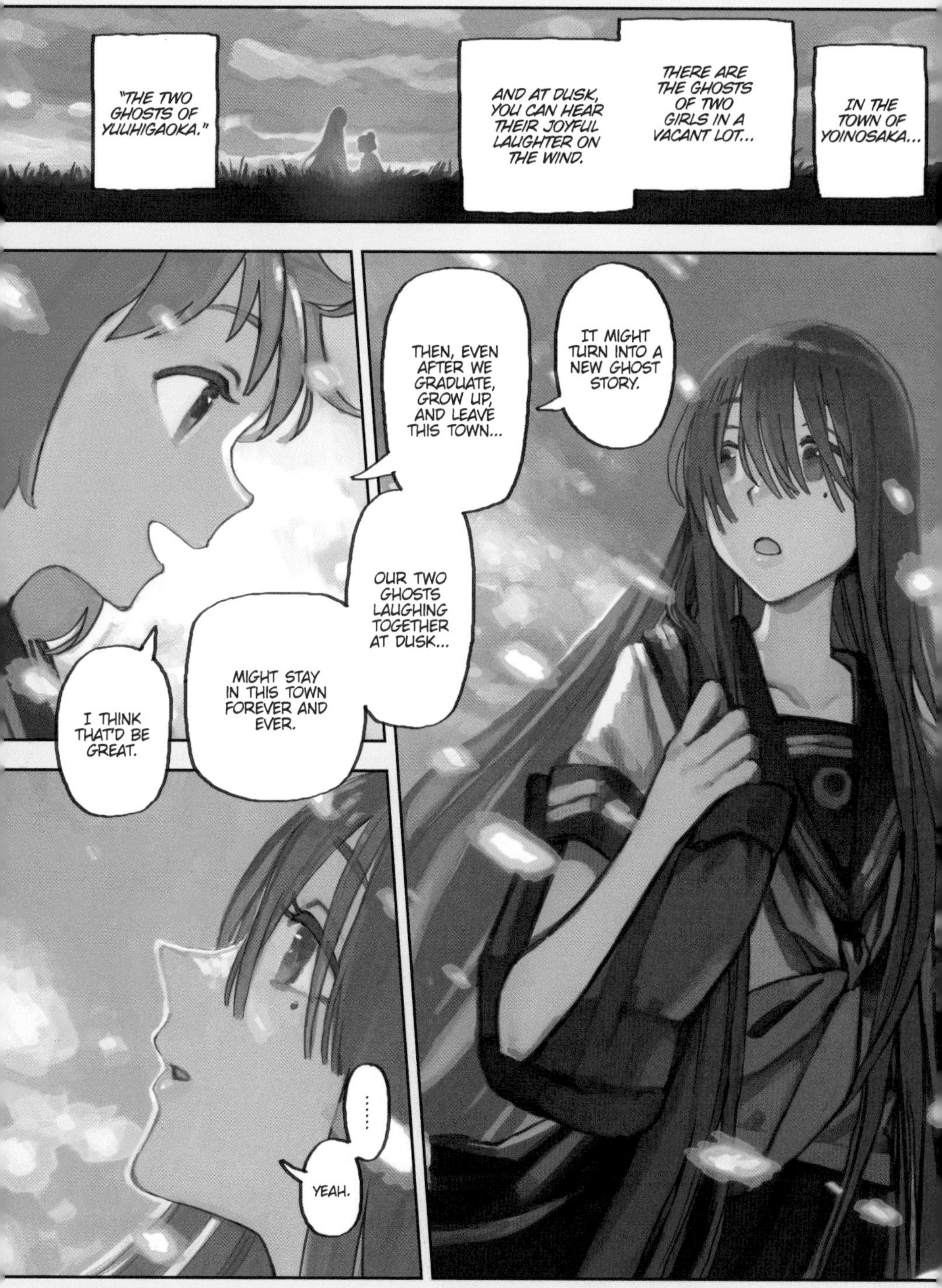
IN THE TOWN OF YOINOSAKA...
THERE ARE THE GHOSTS OF TWO GIRLS IN A VACANT LOT...
AND AT DUSK, YOU CAN HEAR THEIR JOYFUL LAUGHTER ON THE WIND.
"THE TWO GHOSTS OF YUUHIGAOKA."
IT MIGHT TURN INTO A NEW GHOST STORY.
THEN, EVEN AFTER WE GRADUATE, GROW UP, AND LEAVE THIS TOWN...
OUR TWO GHOSTS LAUGHING TOGETHER AT DUSK...
MIGHT STAY IN THIS TOWN FOREVER AND EVER.
I THINK THAT'D BE GREAT.
......
YEAH.

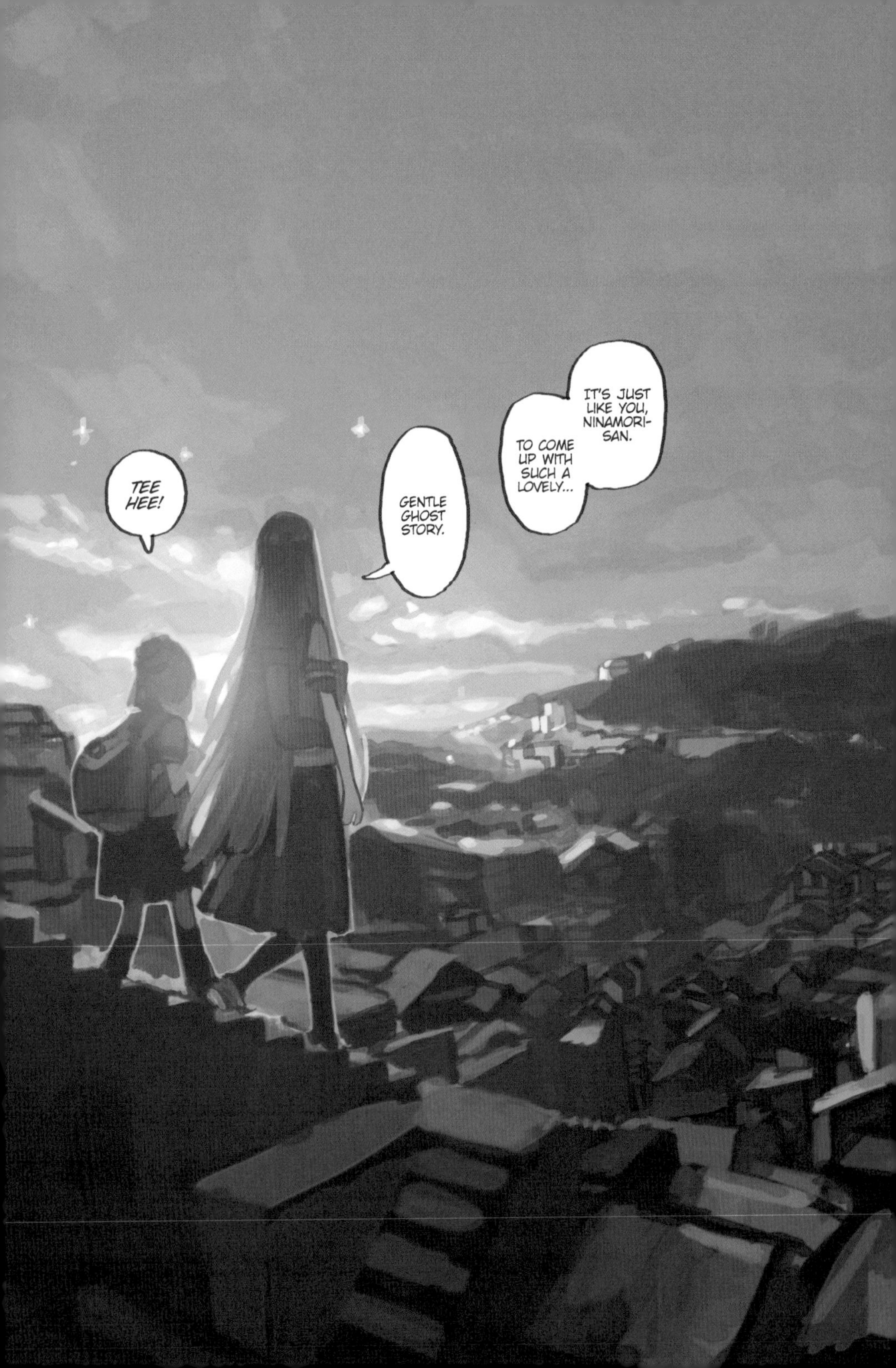
IT'S JUST LIKE YOU, NINAMORI-SAN.
TO COME UP WITH SUCH A LOVELY...
GENTLE GHOST STORY.
TEE HEE!

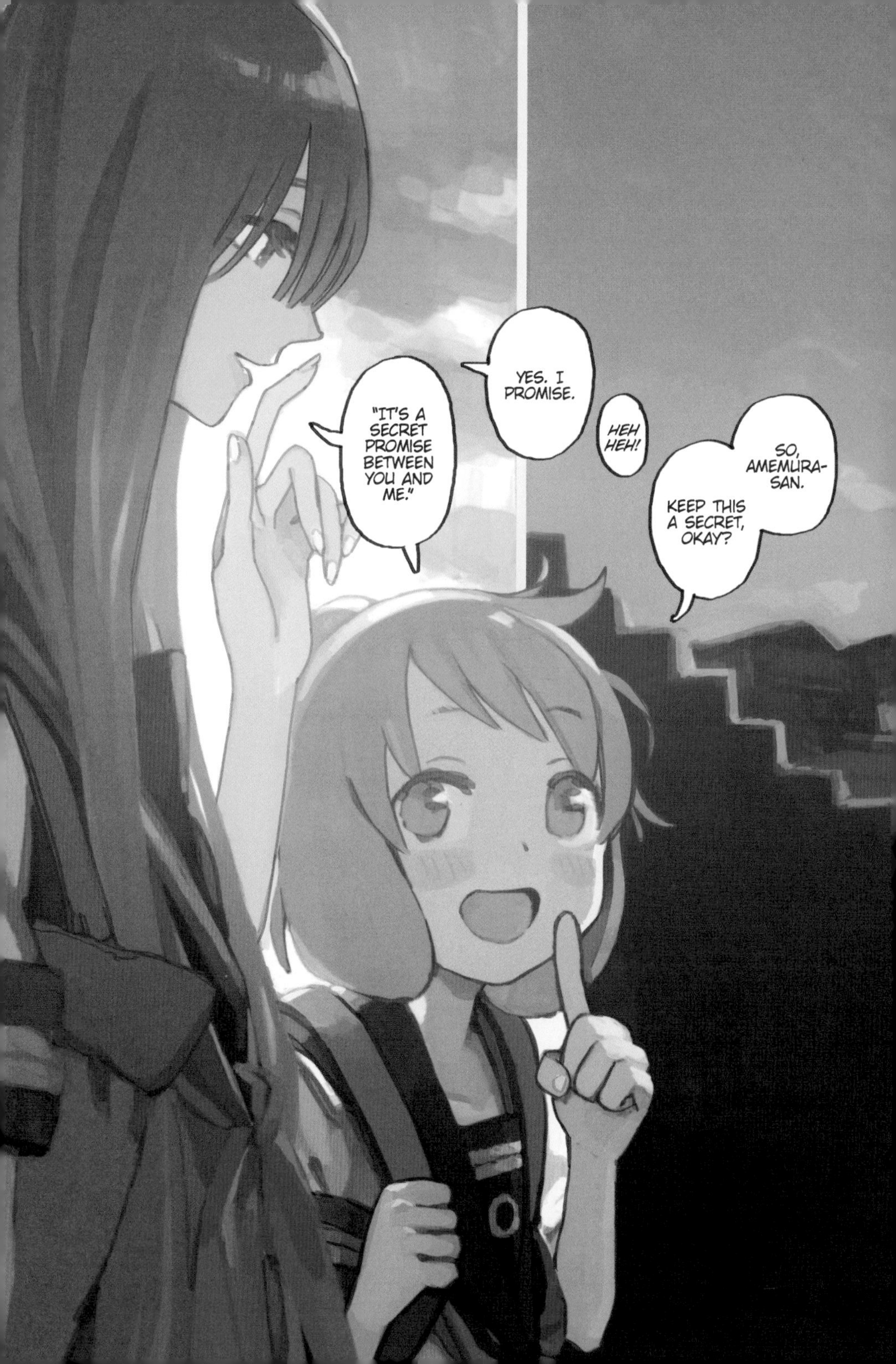
SO, AMEMURA-SAN.
KEEP THIS A SECRET, OKAY?
HEH HEH!
YES. I PROMISE.
"IT'S A SECRET PROMISE BETWEEN YOU AND ME."

Intermission: Good Night Akane-chan @ Coming Home After Chapter 4

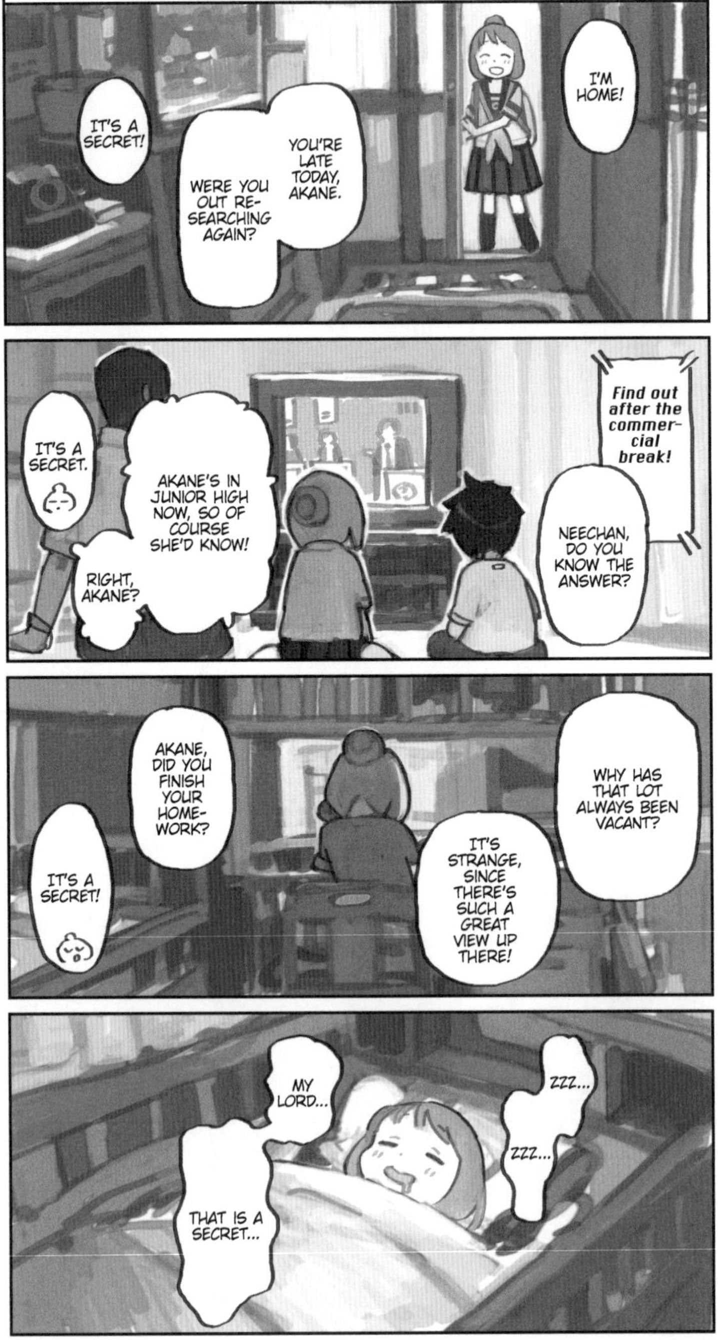
I'M HOME!
YOU'RE LATE TODAY, AKANE.
WERE YOU OUT RE-SEARCHING AGAIN?
IT'S A SECRET!
Find out after the commercial break!
NEECHAN, DO YOU KNOW THE ANSWER?
AKANE'S IN JUNIOR HIGH NOW, SO OF COURSE SHE'D KNOW!
RIGHT, AKANE?
IT'S A SECRET.
WHY HAS THAT LOT ALWAYS BEEN VACANT?
IT'S STRANGE, SINCE THERE'S SUCH A GREAT VIEW UP THERE!
AKANE, DID YOU FINISH YOUR HOME-WORK?
IT'S A SECRET!
ZZZ...
ZZZ...
MY LORD...
THAT IS A SECRET...

NIGHTFALL TRAVELERS

LEAVE ONLY FOOTPRINTS

NIGHTFALL TRAVELERS

LEAVE ONLY FOOTPRINTS

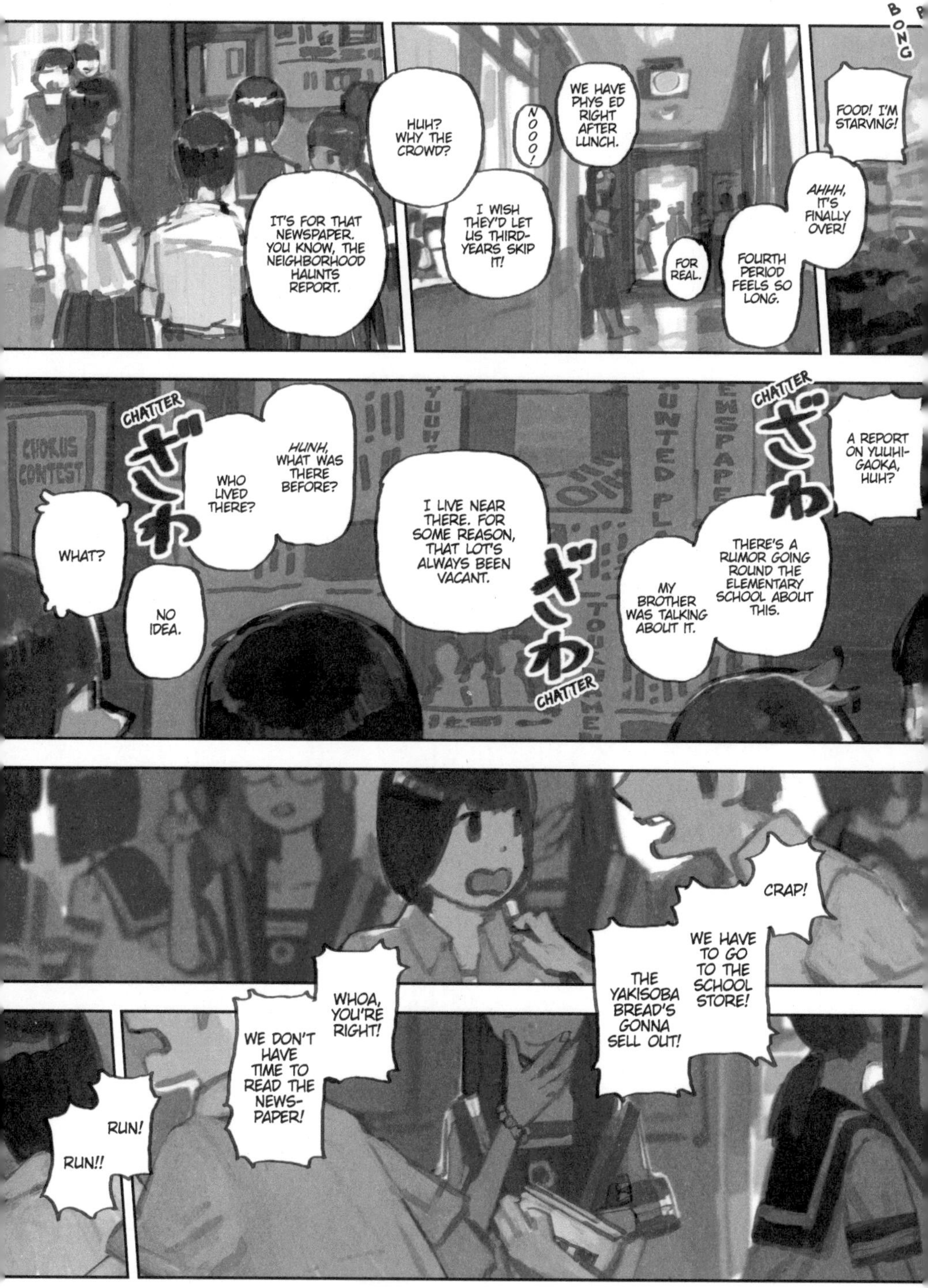
BONG
FOOD! I'M STARVING!
AHHH, IT'S FINALLY OVER!
FOURTH PERIOD FEELS SO LONG.
FOR REAL.
WE HAVE PHYS ED RIGHT AFTER LUNCH.
NOOOO!
I WISH THEY'D LET US THIRD-YEARS SKIP IT!
HUH? WHY THE CROWD?
IT'S FOR THAT NEWSPAPER. YOU KNOW, THE NEIGHBORHOOD HAUNTS REPORT.
CHATTER ざわ
A REPORT ON YUUHI-GAOKA, HUH?
THERE'S A RUMOR GOING ROUND THE ELEMENTARY SCHOOL ABOUT THIS.
MY BROTHER WAS TALKING ABOUT IT.
ざわ CHATTER
I LIVE NEAR THERE. FOR SOME REASON, THAT LOT'S ALWAYS BEEN VACANT.
HUNH, WHAT WAS THERE BEFORE?
WHO LIVED THERE?
CHATTER ざわ
CHORUS CONTEST
WHAT?
NO IDEA.
CRAP!
WE HAVE TO GO TO THE SCHOOL STORE!
THE YAKISOBA BREAD'S GONNA SELL OUT!
WHOA, YOU'RE RIGHT!
WE DON'T HAVE TIME TO READ THE NEWS-PAPER!
RUN!
RUN!!

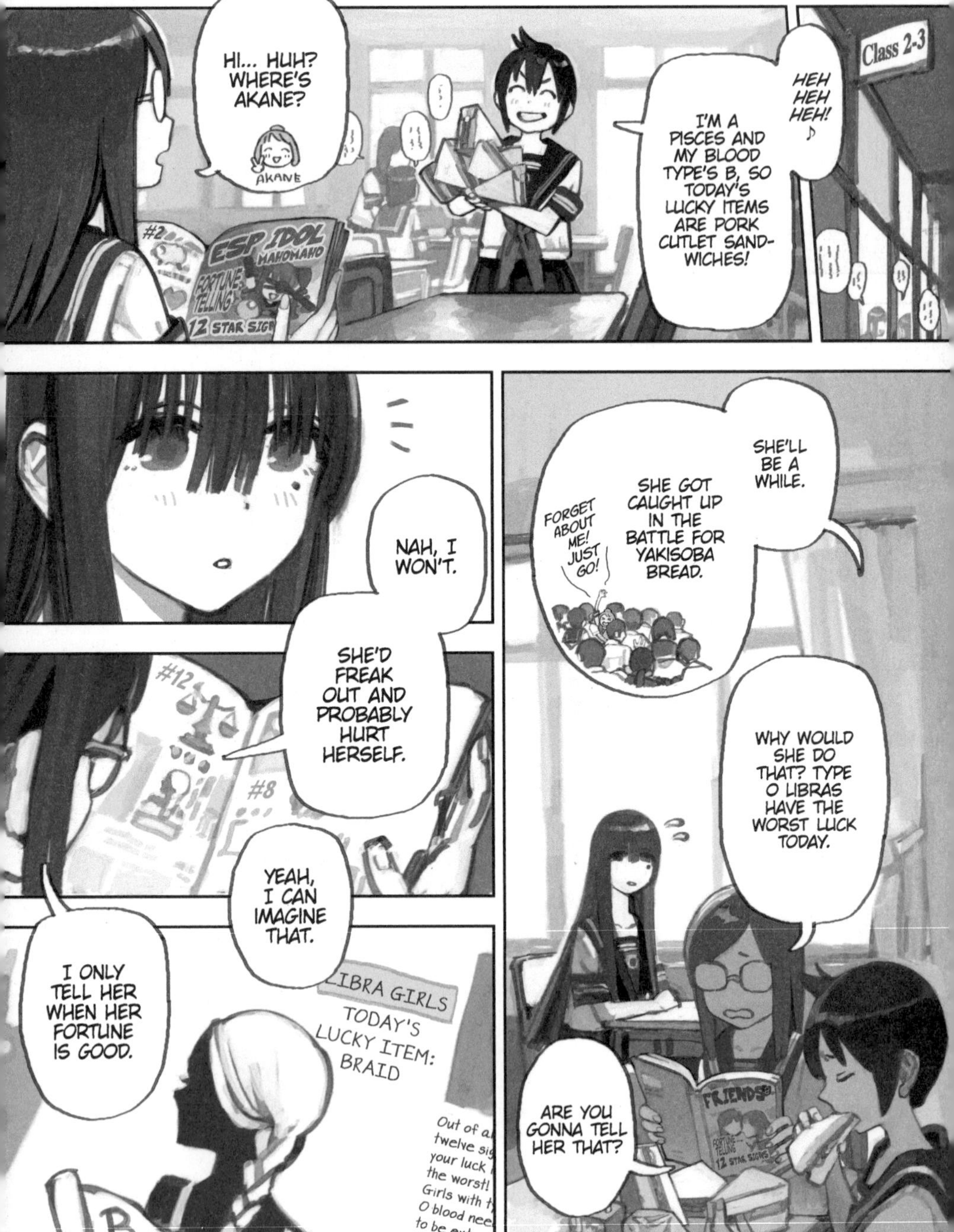
Class 2-3
HEH HEH HEH! ♪
I'M A PISCES AND MY BLOOD TYPE'S B, SO TODAY'S LUCKY ITEMS ARE PORK CUTLET SAND-WICHES!
HI... HUH? WHERE'S AKANE?
AKANE
ESP IDOL MAHOMAHO
FORTUNE TELLING!
12 STAR SIG
SHE'LL BE A WHILE.
SHE GOT CAUGHT UP IN THE BATTLE FOR YAKISOBA BREAD.
FORGET ABOUT ME! JUST GO!
WHY WOULD SHE DO THAT? TYPE O LIBRAS HAVE THE WORST LUCK TODAY.
ARE YOU GONNA TELL HER THAT?
FRIENDS
FORTUNE TELLING
12 STAR SIGNS
NAH, I WON'T.
#12
#8
SHE'D FREAK OUT AND PROBABLY HURT HERSELF.
YEAH, I CAN IMAGINE THAT.
I ONLY TELL HER WHEN HER FORTUNE IS GOOD.
LIBRA GIRLS
TODAY'S LUCKY ITEM: BRAID
Out of a
twelve sig
your luck
the worst!
Girls with t
O blood nee
to be extra
careful!

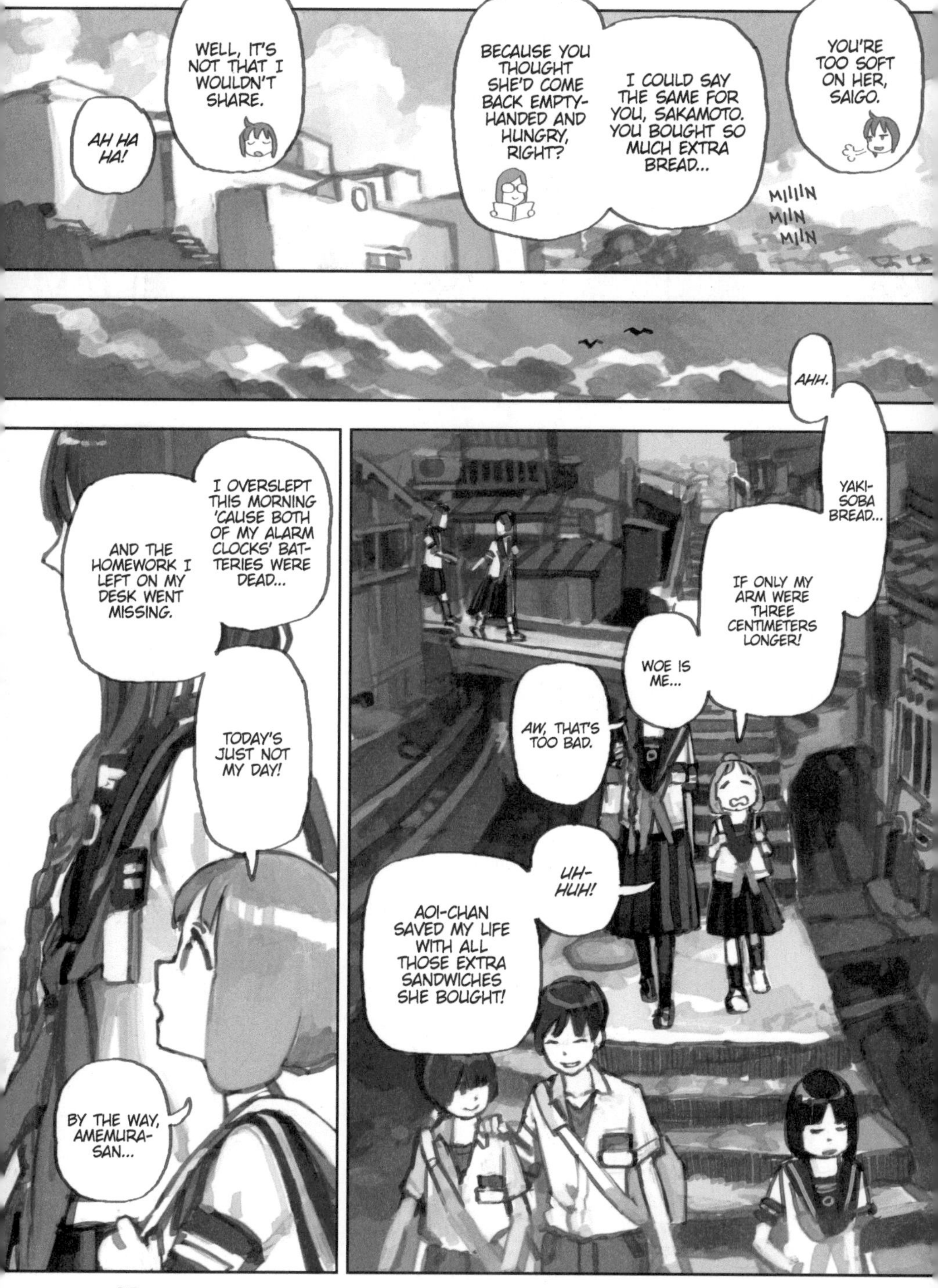
YOU'RE TOO SOFT ON HER, SAIGO.
I COULD SAY THE SAME FOR YOU, SAKAMOTO. YOU BOUGHT SO MUCH EXTRA BREAD...
BECAUSE YOU THOUGHT SHE'D COME BACK EMPTY-HANDED AND HUNGRY, RIGHT?
MIIIN
MIIN
MIIN
WELL, IT'S NOT THAT I WOULDN'T SHARE.
AH HA HA!
AHH.
YAKI-SOBA BREAD...
IF ONLY MY ARM WERE THREE CENTIMETERS LONGER!
WOE IS ME...
AW, THAT'S TOO BAD.
UH-HUH!
AOI-CHAN SAVED MY LIFE WITH ALL THOSE EXTRA SANDWICHES SHE BOUGHT!
I OVERSLEPT THIS MORNING 'CAUSE BOTH OF MY ALARM CLOCKS' BATTERIES WERE DEAD...
AND THE HOMEWORK I LEFT ON MY DESK WENT MISSING.
TODAY'S JUST NOT MY DAY!
BY THE WAY, AMEMURA-SAN...

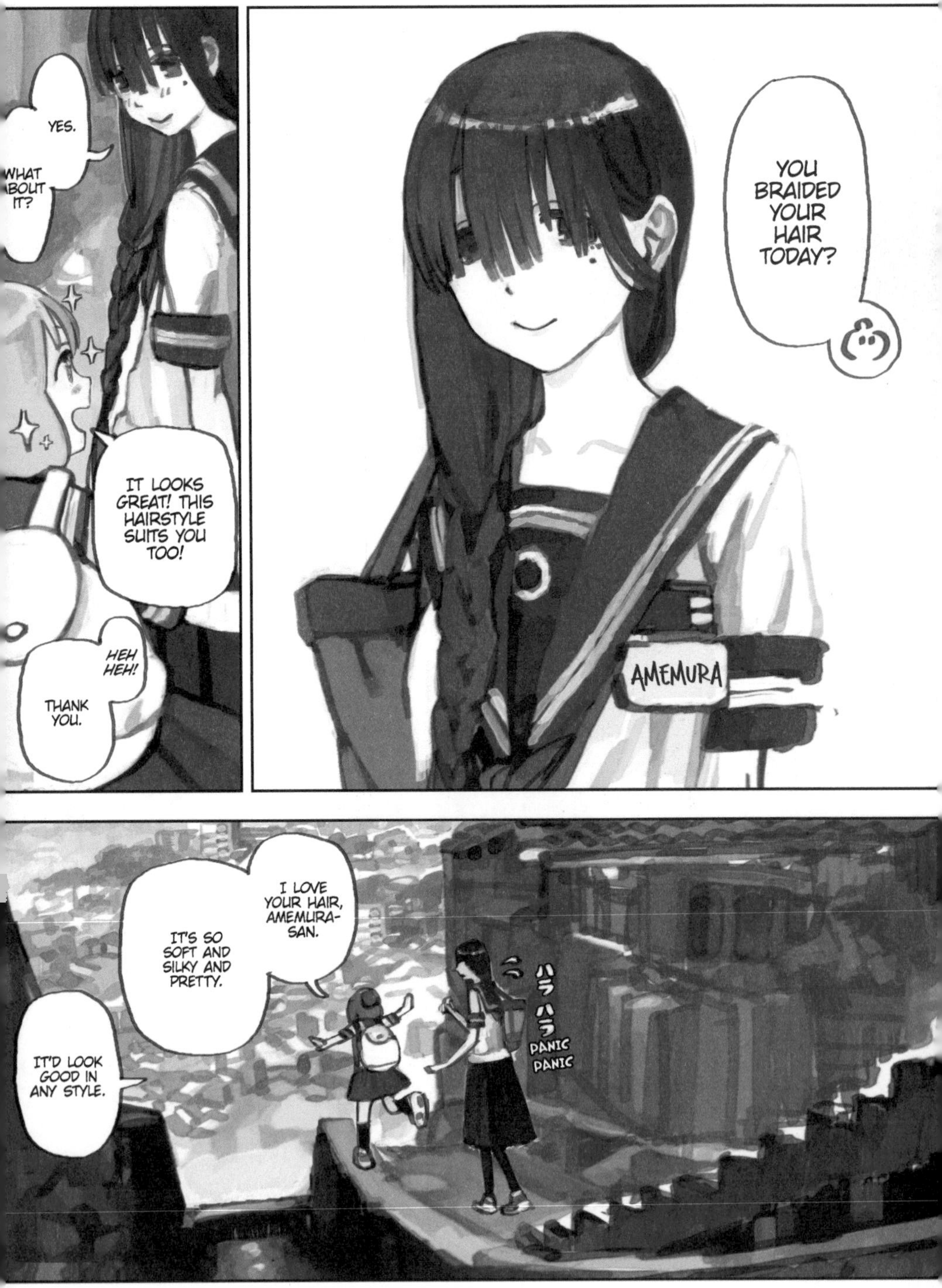
YOU BRAIDED YOUR HAIR TODAY?
AMEMURA
YES.
WHAT ABOUT IT?
IT LOOKS GREAT! THIS HAIRSTYLE SUITS YOU TOO!
HEH HEH!
THANK YOU.
I LOVE YOUR HAIR, AMEMURA-SAN.
IT'S SO SOFT AND SILKY AND PRETTY.
ハラハラ
PANIC PANIC
IT'D LOOK GOOD IN ANY STYLE.

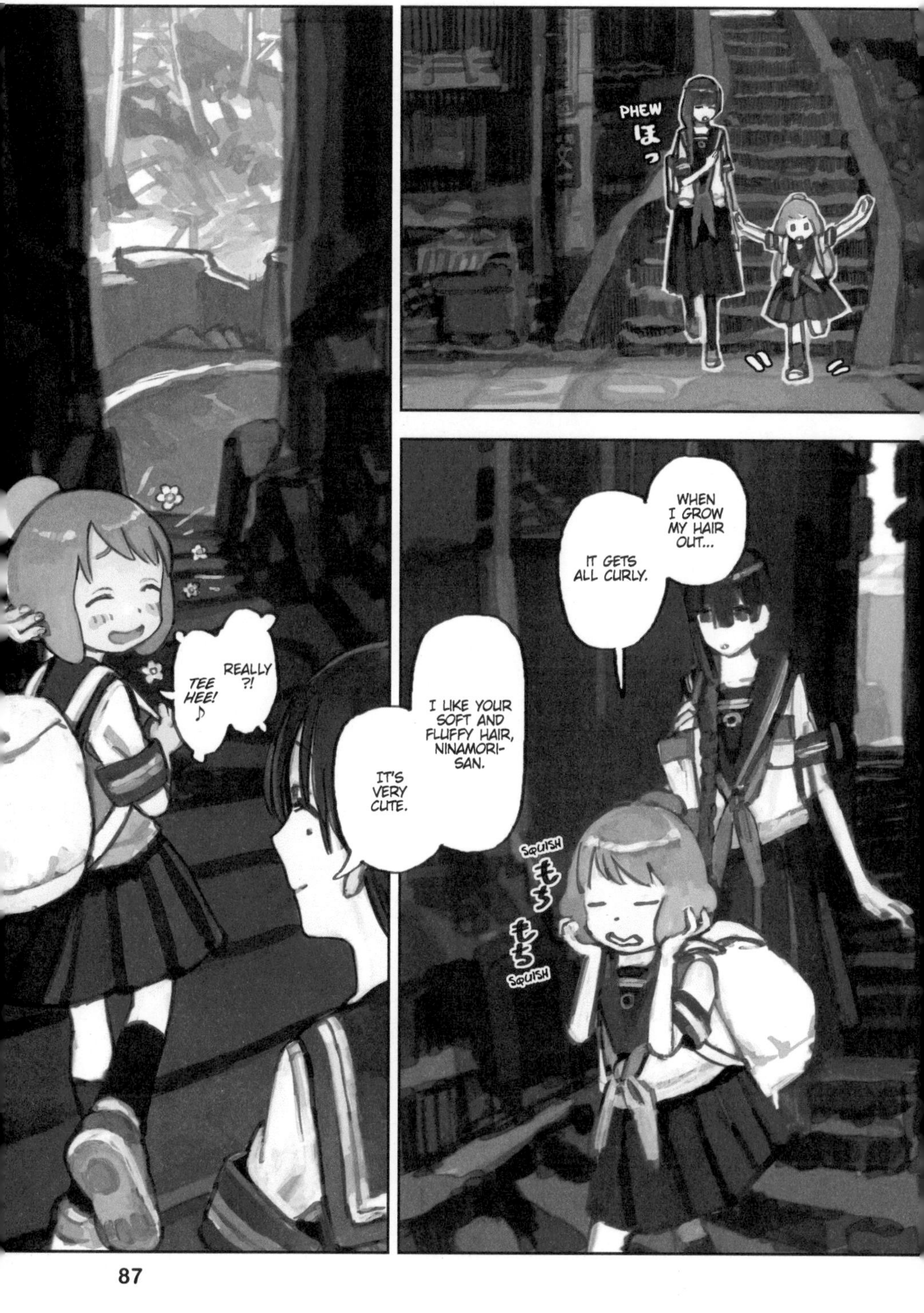
PHEW
ほっ
WHEN I GROW MY HAIR OUT...
IT GETS ALL CURLY.
SQUISH
もち もち
SQUISH
I LIKE YOUR SOFT AND FLUFFY HAIR, NINAMORI-SAN.
IT'S VERY CUTE.
REALLY ?!
TEE HEE! ♪

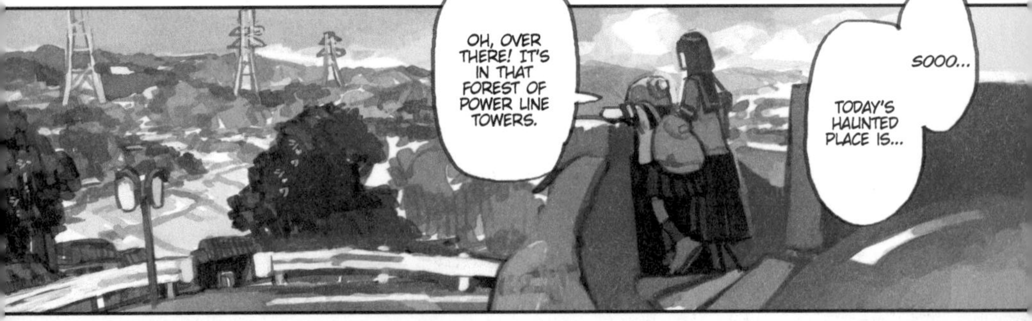
SOOO...
TODAY'S HAUNTED PLACE IS...
OH, OVER THERE! IT'S IN THAT FOREST OF POWER LINE TOWERS.

Chapter 5: The Ghost on the Surface of Rokkotsu Pond

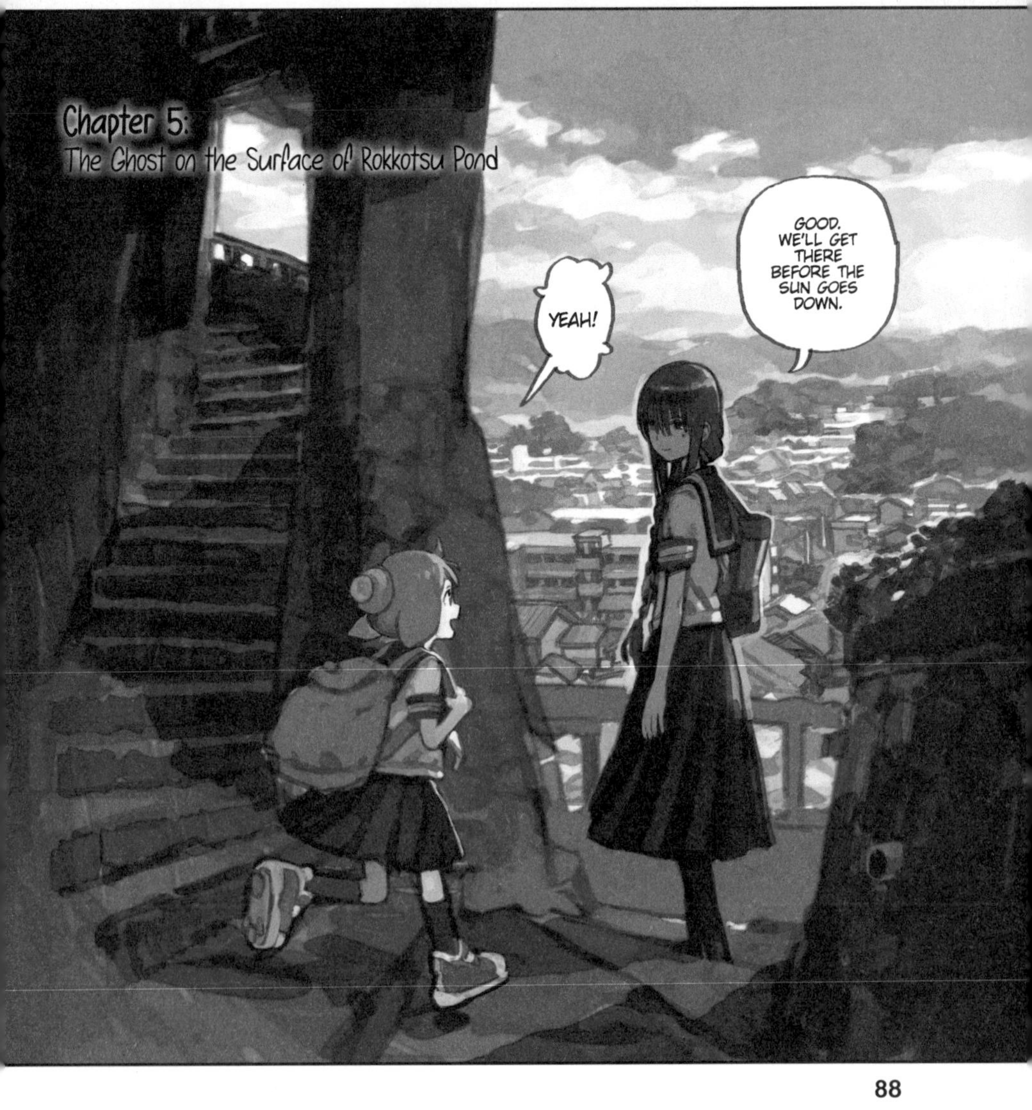
GOOD. WE'LL GET THERE BEFORE THE SUN GOES DOWN.
YEAH!

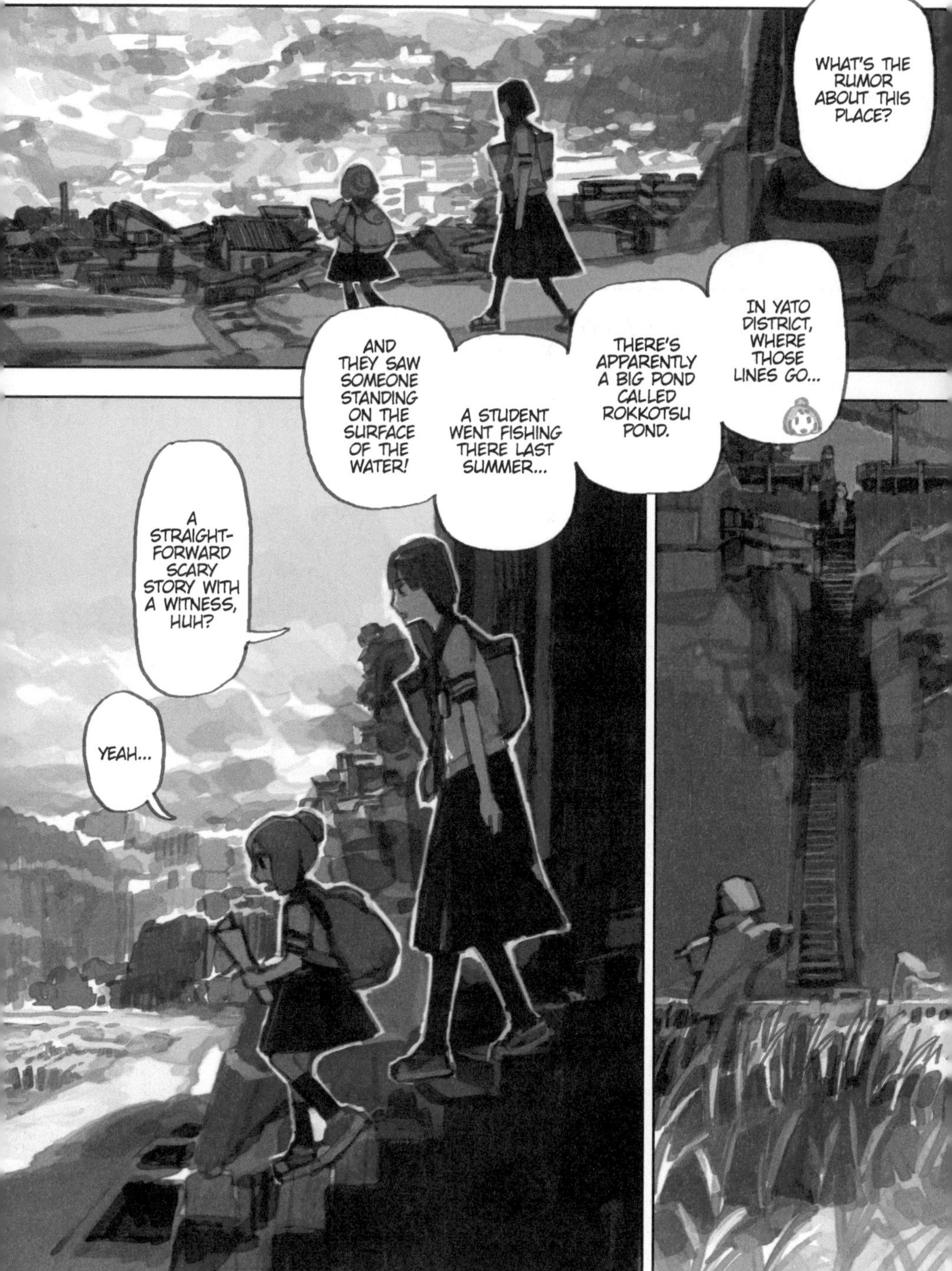
WHAT'S THE RUMOR ABOUT THIS PLACE?
IN YATO DISTRICT, WHERE THOSE LINES GO...
THERE'S APPARENTLY A BIG POND CALLED ROKKOTSU POND.
A STUDENT WENT FISHING THERE LAST SUMMER...
AND THEY SAW SOMEONE STANDING ON THE SURFACE OF THE WATER!
A STRAIGHT-FORWARD SCARY STORY WITH A WITNESS, HUH?
YEAH...

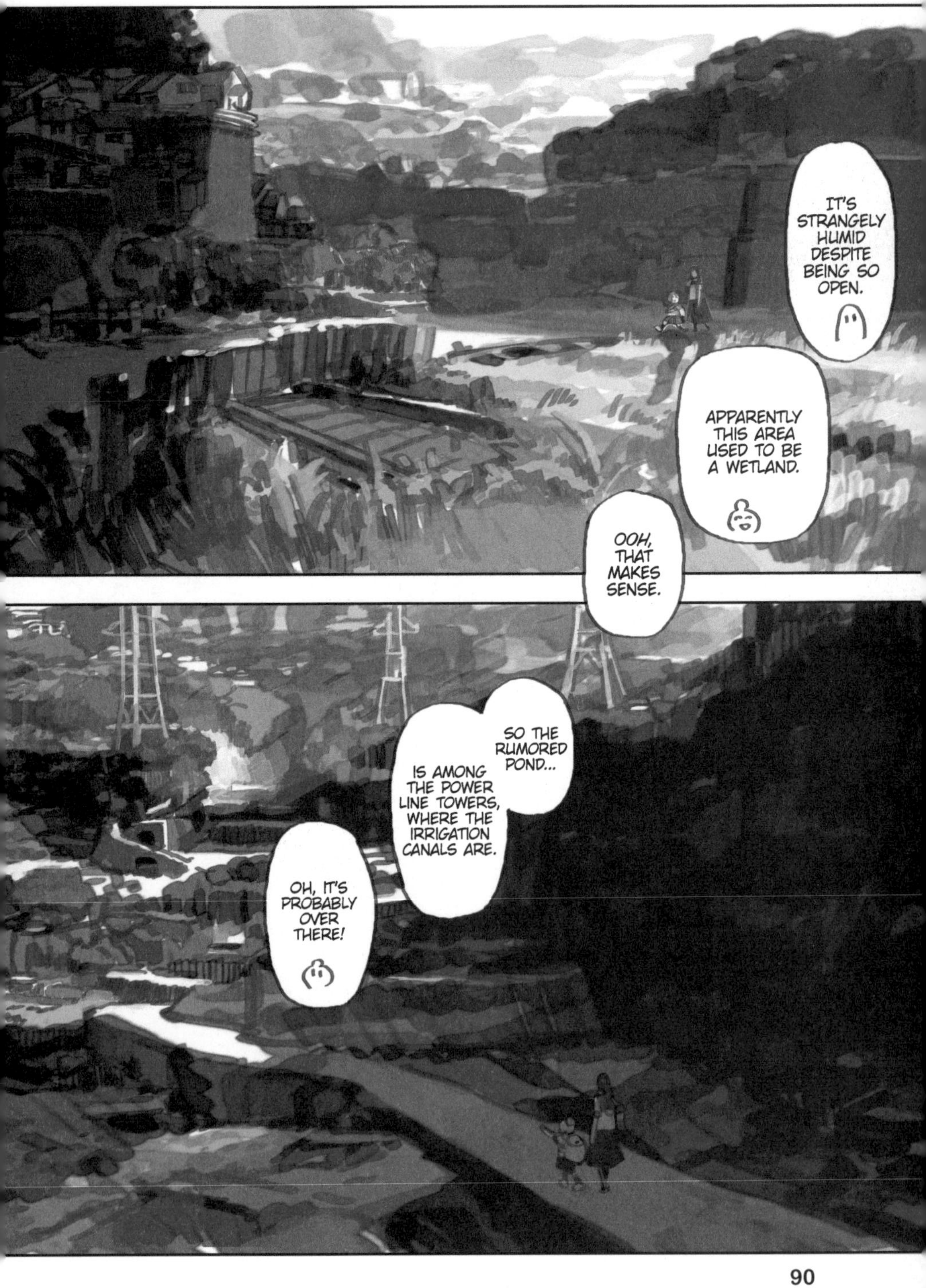
IT'S STRANGELY HUMID DESPITE BEING SO OPEN.
APPARENTLY THIS AREA USED TO BE A WETLAND.
OOH, THAT MAKES SENSE.
SO THE RUMORED POND...
IS AMONG THE POWER LINE TOWERS, WHERE THE IRRIGATION CANALS ARE.
OH, IT'S PROBABLY OVER THERE!

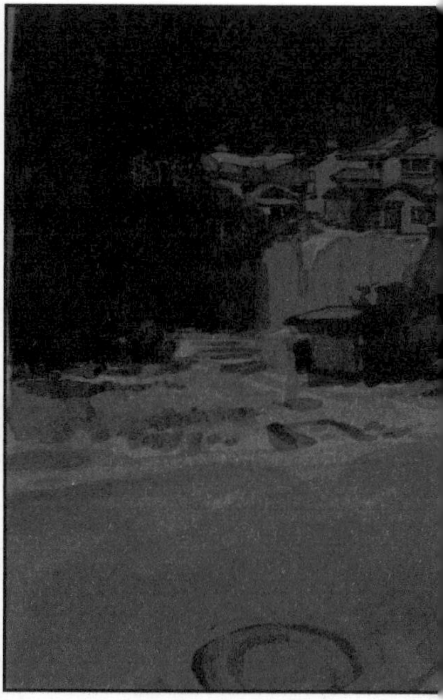

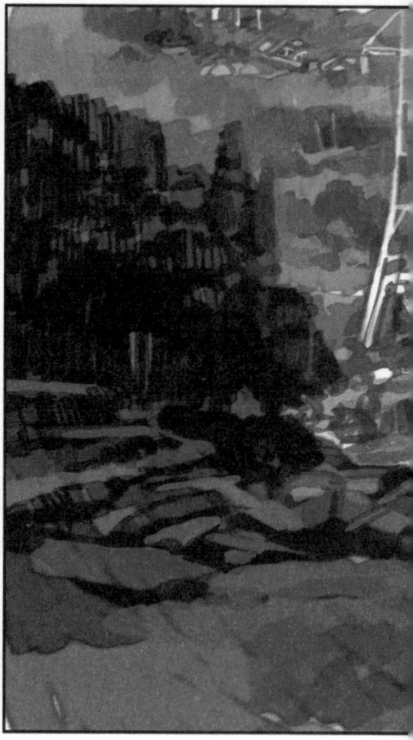

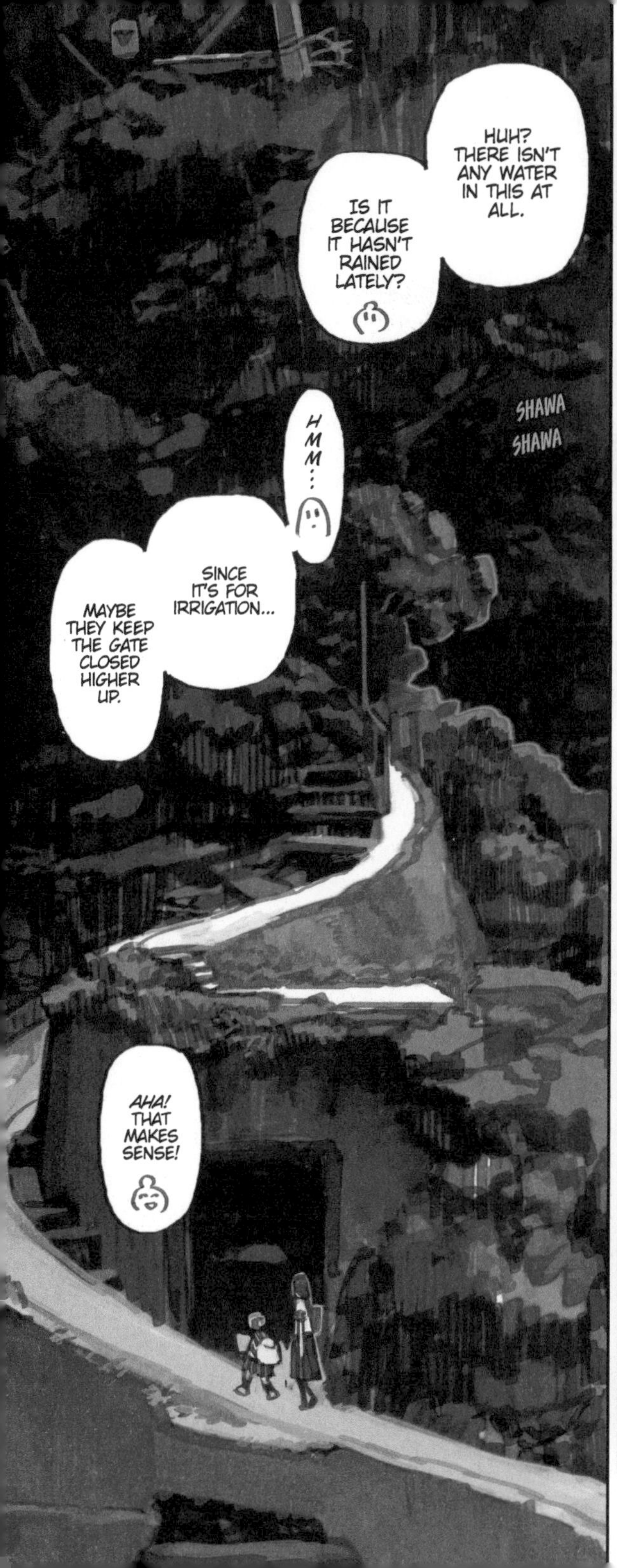
HUH? THERE ISN'T ANY WATER IN THIS AT ALL.
IS IT BECAUSE IT HASN'T RAINED LATELY?
SHAWA SHAWA
HMM...
SINCE IT'S FOR IRRIGATION...
MAYBE THEY KEEP THE GATE CLOSED HIGHER UP.
AHA! THAT MAKES SENSE!

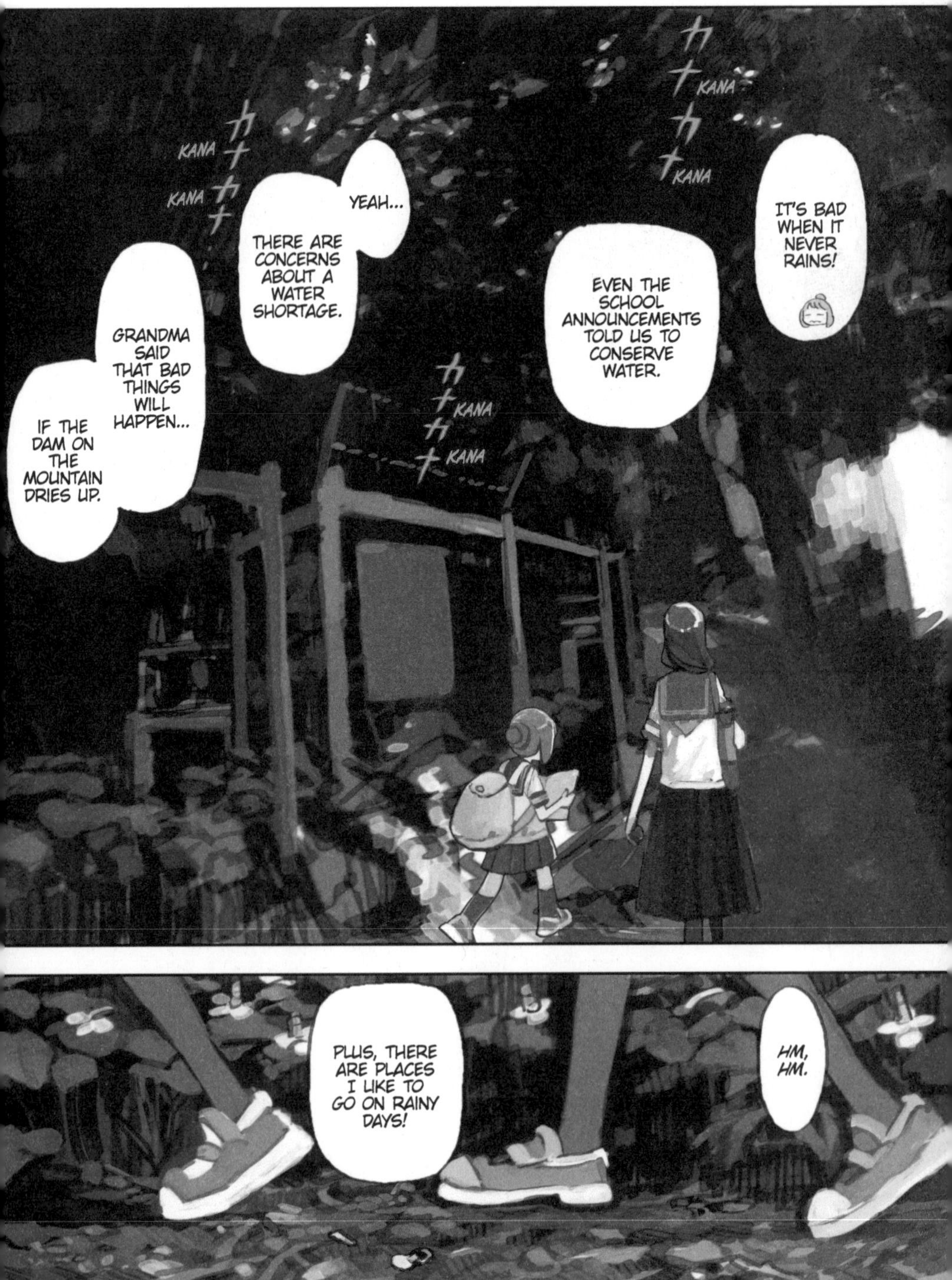
KANA
KANA
IT'S BAD WHEN IT NEVER RAINS!
EVEN THE SCHOOL ANNOUNCEMENTS TOLD US TO CONSERVE WATER.
YEAH...
THERE ARE CONCERNS ABOUT A WATER SHORTAGE.
KANA
KANA
GRANDMA SAID THAT BAD THINGS WILL HAPPEN...
IF THE DAM ON THE MOUNTAIN DRIES UP.
KANA
KANA
HM, HM.
PLUS, THERE ARE PLACES I LIKE TO GO ON RAINY DAYS!

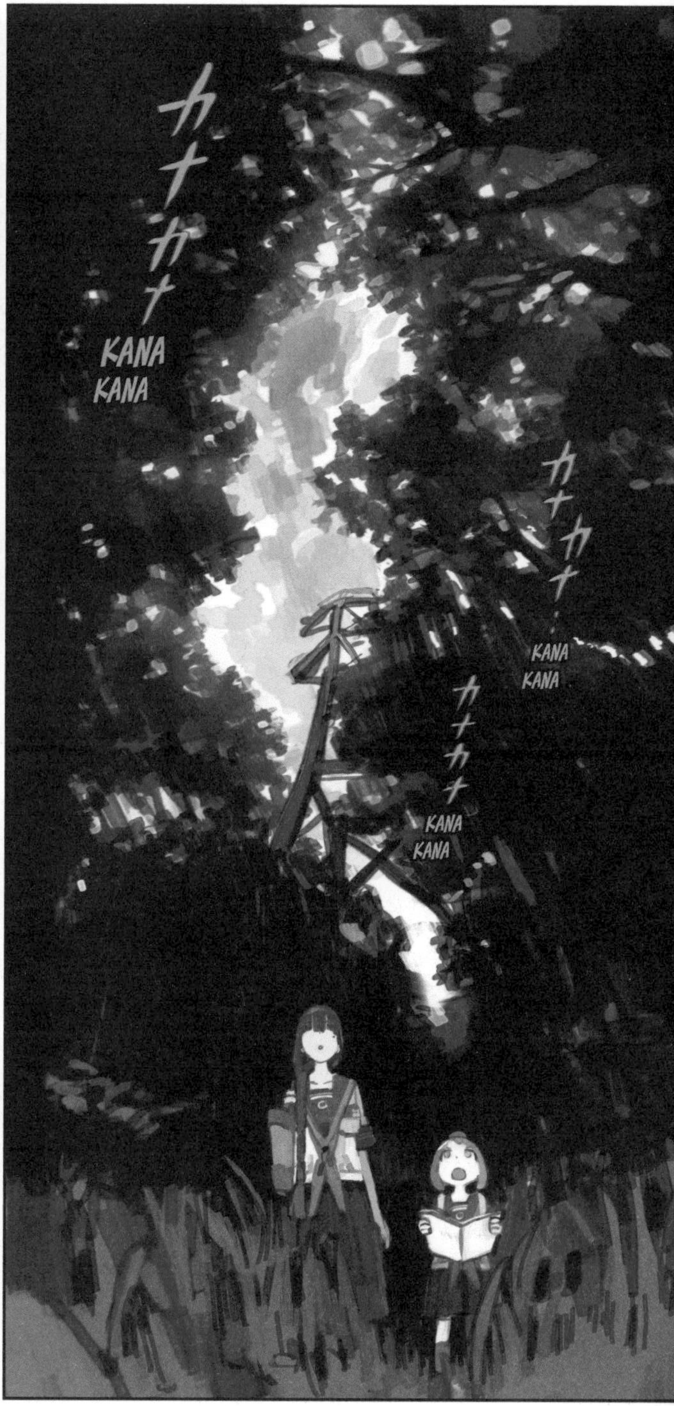
カナカナ
KANA
KANA
カナカナ
KANA
KANA
カナカナ
KANA
KANA
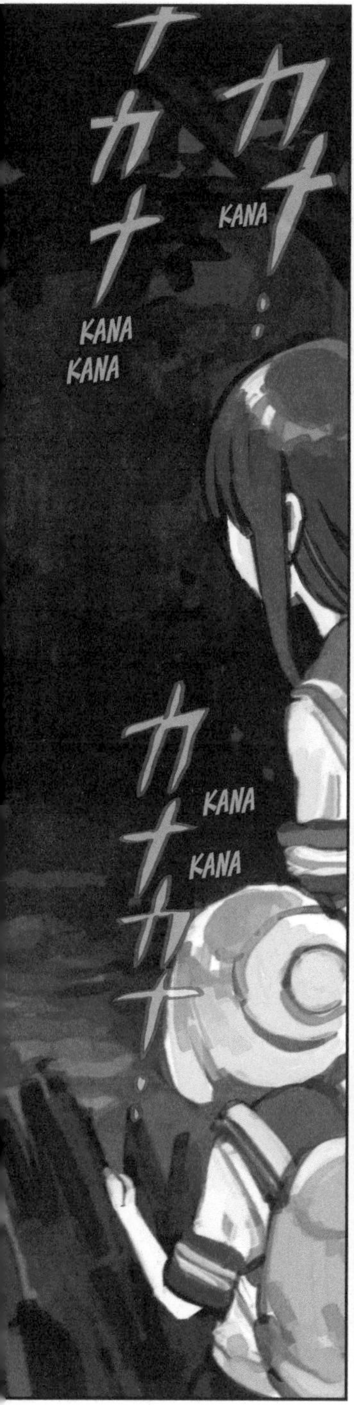
カナ
KANA
ナカナ
KANA
KANA
カナカナ
KANA
KANA

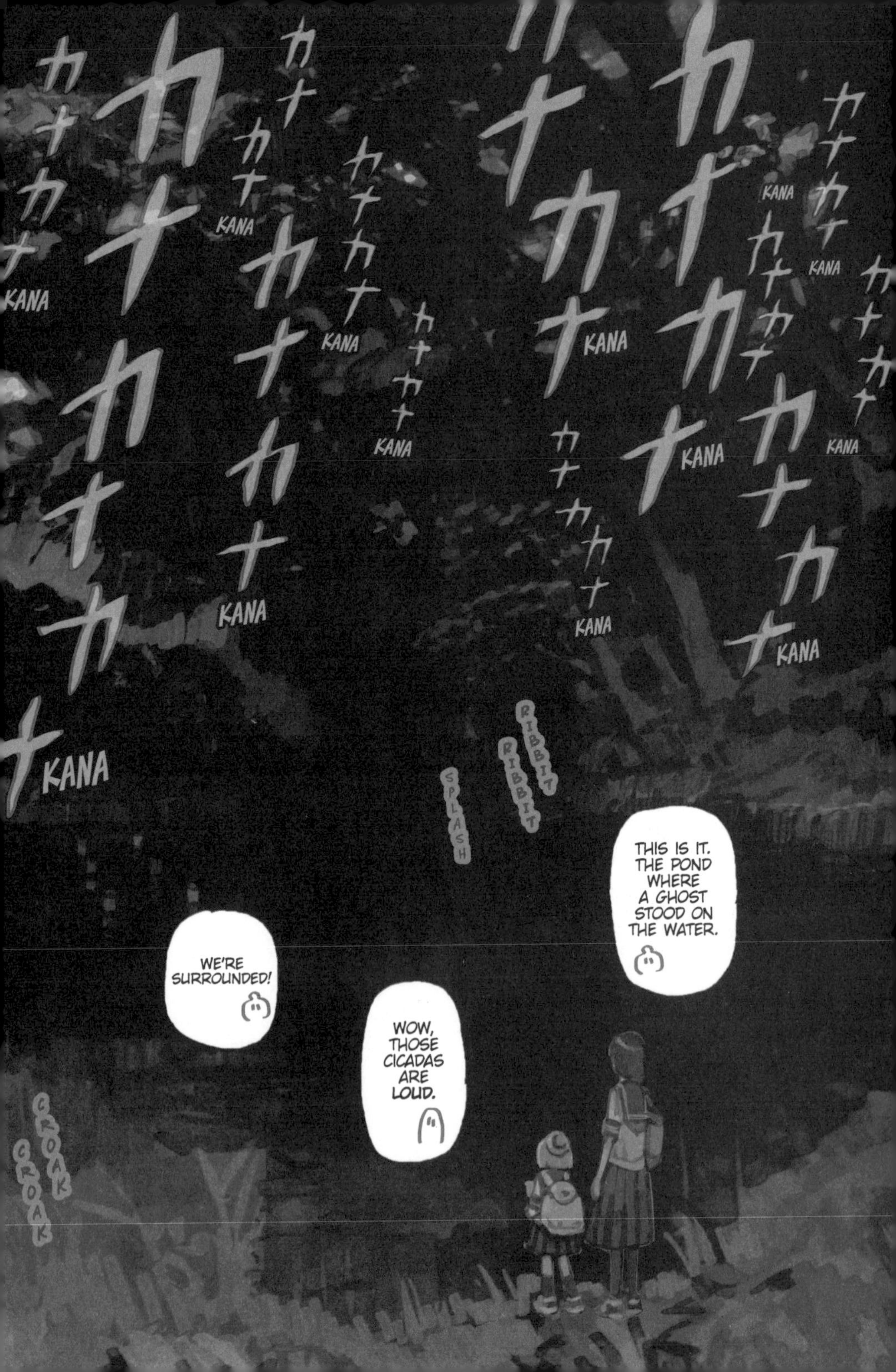
カナカナ
KANA
カナカナ
KANA
カナカナカナ
KANA
カナカナカナ
KANA
カナカナ
KANA
カナカナ
KANA
カナカナ
KANA
カナカナ
KANA
カナカナカナ
KANA
カナカナ
KANA
カナカナ
KANA
カナカナカナ
KANA
RIBBIT
RIBBIT
SPLASH
THIS IS IT. THE POND WHERE A GHOST STOOD ON THE WATER.
WOW, THOSE CICADAS ARE LOUD.
WE'RE SURROUNDED!
CROAK
CROAK

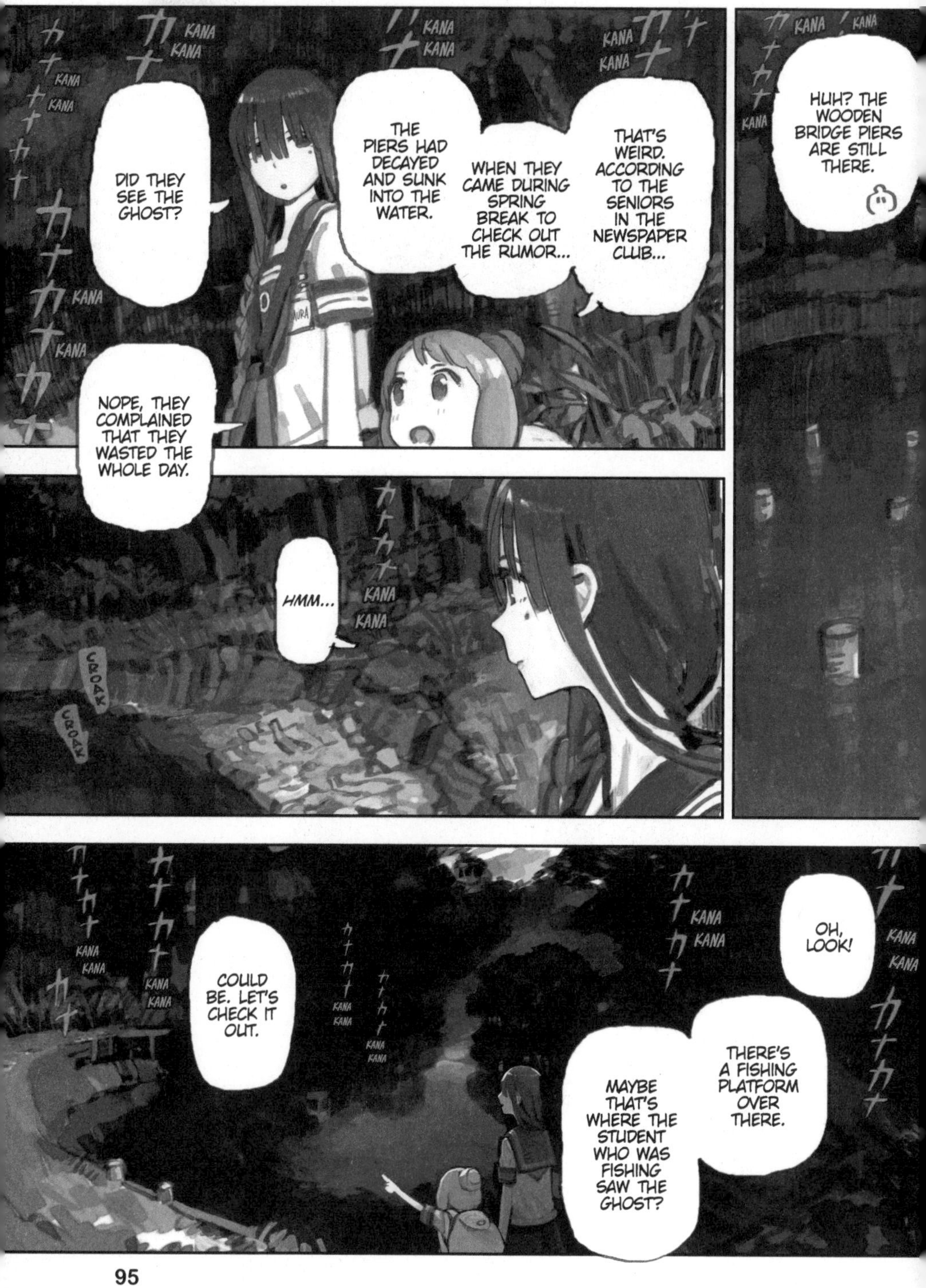
KANA KANA
HUH? THE WOODEN BRIDGE PIERS ARE STILL THERE.
KANA KANA
THAT'S WEIRD. ACCORDING TO THE SENIORS IN THE NEWSPAPER CLUB...
WHEN THEY CAME DURING SPRING BREAK TO CHECK OUT THE RUMOR...
THE PIERS HAD DECAYED AND SUNK INTO THE WATER.
DID THEY SEE THE GHOST?
KANA KANA
NOPE, THEY COMPLAINED THAT THEY WASTED THE WHOLE DAY.
KANA KANA
HMM...
CROAK CROAK
KANA KANA
OH, LOOK!
THERE'S A FISHING PLATFORM OVER THERE.
MAYBE THAT'S WHERE THE STUDENT WHO WAS FISHING SAW THE GHOST?
COULD BE. LET'S CHECK IT OUT.

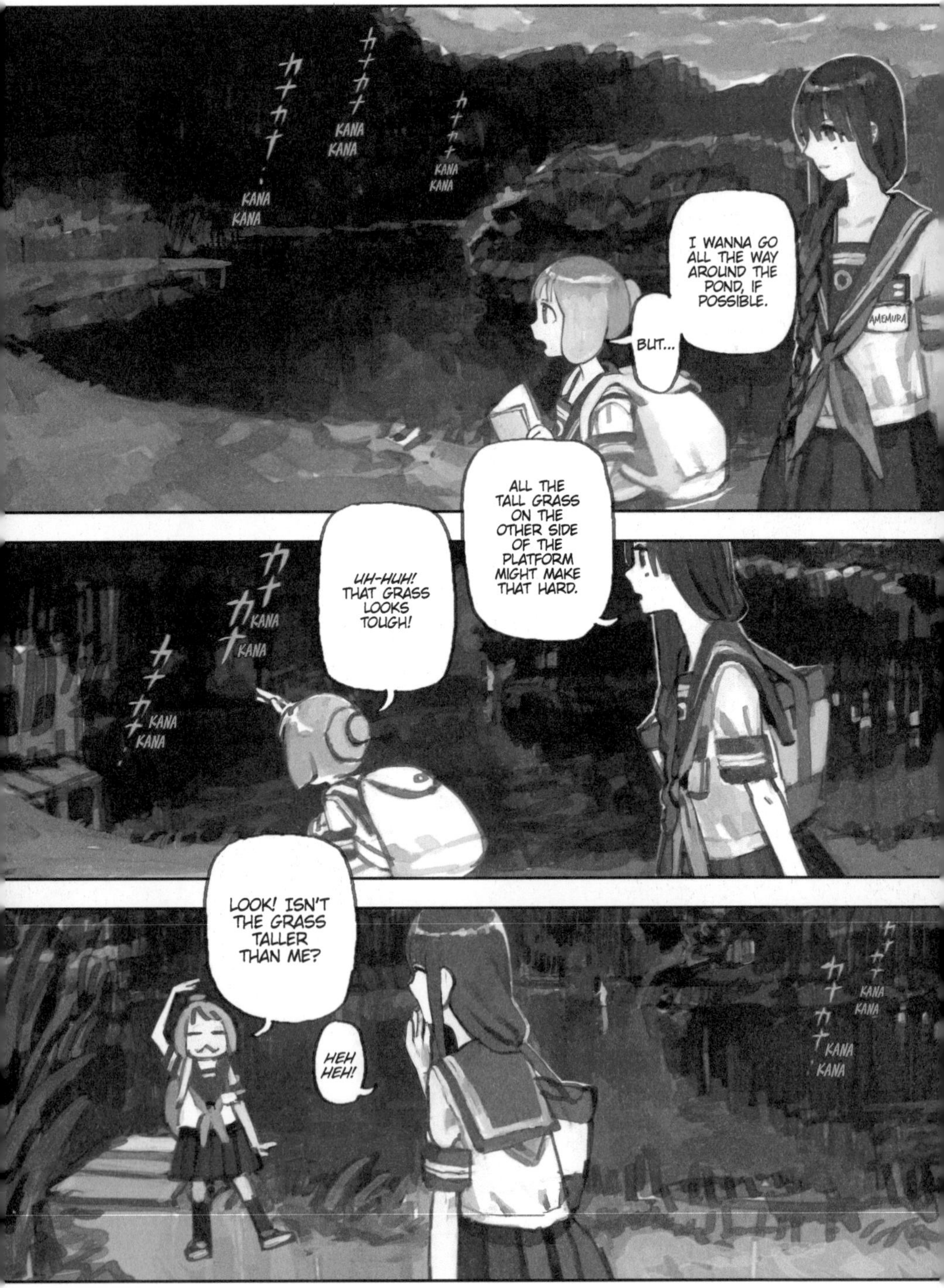
AMEMURA
I WANNA GO ALL THE WAY AROUND THE POND, IF POSSIBLE.
BUT...
KANA KANA
KANA KANA
KANA KANA
ALL THE TALL GRASS ON THE OTHER SIDE OF THE PLATFORM MIGHT MAKE THAT HARD.
UH-HUH! THAT GRASS LOOKS TOUGH!
KANA KANA
KANA KANA
KANA KANA
KANA KANA
LOOK! ISN'T THE GRASS TALLER THAN ME?
HEH HEH!

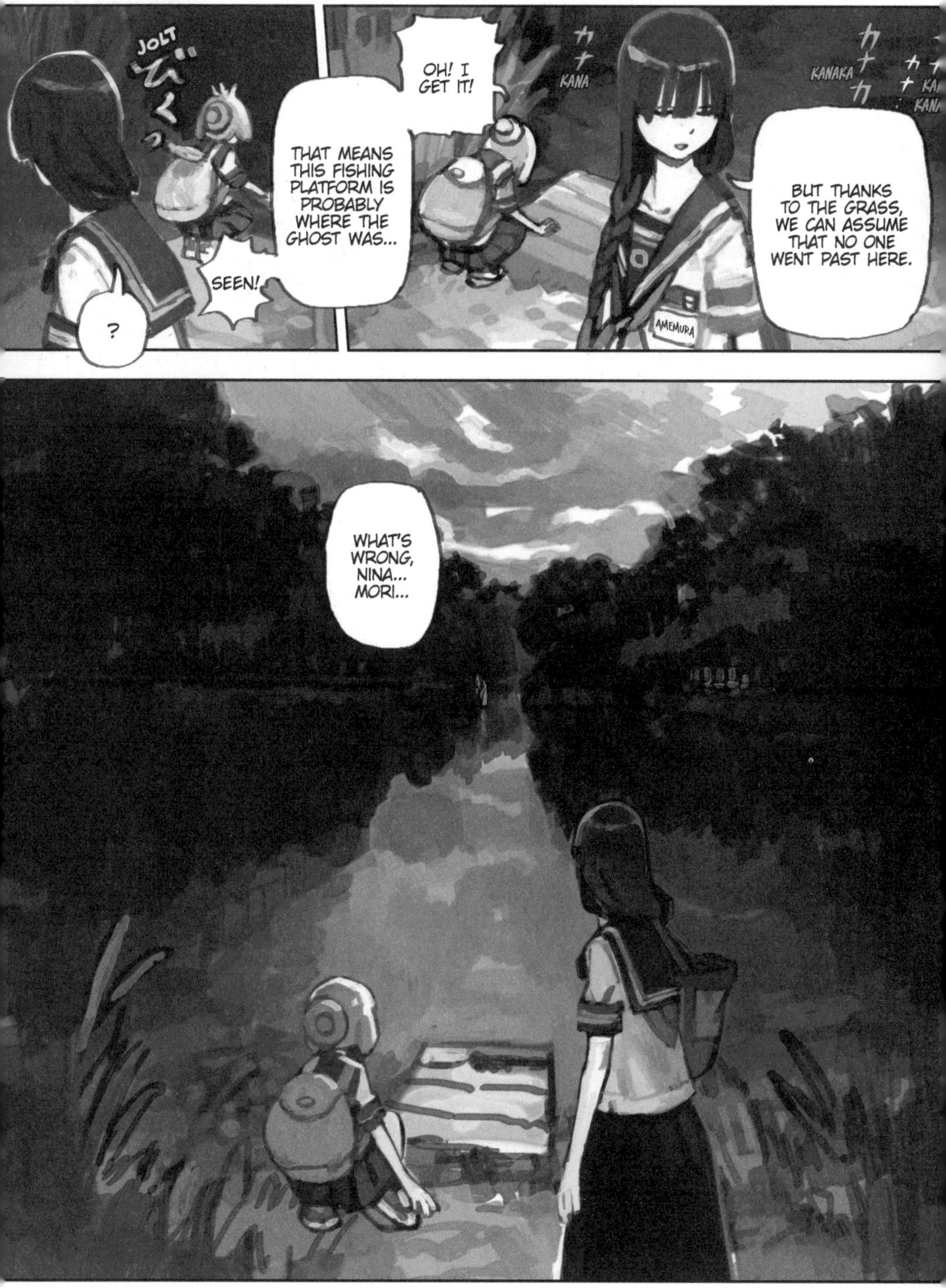
カナ
KANA
カナカ
KANAKA
BUT THANKS TO THE GRASS, WE CAN ASSUME THAT NO ONE WENT PAST HERE.
OH! I GET IT!
THAT MEANS THIS FISHING PLATFORM IS PROBABLY WHERE THE GHOST WAS...
AMEMURA
SEEN!
JOLT
びくっ
?
WHAT'S WRONG, NINA... MORI...

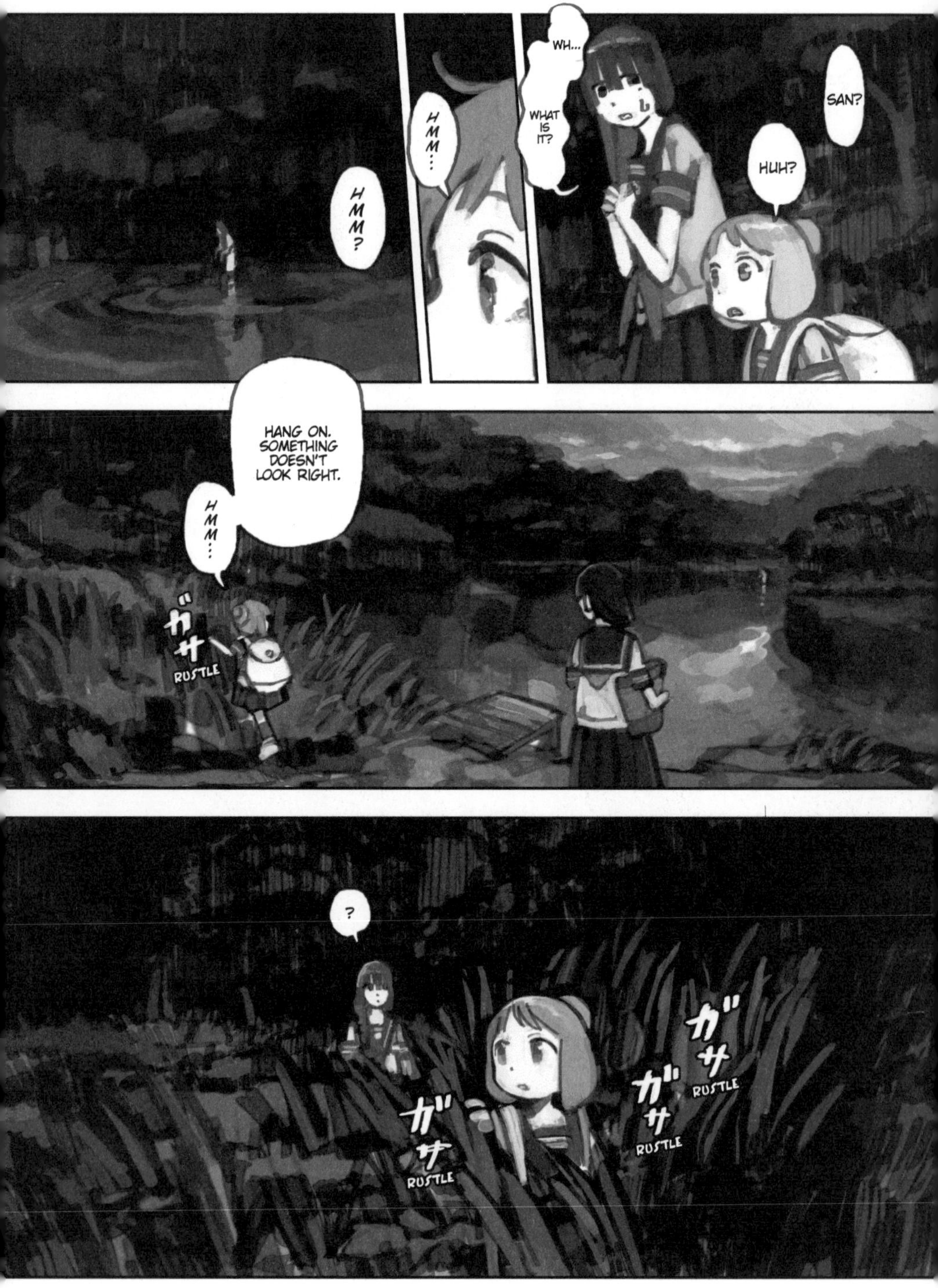
SAN?
HUH?
WH...
WHAT IS IT?
HMM...
HMM?
HANG ON. SOMETHING DOESN'T LOOK RIGHT.
HMM...
ガサ
RUSTLE
ガサ
RUSTLE
ガサ
RUSTLE
?
ガサ
RUSTLE

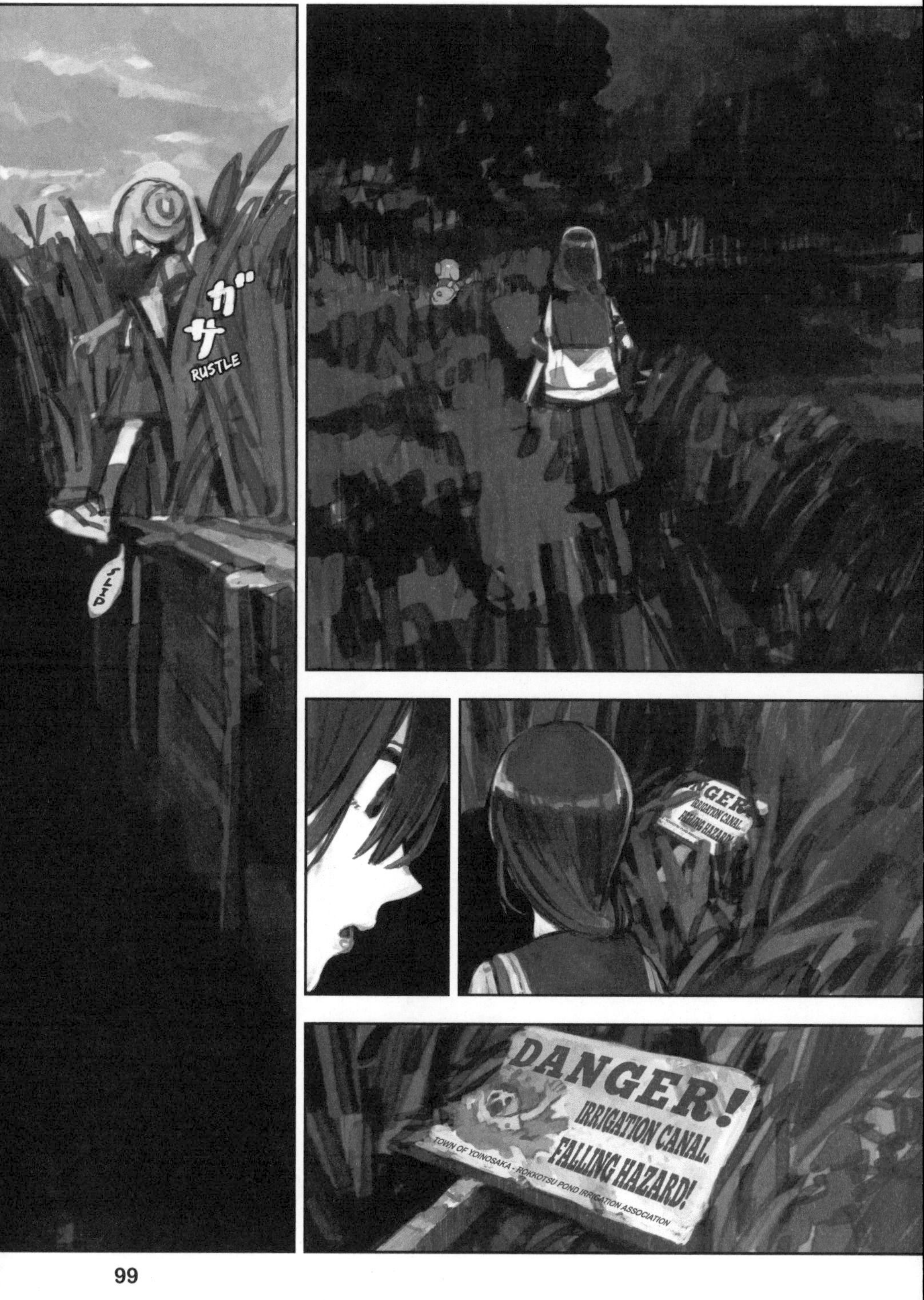
IRRIGATION CANAL.
FALLING HAZARD!
DANGER!
IRRIGATION CANAL.
FALLING HAZARD!
TOWN OF YOINOSAKA - ROKKOTSU POND IRRIGATION ASSOCIATION
ガサ
RUSTLE
SLIP

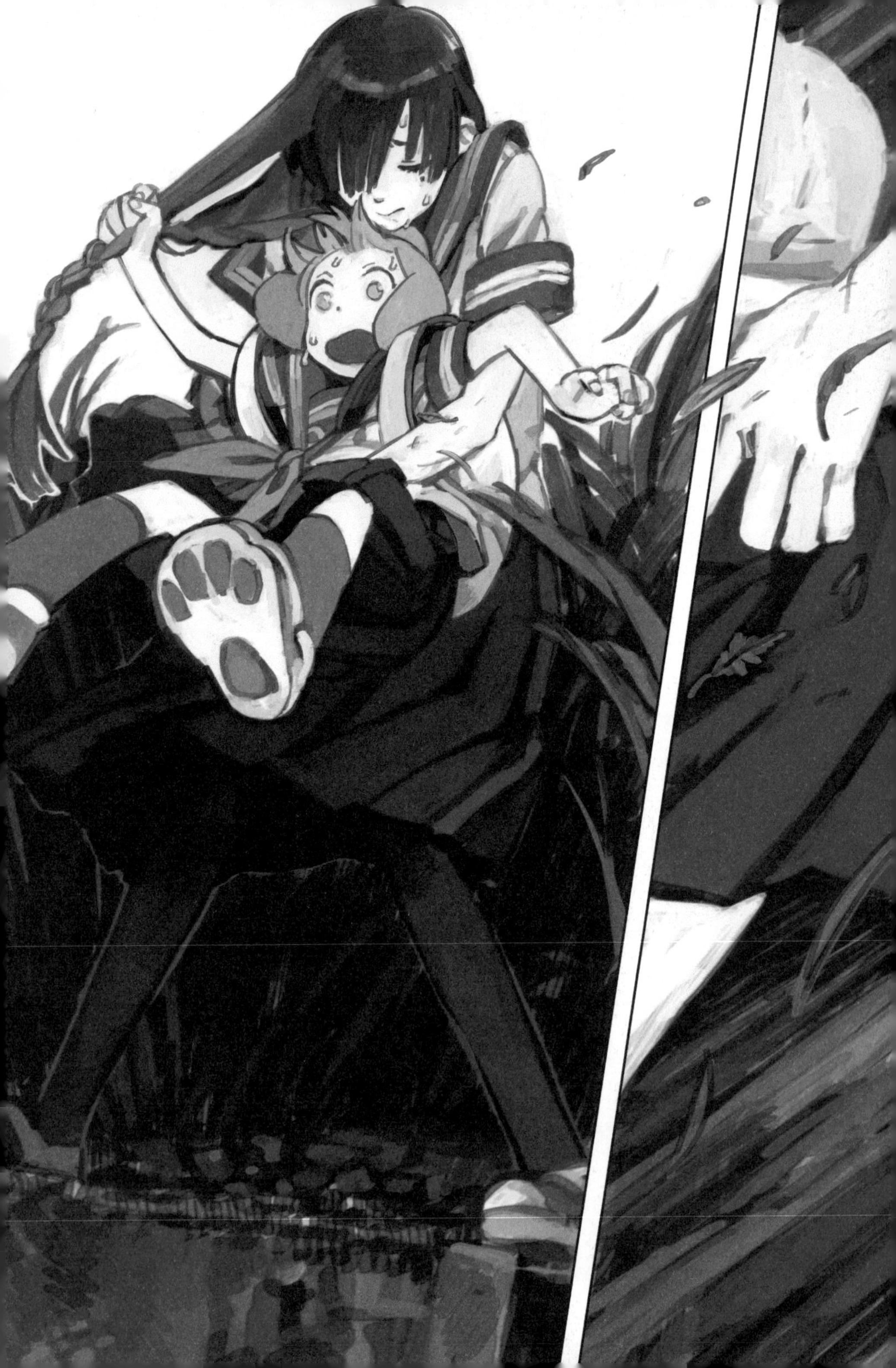

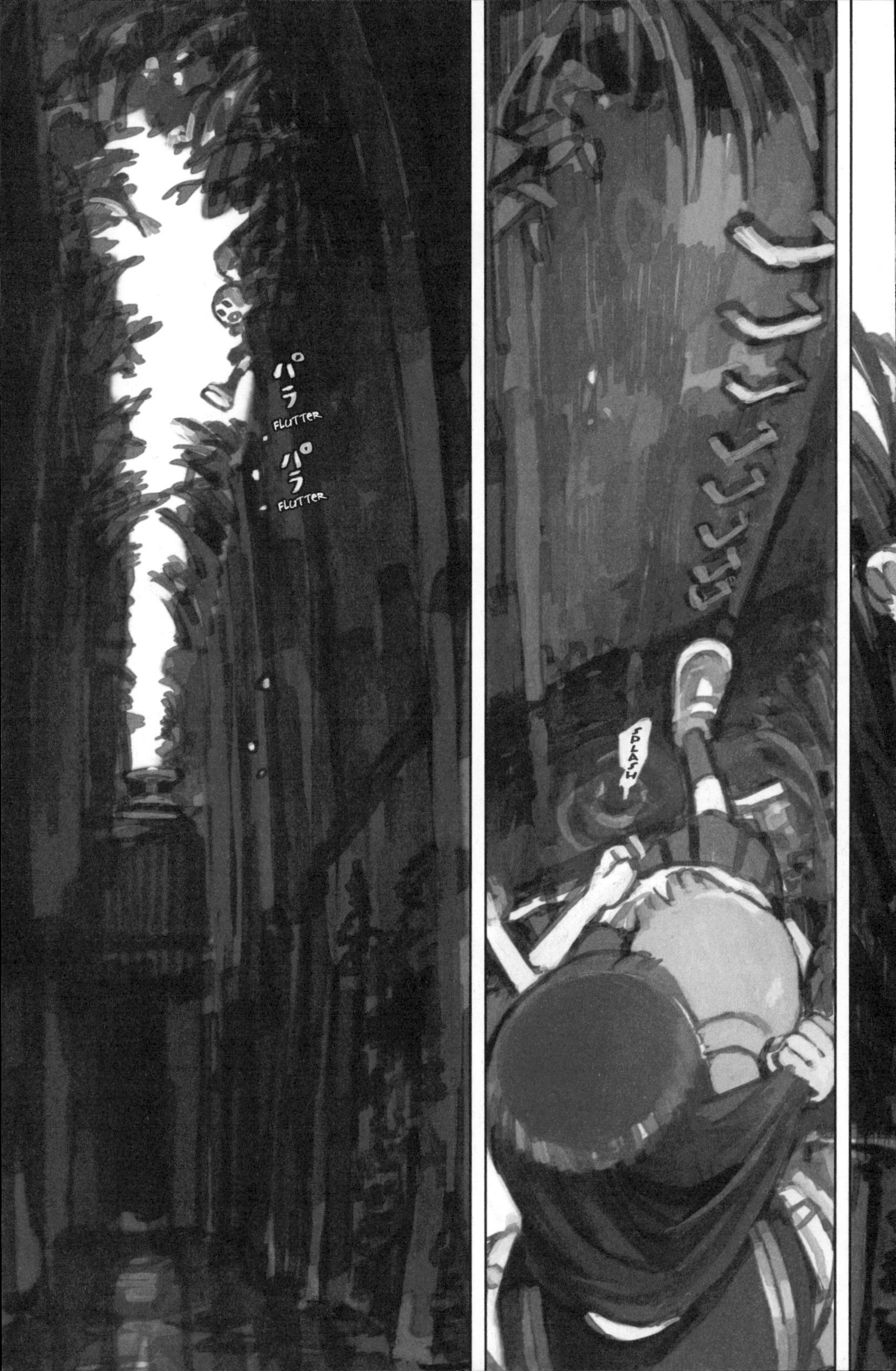
SPLASH
パラ
FLUTTER
パラ
FLUTTER

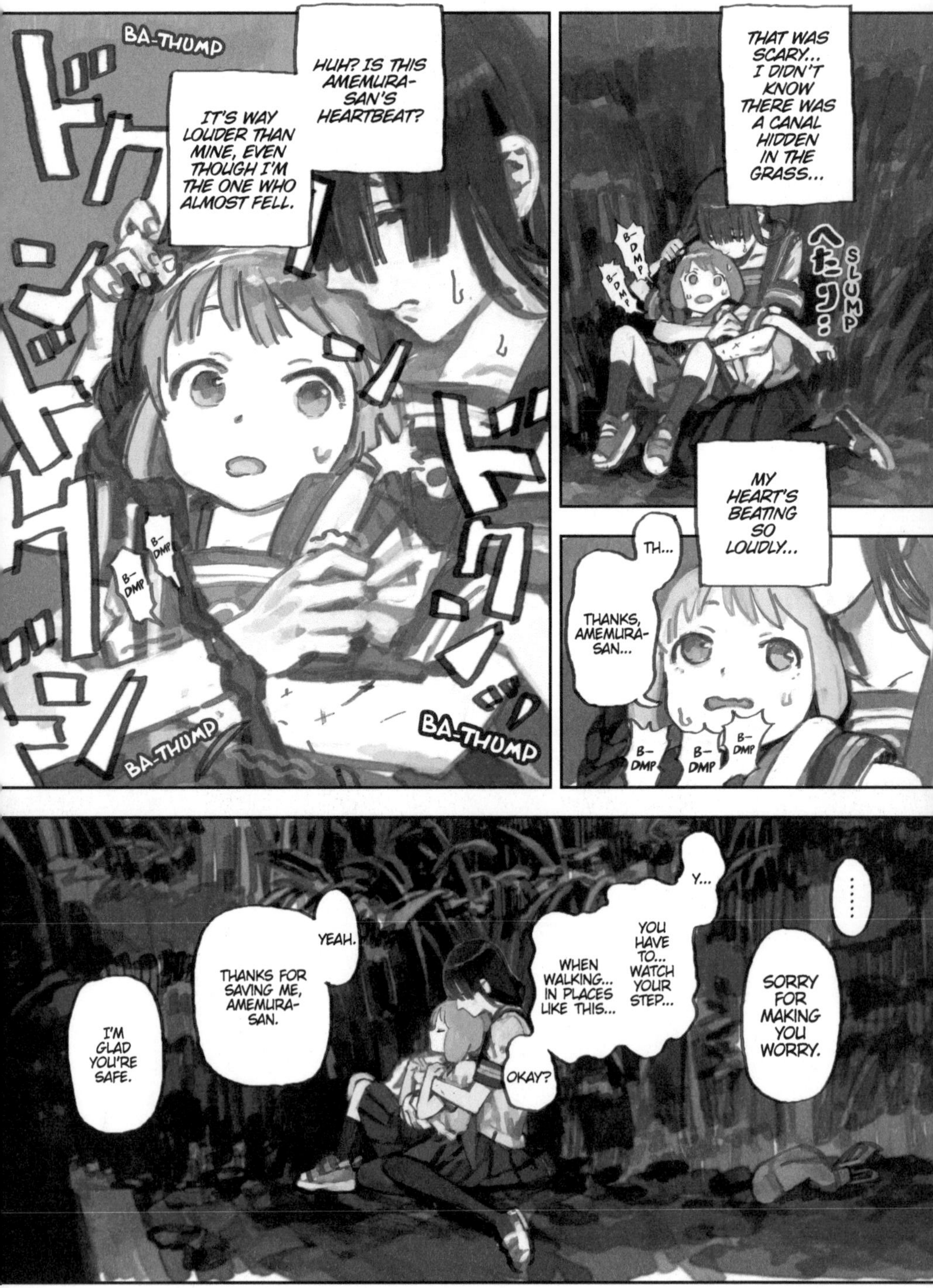
THAT WAS SCARY... I DIDN'T KNOW THERE WAS A CANAL HIDDEN IN THE GRASS...
B-DMP
B-DMP
へたり…
SLUMP
MY HEART'S BEATING SO LOUDLY...
TH...
THANKS, AMEMURA-SAN...
B-DMP
B-DMP
B-DMP
HUH? IS THIS AMEMURA-SAN'S HEARTBEAT?
IT'S WAY LOUDER THAN MINE, EVEN THOUGH I'M THE ONE WHO ALMOST FELL.
BA-THUMP
B-DMP
B-DMP
BA-THUMP
BA-THUMP
......
SORRY FOR MAKING YOU WORRY.
Y...
YOU HAVE TO... WATCH YOUR STEP...
WHEN WALKING... IN PLACES LIKE THIS...
OKAY?
YEAH.
THANKS FOR SAVING ME, AMEMURA-SAN.
I'M GLAD YOU'RE SAFE.

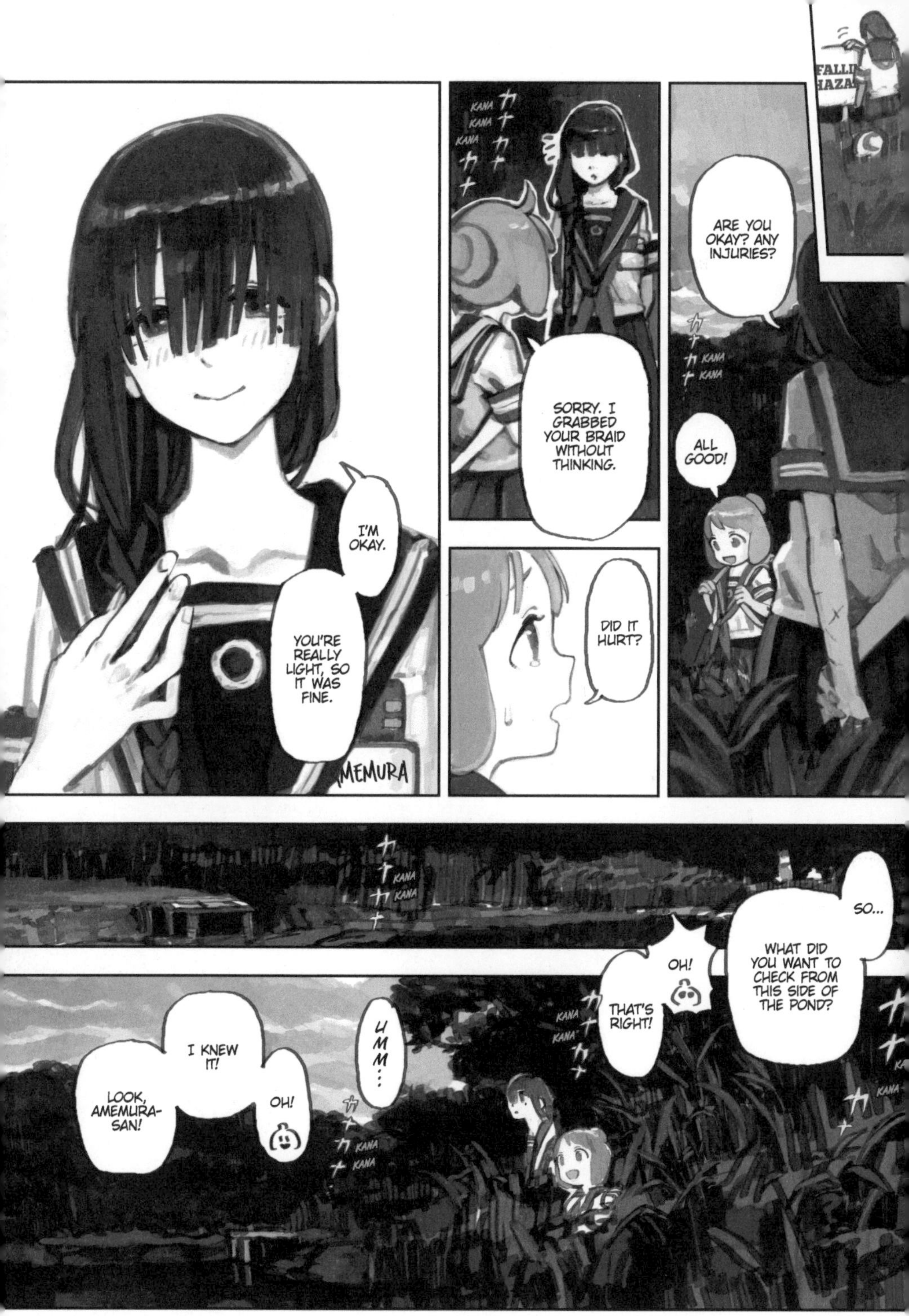
ARE YOU OKAY? ANY INJURIES?
KANA KANA
ALL GOOD!
KANA KANA KANA
SORRY. I GRABBED YOUR BRAID WITHOUT THINKING.
DID IT HURT?
I'M OKAY.
YOU'RE REALLY LIGHT, SO IT WAS FINE.
KANA KANA
SO...
WHAT DID YOU WANT TO CHECK FROM THIS SIDE OF THE POND?
KANA
OH!
THAT'S RIGHT!
KANA KANA
UMM...
I KNEW IT!
OH!
LOOK, AMEMURA-SAN!
KANA KANA

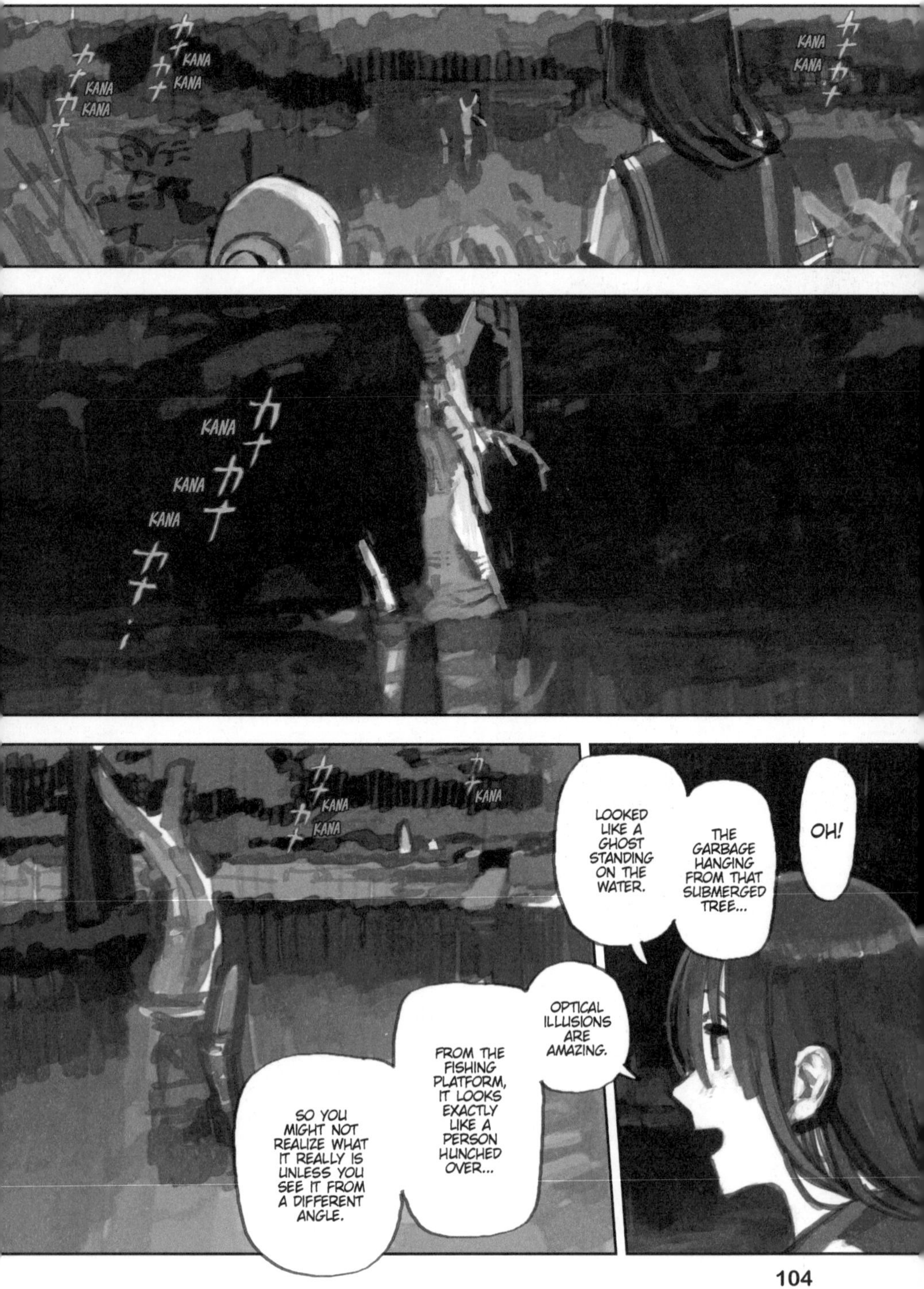
カナカナ KANA KANA
カナカナ KANA KANA
カナカナ KANA KANA
カナカナカナ KANA KANA KANA
OH!
THE GARBAGE HANGING FROM THAT SUBMERGED TREE...
LOOKED LIKE A GHOST STANDING ON THE WATER.
OPTICAL ILLUSIONS ARE AMAZING.
FROM THE FISHING PLATFORM, IT LOOKS EXACTLY LIKE A PERSON HUNCHED OVER...
SO YOU MIGHT NOT REALIZE WHAT IT REALLY IS UNLESS YOU SEE IT FROM A DIFFERENT ANGLE.
カ KANA
カナカナ KANA KANA

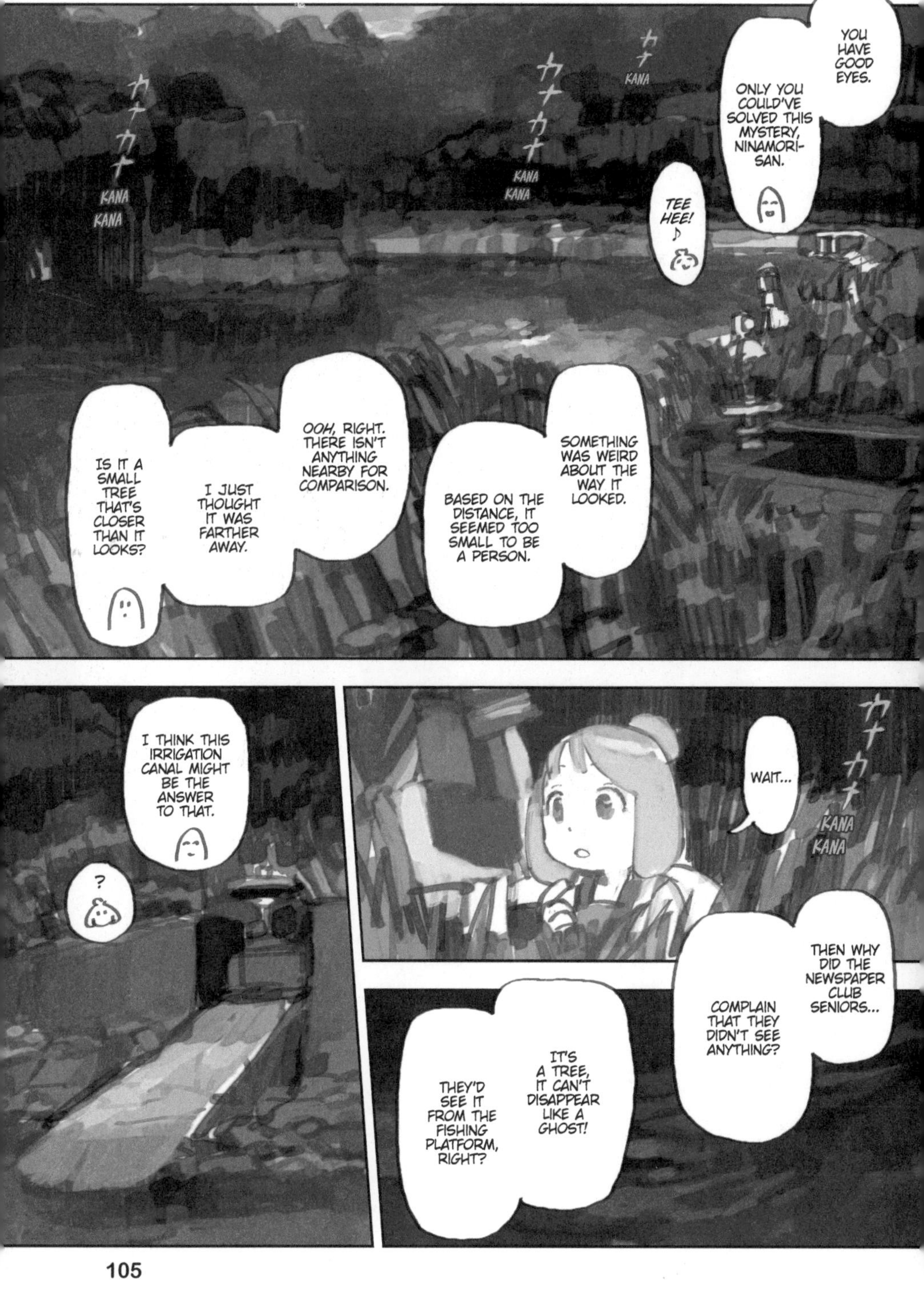
YOU HAVE GOOD EYES.
ONLY YOU COULD'VE SOLVED THIS MYSTERY, NINAMORI-SAN.
TEE HEE! ♪
KANA
KANA KANA
KANA KANA
SOMETHING WAS WEIRD ABOUT THE WAY IT LOOKED.
BASED ON THE DISTANCE, IT SEEMED TOO SMALL TO BE A PERSON.
OOH, RIGHT. THERE ISN'T ANYTHING NEARBY FOR COMPARISON.
I JUST THOUGHT IT WAS FARTHER AWAY.
IS IT A SMALL TREE THAT'S CLOSER THAN IT LOOKS?
WAIT...
KANA KANA
THEN WHY DID THE NEWSPAPER CLUB SENIORS...
COMPLAIN THAT THEY DIDN'T SEE ANYTHING?
IT'S A TREE, IT CAN'T DISAPPEAR LIKE A GHOST!
THEY'D SEE IT FROM THE FISHING PLATFORM, RIGHT?
I THINK THIS IRRIGATION CANAL MIGHT BE THE ANSWER TO THAT.
?

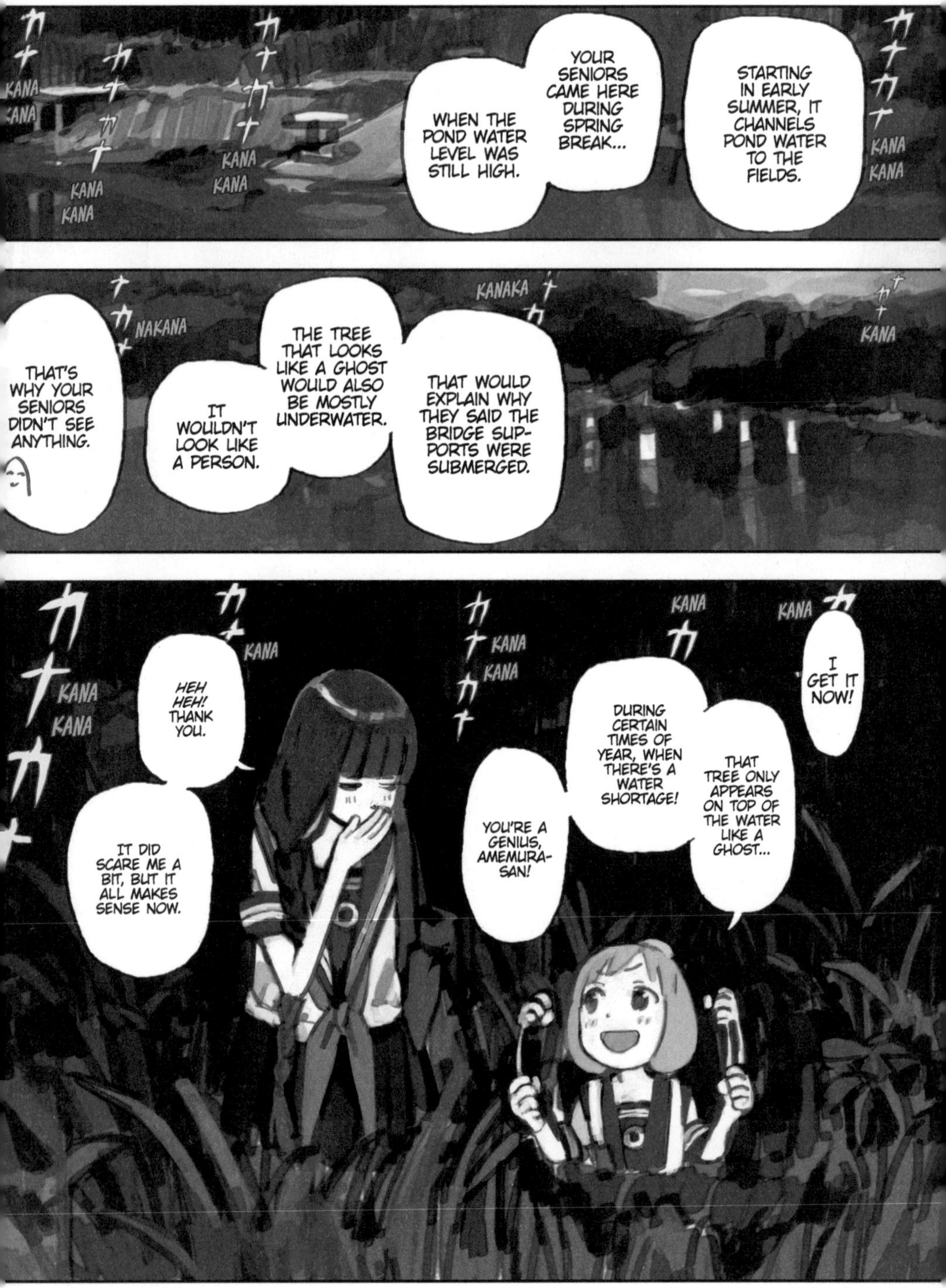
KANA KANA
STARTING IN EARLY SUMMER, IT CHANNELS POND WATER TO THE FIELDS.
YOUR SENIORS CAME HERE DURING SPRING BREAK...
WHEN THE POND WATER LEVEL WAS STILL HIGH.
KANA KANA
KANA KANA
KANA
KANA
KANAKA
THAT WOULD EXPLAIN WHY THEY SAID THE BRIDGE SUP-PORTS WERE SUBMERGED.
THE TREE THAT LOOKS LIKE A GHOST WOULD ALSO BE MOSTLY UNDERWATER.
IT WOULDN'T LOOK LIKE A PERSON.
NAKANA
THAT'S WHY YOUR SENIORS DIDN'T SEE ANYTHING.
KANA
KANA
I GET IT NOW!
THAT TREE ONLY APPEARS ON TOP OF THE WATER LIKE A GHOST...
DURING CERTAIN TIMES OF YEAR, WHEN THERE'S A WATER SHORTAGE!
YOU'RE A GENIUS, AMEMURA-SAN!
KANA KANA
KANA
HEH HEH! THANK YOU.
IT DID SCARE ME A BIT, BUT IT ALL MAKES SENSE NOW.
KANA KANA

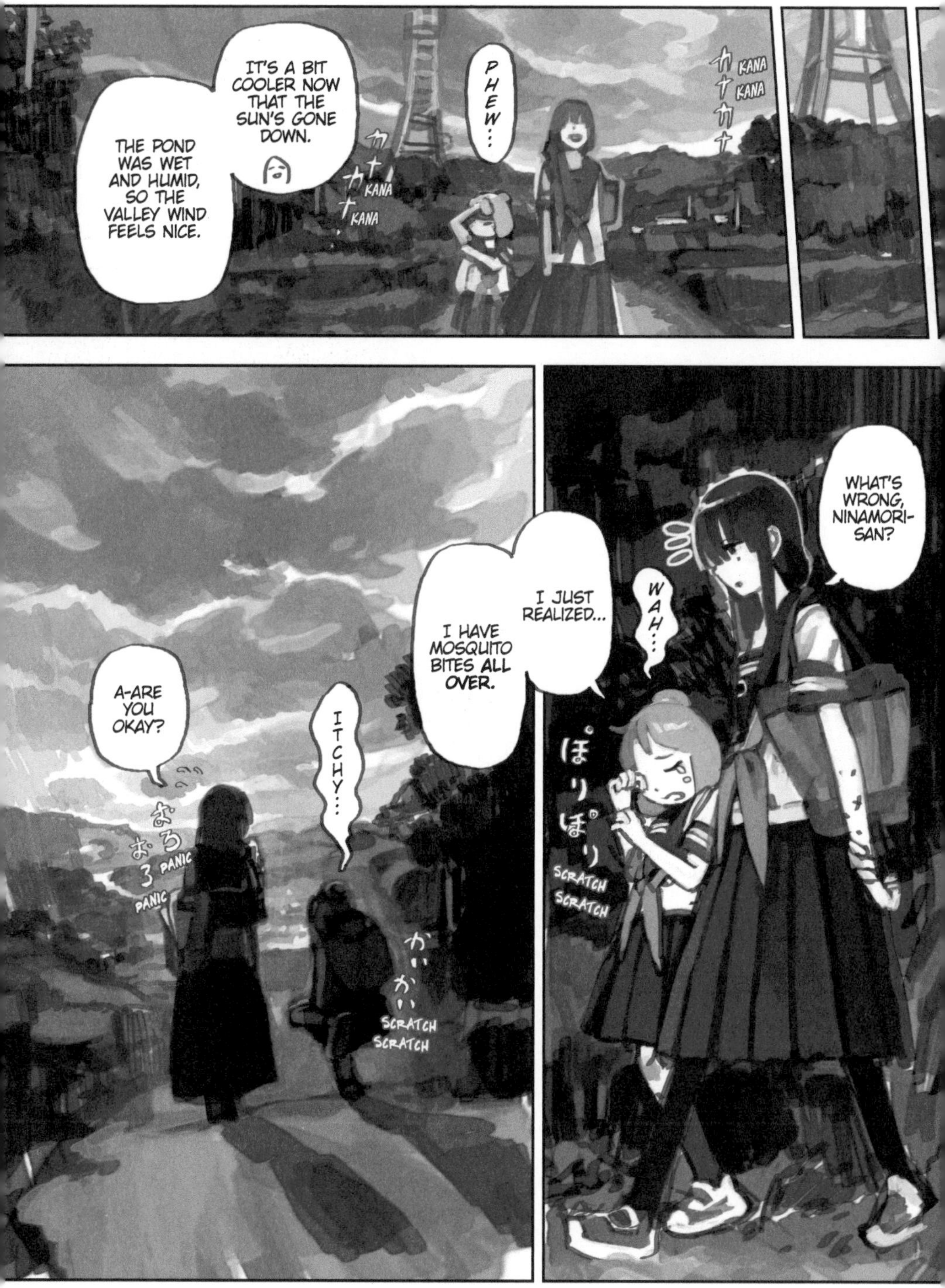
カナカナ KANA KANA
PHEW...
IT'S A BIT COOLER NOW THAT THE SUN'S GONE DOWN.
THE POND WAS WET AND HUMID, SO THE VALLEY WIND FEELS NICE.
カナカナ KANA KANA
WHAT'S WRONG, NINAMORI-SAN?
WAH...
I JUST REALIZED...
I HAVE MOSQUITO BITES **ALL OVER.**
ぽりぽり SCRATCH SCRATCH
ITCHY...
A-ARE YOU OKAY?
おろおろ PANIC PANIC
かいかい SCRATCH SCRATCH

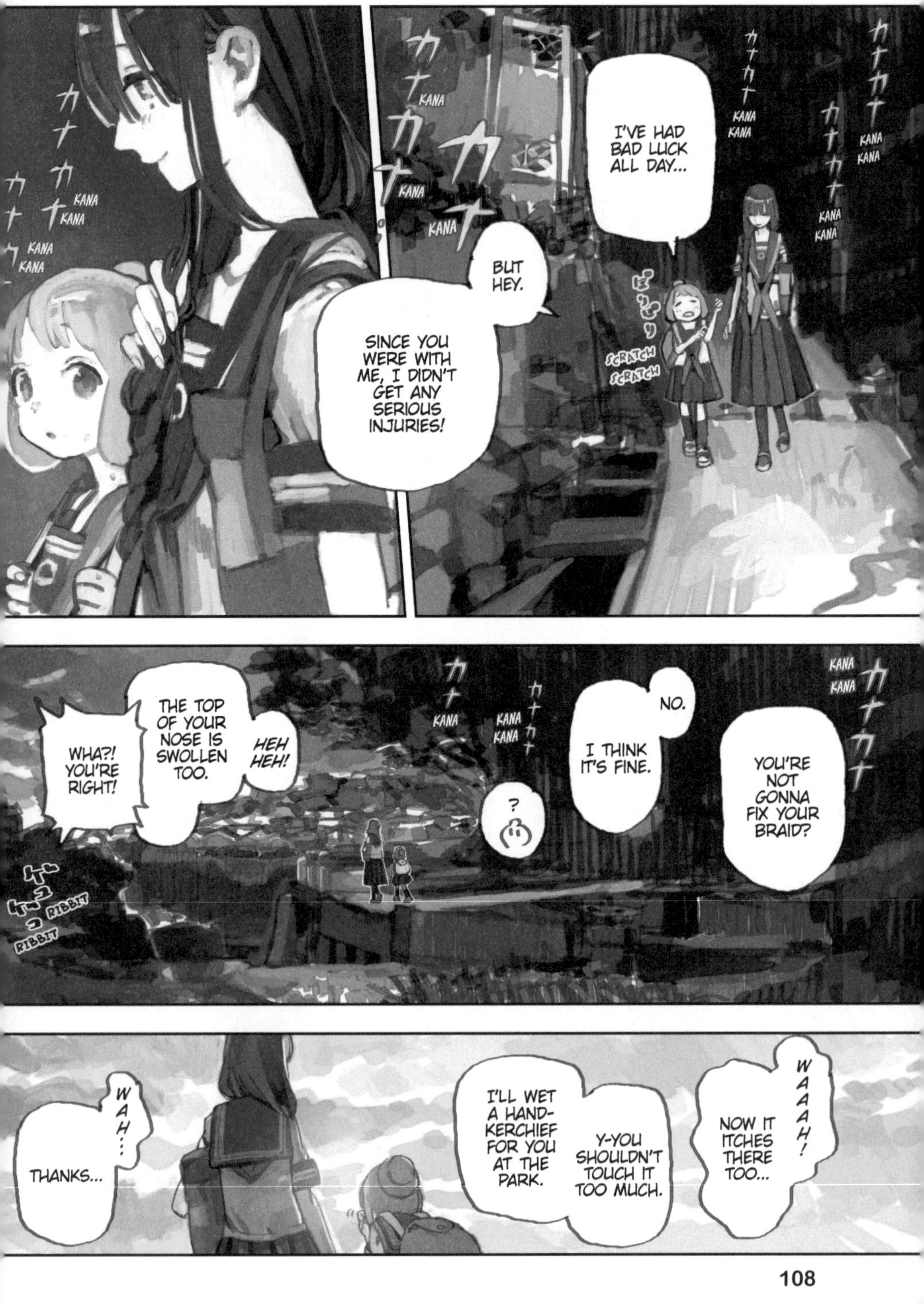
KANA KANA
I'VE HAD BAD LUCK ALL DAY...
SCRATCH SCRATCH
BUT HEY.
SINCE YOU WERE WITH ME, I DIDN'T GET ANY SERIOUS INJURIES!
KANA KANA
KANA KANA
YOU'RE NOT GONNA FIX YOUR BRAID?
NO.
I THINK IT'S FINE.
KANA KANA
?
HEH HEH!
THE TOP OF YOUR NOSE IS SWOLLEN TOO.
WHA?! YOU'RE RIGHT!
RIBBIT RIBBIT
NOW IT ITCHES THERE TOO...
WAAAAH!
Y-YOU SHOULDN'T TOUCH IT TOO MUCH.
I'LL WET A HAND-KERCHIEF FOR YOU AT THE PARK.
WAAH...
THANKS...

NIGHTFALL TRAVELERS

LEAVE ONLY FOOTPRINTS

NIGHTFALL TRAVELERS

LEAVE ONLY FOOTPRINTS

Intermission: Good Night Akane-chan @ Coming Home After Chapter 5

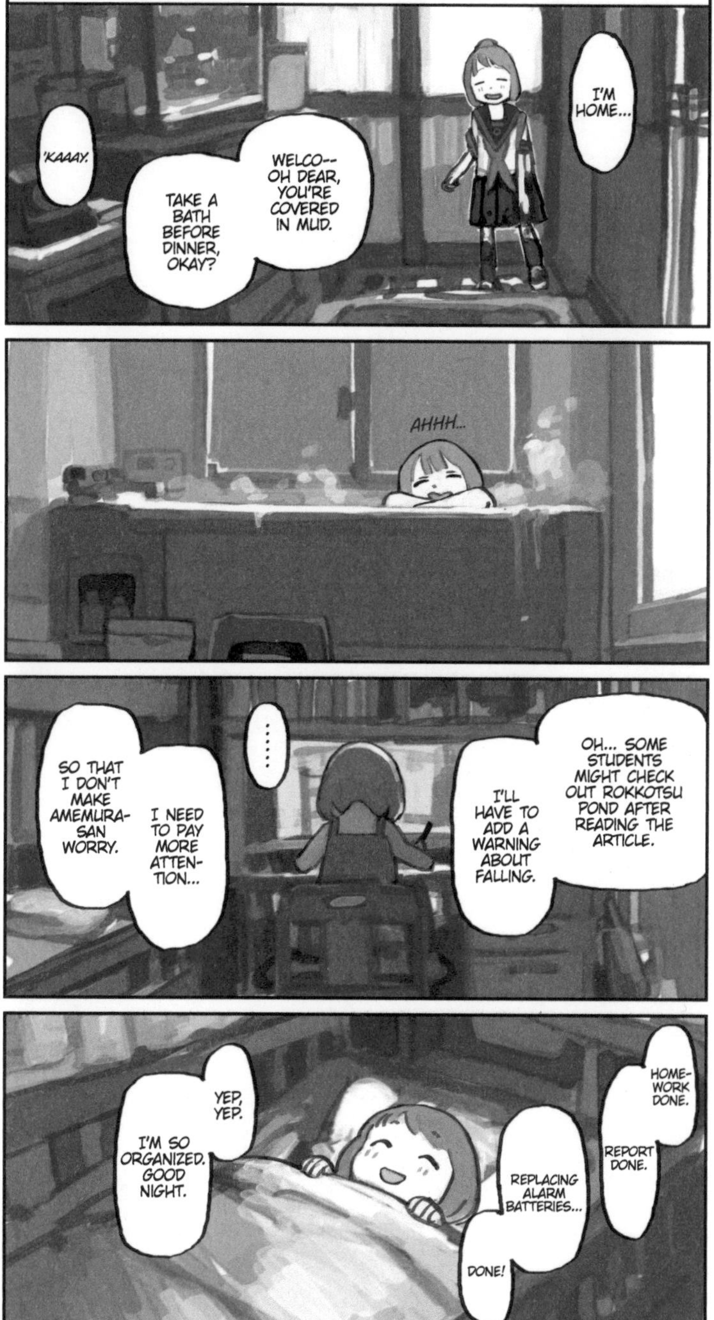
I'M HOME...
WELCO-- OH DEAR, YOU'RE COVERED IN MUD.
TAKE A BATH BEFORE DINNER, OKAY?
'KAAAY.
AHHH...
OH... SOME STUDENTS MIGHT CHECK OUT ROKKOTSU POND AFTER READING THE ARTICLE.
I'LL HAVE TO ADD A WARNING ABOUT FALLING.
......
I NEED TO PAY MORE ATTEN-TION...
SO THAT I DON'T MAKE AMEMURA-SAN WORRY.
HOME-WORK DONE.
REPORT DONE.
REPLACING ALARM BATTERIES...
DONE!
YEP, YEP.
I'M SO ORGANIZED. GOOD NIGHT.

NIGHTFALL TRAVELERS

LEAVE ONLY FOOTPRINTS

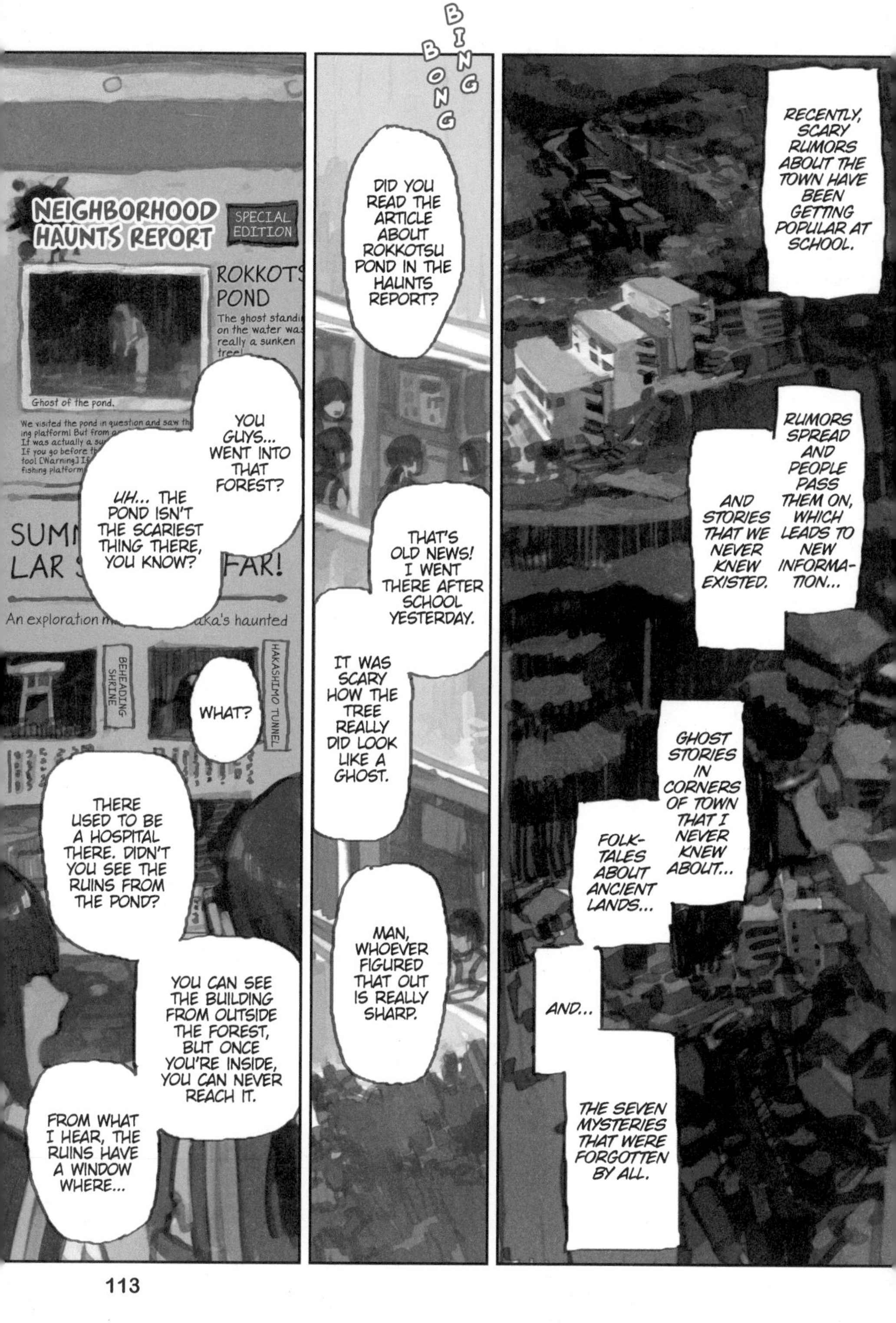
RECENTLY, SCARY RUMORS ABOUT THE TOWN HAVE BEEN GETTING POPULAR AT SCHOOL.
RUMORS SPREAD AND PEOPLE PASS THEM ON, WHICH LEADS TO NEW INFORMATION...
AND STORIES THAT WE NEVER KNEW EXISTED.
GHOST STORIES IN CORNERS OF TOWN THAT I NEVER KNEW ABOUT...
FOLKTALES ABOUT ANCIENT LANDS...
AND...
THE SEVEN MYSTERIES THAT WERE FORGOTTEN BY ALL.
BING BONG
DID YOU READ THE ARTICLE ABOUT ROKKOTSU POND IN THE HAUNTS REPORT?
THAT'S OLD NEWS! I WENT THERE AFTER SCHOOL YESTERDAY.
IT WAS SCARY HOW THE TREE REALLY DID LOOK LIKE A GHOST.
MAN, WHOEVER FIGURED THAT OUT IS REALLY SHARP.
NEIGHBORHOOD HAUNTS REPORT
SPECIAL EDITION
Ghost of the pond.
BEHEADING SHRINE
HAKASHIMO TUNNEL
YOU GUYS... WENT INTO THAT FOREST?
UH... THE POND ISN'T THE SCARIEST THING THERE, YOU KNOW?
WHAT?
THERE USED TO BE A HOSPITAL THERE. DIDN'T YOU SEE THE RUINS FROM THE POND?
YOU CAN SEE THE BUILDING FROM OUTSIDE THE FOREST, BUT ONCE YOU'RE INSIDE, YOU CAN NEVER REACH IT.
FROM WHAT I HEAR, THE RUINS HAVE A WINDOW WHERE...

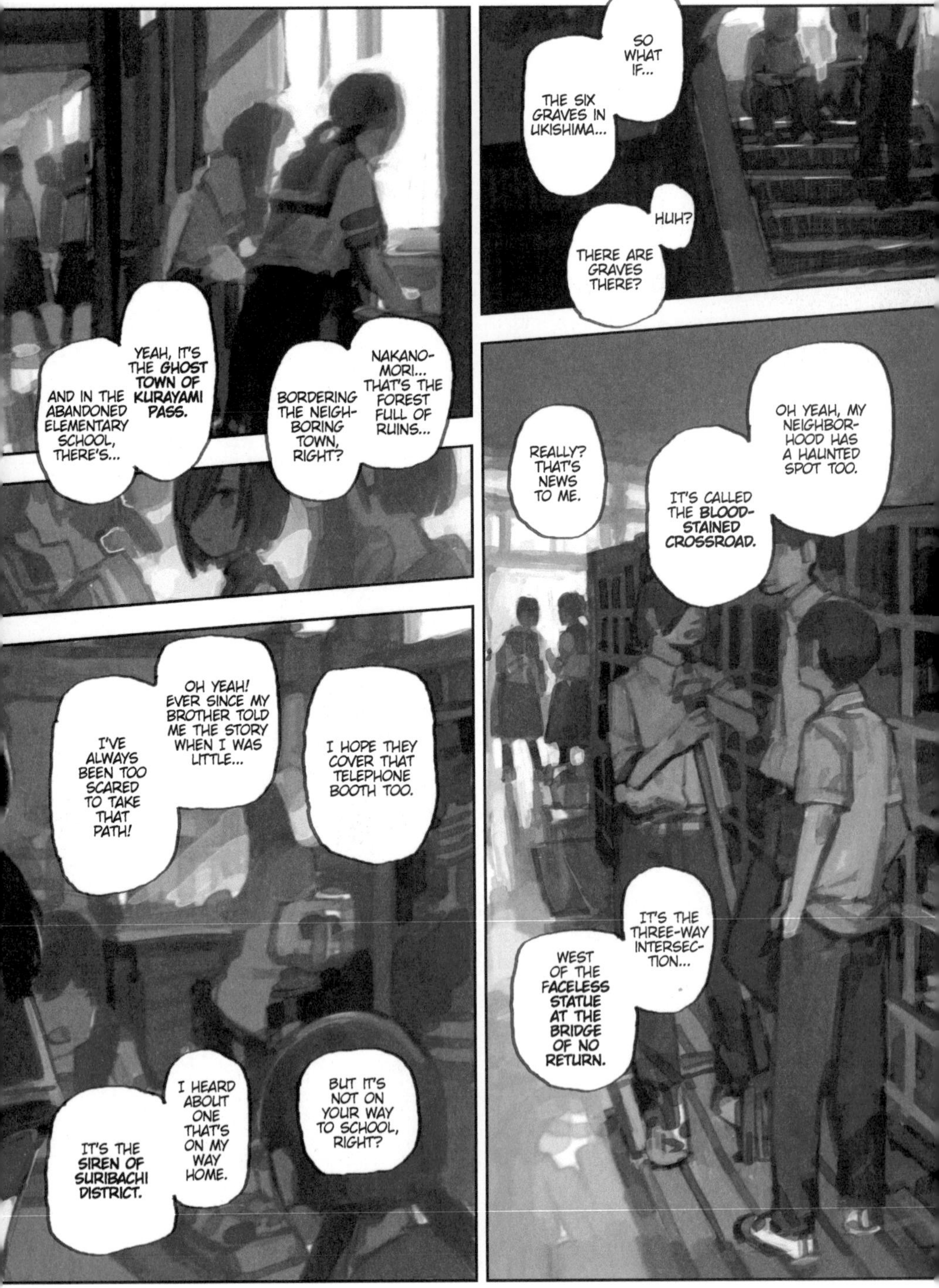
SO WHAT IF...
THE SIX GRAVES IN UKISHIMA...
HUH?
THERE ARE GRAVES THERE?
OH YEAH, MY NEIGHBOR-HOOD HAS A HAUNTED SPOT TOO.
REALLY? THAT'S NEWS TO ME.
IT'S CALLED THE BLOOD-STAINED CROSSROAD.
IT'S THE THREE-WAY INTERSEC-TION...
WEST OF THE FACELESS STATUE AT THE BRIDGE OF NO RETURN.
NAKANO-MORI... THAT'S THE FOREST FULL OF RUINS...
BORDERING THE NEIGH-BORING TOWN, RIGHT?
YEAH, IT'S THE GHOST TOWN OF KURAYAMI PASS.
AND IN THE ABANDONED ELEMENTARY SCHOOL, THERE'S...
I HOPE THEY COVER THAT TELEPHONE BOOTH TOO.
OH YEAH! EVER SINCE MY BROTHER TOLD ME THE STORY WHEN I WAS LITTLE...
I'VE ALWAYS BEEN TOO SCARED TO TAKE THAT PATH!
BUT IT'S NOT ON YOUR WAY TO SCHOOL, RIGHT?
I HEARD ABOUT ONE THAT'S ON MY WAY HOME.
IT'S THE SIREN OF SURIBACHI DISTRICT.

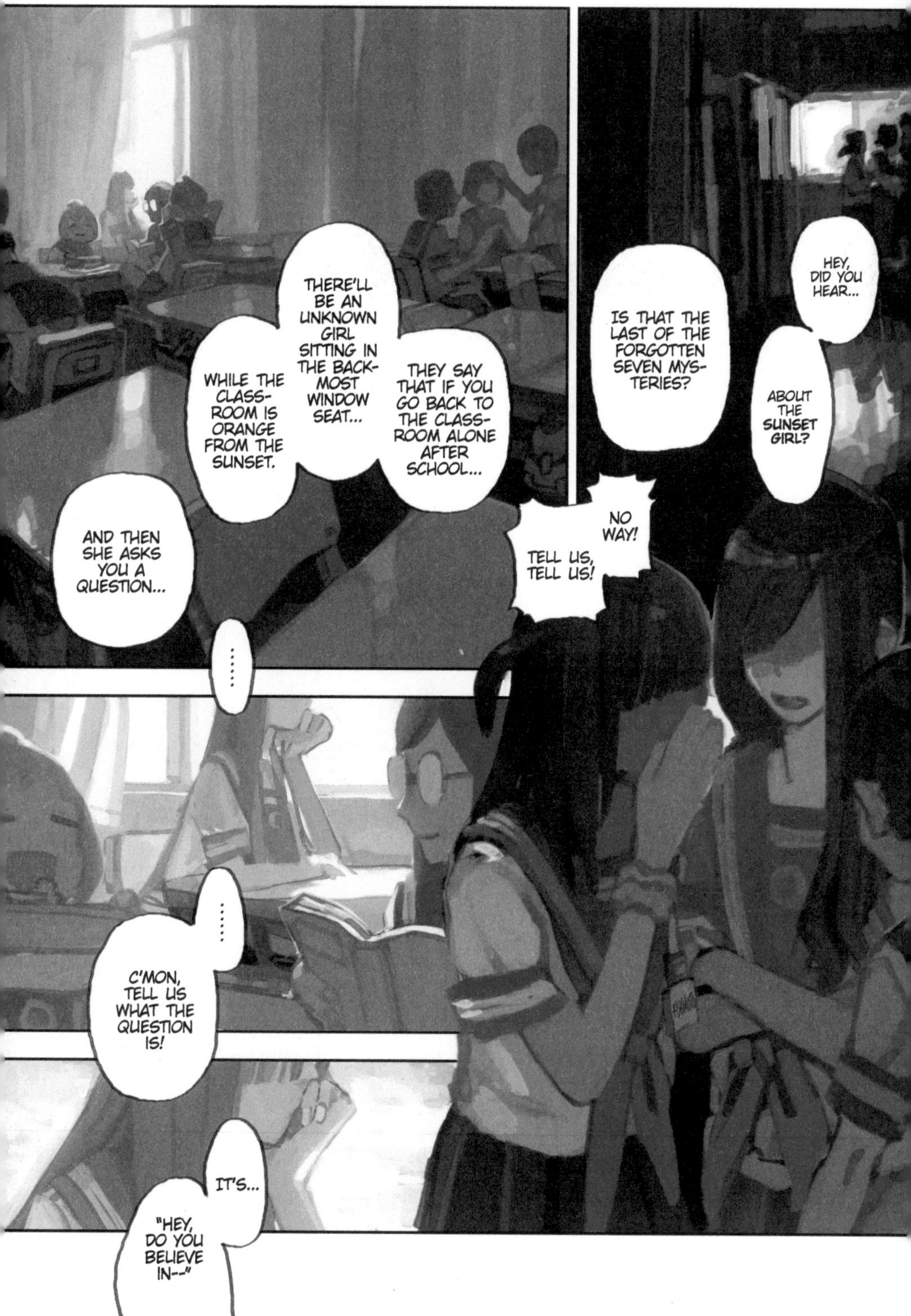
HEY, DID YOU HEAR...
ABOUT THE SUNSET GIRL?
IS THAT THE LAST OF THE FORGOTTEN SEVEN MYSTERIES?
NO WAY!
TELL US, TELL US!
THEY SAY THAT IF YOU GO BACK TO THE CLASSROOM ALONE AFTER SCHOOL...
THERE'LL BE AN UNKNOWN GIRL SITTING IN THE BACKMOST WINDOW SEAT...
WHILE THE CLASSROOM IS ORANGE FROM THE SUNSET.
AND THEN SHE ASKS YOU A QUESTION...
......
......
C'MON, TELL US WHAT THE QUESTION IS!
IT'S...
"HEY, DO YOU BELIEVE IN--"

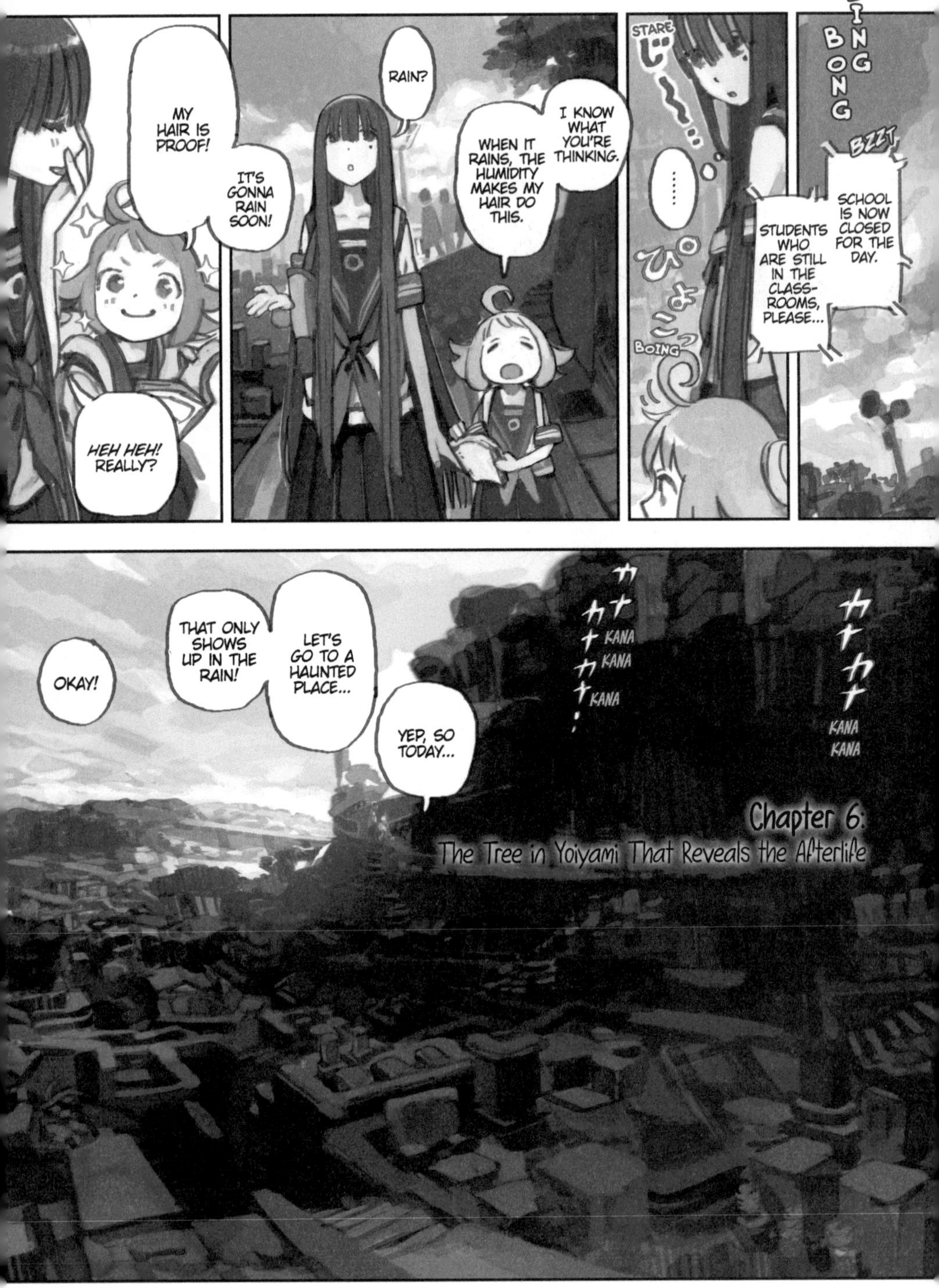
BING BONG
BZZT
SCHOOL IS NOW CLOSED FOR THE DAY.
STUDENTS WHO ARE STILL IN THE CLASS-ROOMS, PLEASE...
STARE
じ～…
......
ぴょこっ
BOING
I KNOW WHAT YOU'RE THINKING.
WHEN IT RAINS, THE HUMIDITY MAKES MY HAIR DO THIS.
RAIN?
IT'S GONNA RAIN SOON!
MY HAIR IS PROOF!
HEH HEH! REALLY?
カナカナ
KANA KANA
カナカナ
KANA KANA
カナ
KANA
YEP, SO TODAY...
LET'S GO TO A HAUNTED PLACE...
THAT ONLY SHOWS UP IN THE RAIN!
OKAY!
Chapter 6:
The Tree in Yoiyami That Reveals the Afterlife

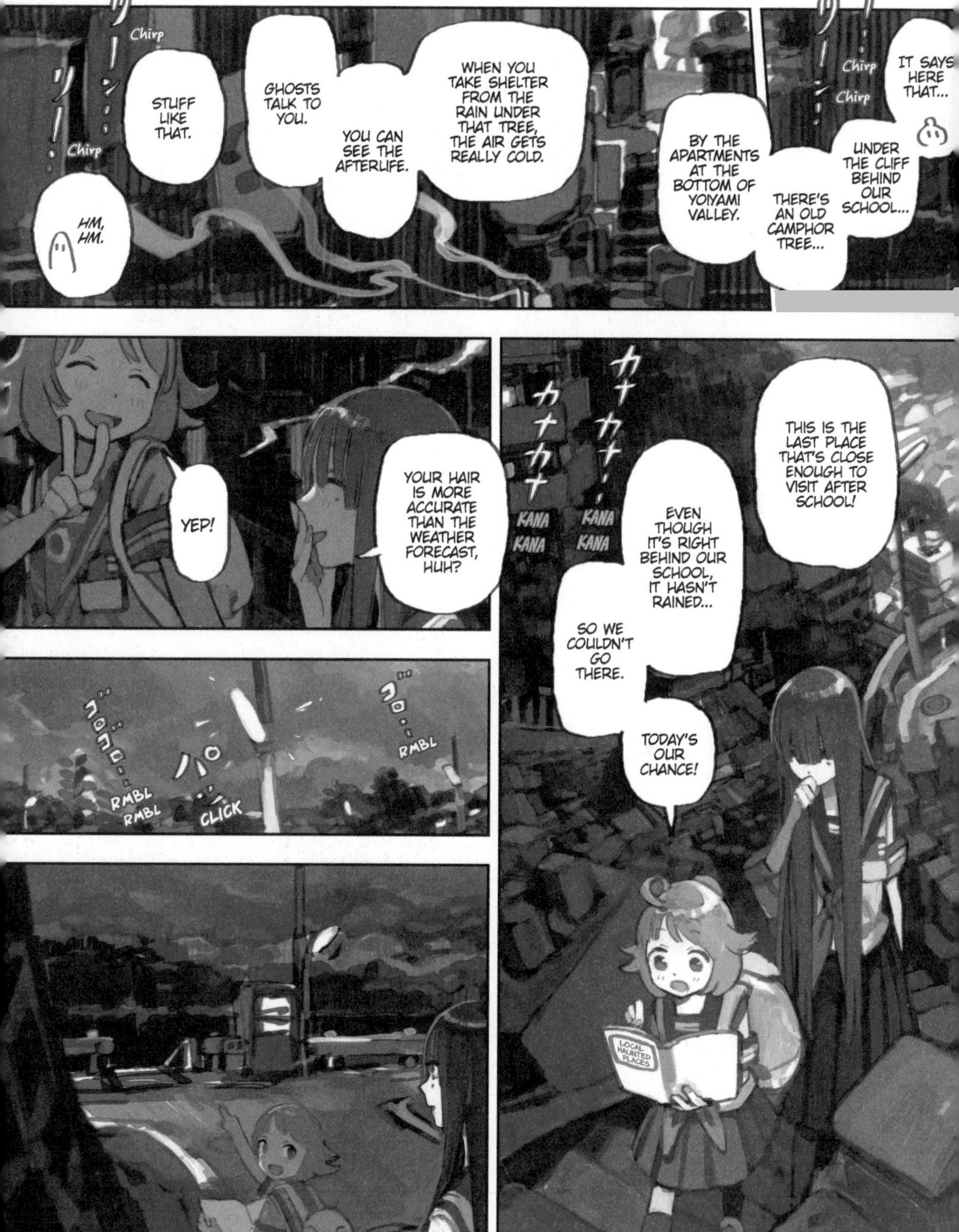
Chirp
Chirp
IT SAYS HERE THAT...
UNDER THE CLIFF BEHIND OUR SCHOOL...
THERE'S AN OLD CAMPHOR TREE...
BY THE APARTMENTS AT THE BOTTOM OF YOIYAMI VALLEY.
WHEN YOU TAKE SHELTER FROM THE RAIN UNDER THAT TREE, THE AIR GETS REALLY COLD.
YOU CAN SEE THE AFTERLIFE.
GHOSTS TALK TO YOU.
Chirp
STUFF LIKE THAT.
Chirp
HM, HM.
THIS IS THE LAST PLACE THAT'S CLOSE ENOUGH TO VISIT AFTER SCHOOL!
KANA KANA
KANA KANA
EVEN THOUGH IT'S RIGHT BEHIND OUR SCHOOL, IT HASN'T RAINED...
SO WE COULDN'T GO THERE.
TODAY'S OUR CHANCE!
LOCAL HAUNTED PLACES
YOUR HAIR IS MORE ACCURATE THAN THE WEATHER FORECAST, HUH?
YEP!
RMBL
CLICK
RMBL RMBL

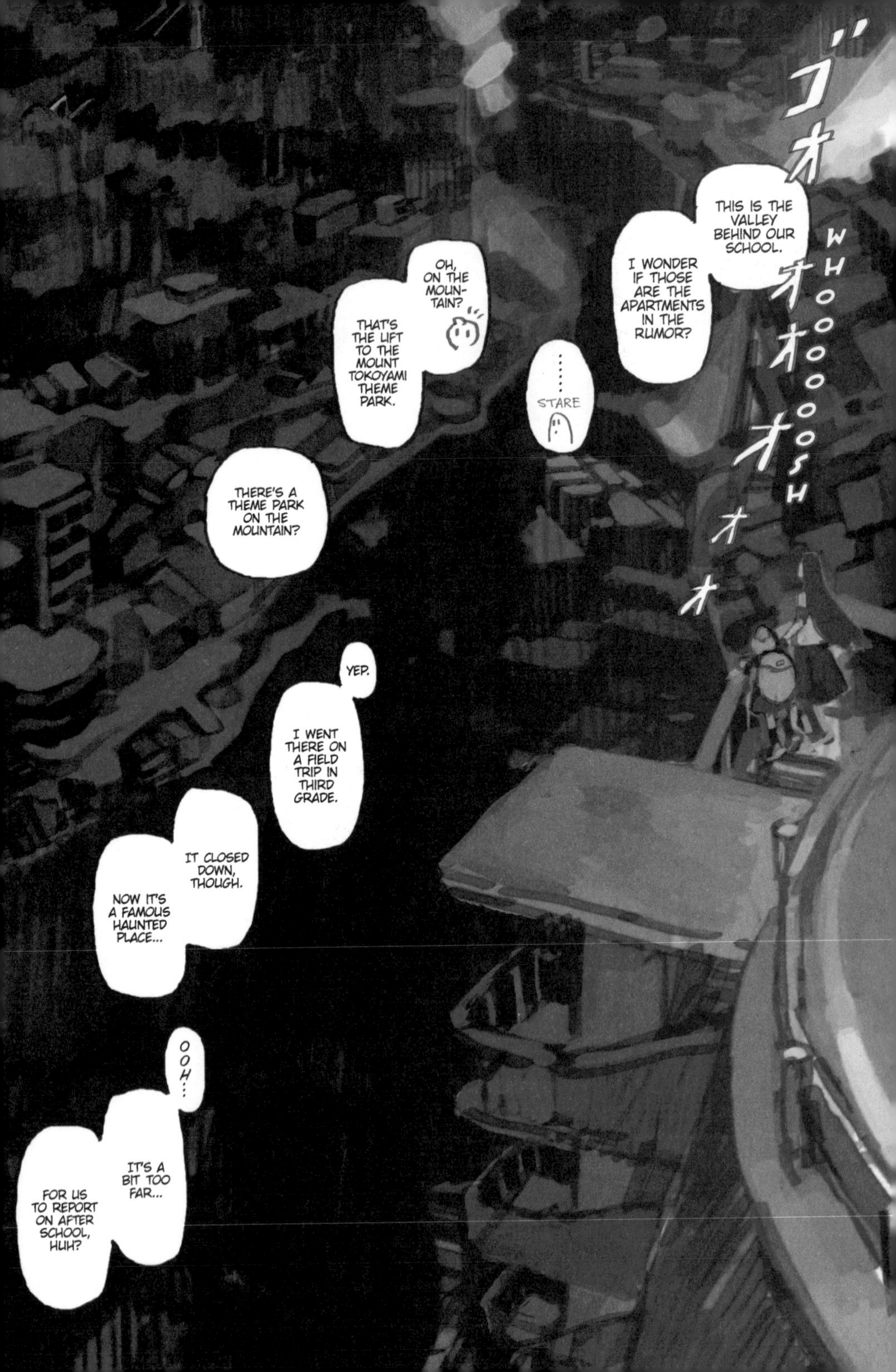

ゴオオオオオオ
WHOOOOOOOSH
THIS IS THE VALLEY BEHIND OUR SCHOOL.
I WONDER IF THOSE ARE THE APARTMENTS IN THE RUMOR?
......
STARE
OH, ON THE MOUNTAIN?
THAT'S THE LIFT TO THE MOUNT TOKOYAMI THEME PARK.
THERE'S A THEME PARK ON THE MOUNTAIN?
YEP.
I WENT THERE ON A FIELD TRIP IN THIRD GRADE.
IT CLOSED DOWN, THOUGH.
NOW IT'S A FAMOUS HAUNTED PLACE...
OOH...
IT'S A BIT TOO FAR...
FOR US TO REPORT ON AFTER SCHOOL, HUH?

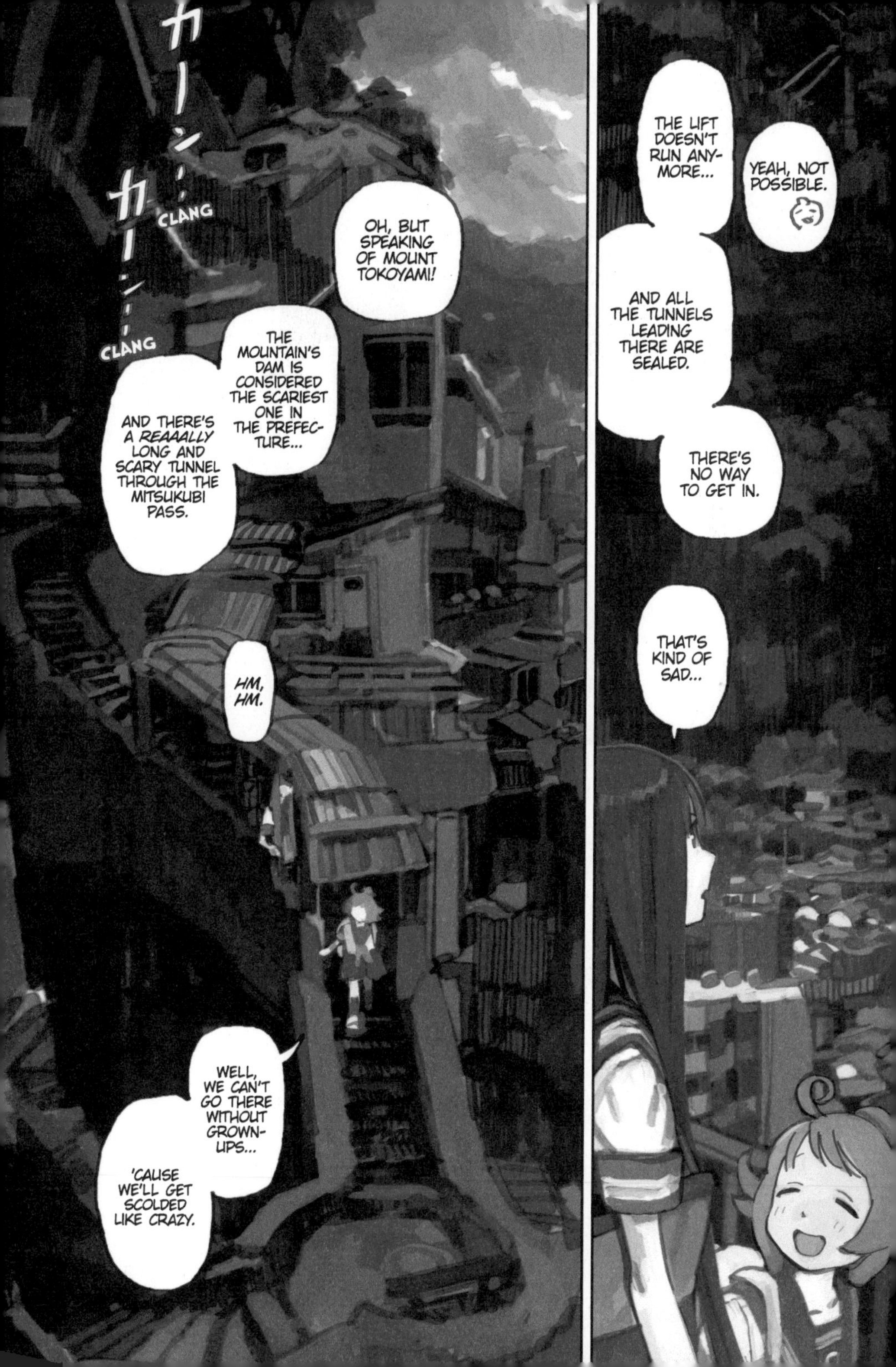
THE LIFT DOESN'T RUN ANY-MORE...
YEAH, NOT POSSIBLE.
AND ALL THE TUNNELS LEADING THERE ARE SEALED.
THERE'S NO WAY TO GET IN.
THAT'S KIND OF SAD...
CLANG
CLANG
OH, BUT SPEAKING OF MOUNT TOKOYAMI!
THE MOUNTAIN'S DAM IS CONSIDERED THE SCARIEST ONE IN THE PREFEC-TURE...
AND THERE'S A *REAAALLY* LONG AND SCARY TUNNEL THROUGH THE MITSUKUBI PASS.
HM, HM.
WELL, WE CAN'T GO THERE WITHOUT GROWN-UPS...
'CAUSE WE'LL GET SCOLDED LIKE CRAZY.

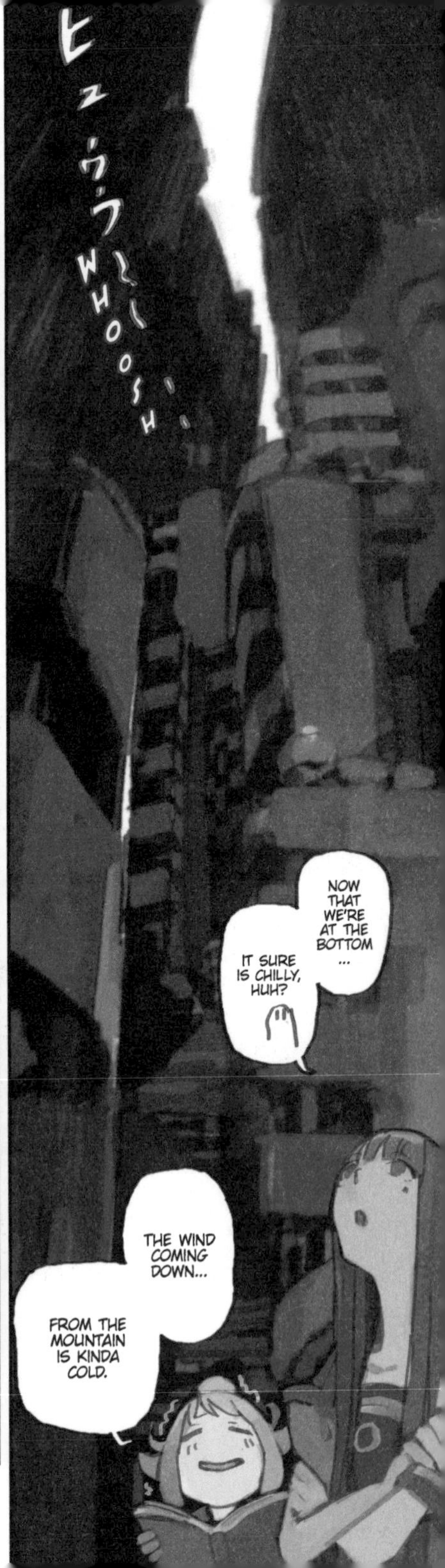
WHOOOSH
NOW THAT WE'RE AT THE BOTTOM...
IT SURE IS CHILLY, HUH?
THE WIND COMING DOWN...
FROM THE MOUNTAIN IS KINDA COLD.

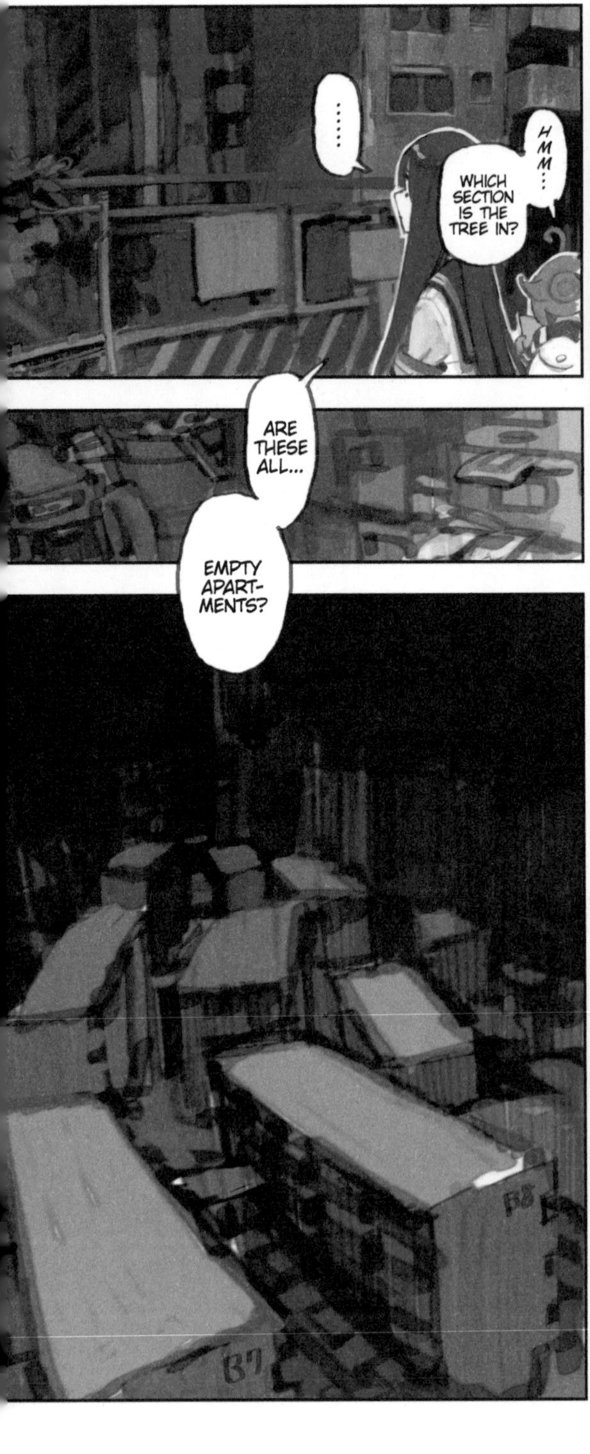
HMM... WHICH SECTION IS THE TREE IN?
......
ARE THESE ALL...
EMPTY APARTMENTS?
B8
B7

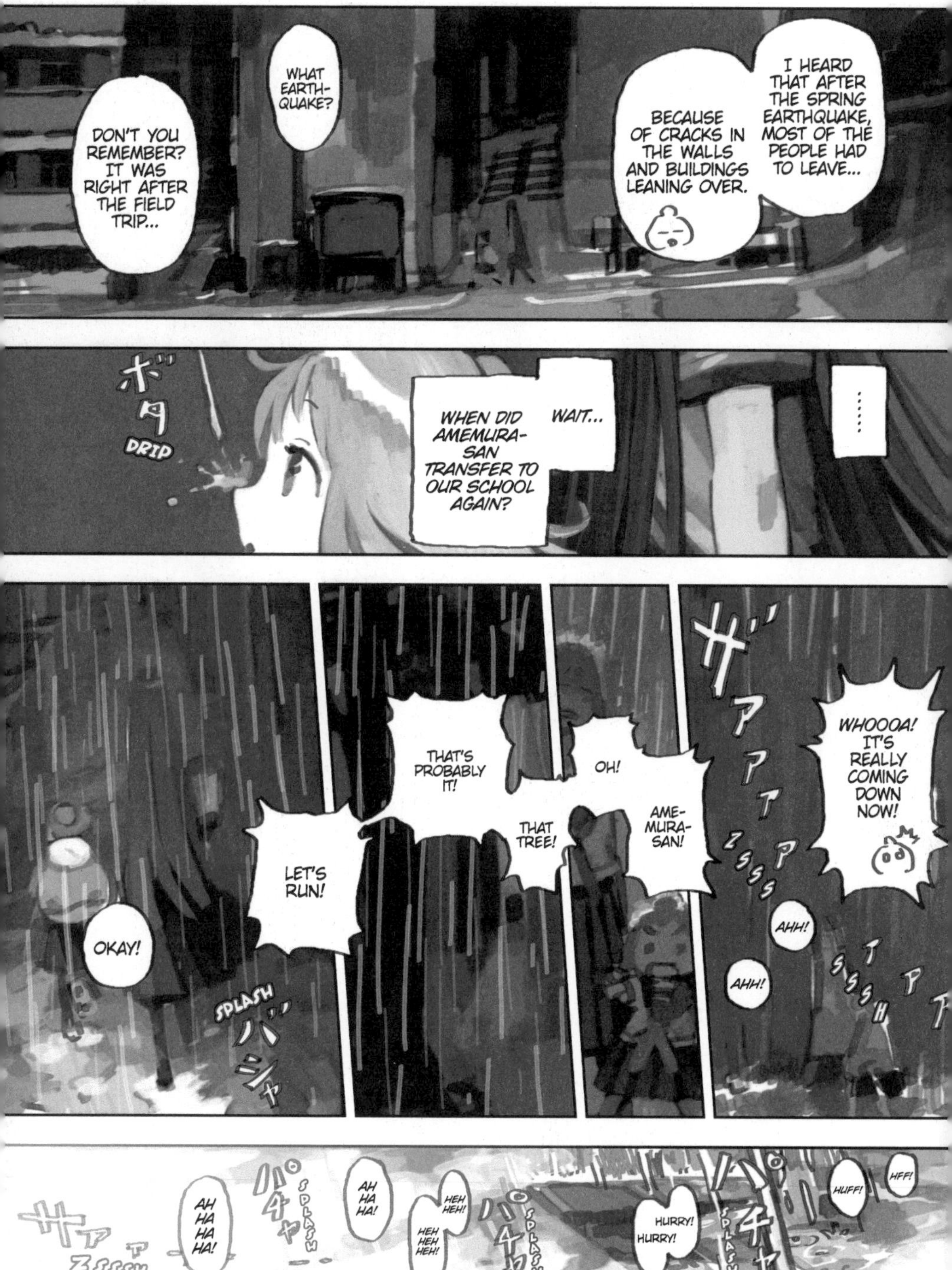
I HEARD THAT AFTER THE SPRING EARTHQUAKE, MOST OF THE PEOPLE HAD TO LEAVE...
BECAUSE OF CRACKS IN THE WALLS AND BUILDINGS LEANING OVER.
WHAT EARTHQUAKE?
DON'T YOU REMEMBER? IT WAS RIGHT AFTER THE FIELD TRIP...
......
WAIT...
WHEN DID AMEMURA-SAN TRANSFER TO OUR SCHOOL AGAIN?
ボタ
DRIP
ザァァァ
ZSSSP
WHOOOA! IT'S REALLY COMING DOWN NOW!
AHH!
AHH!
TSSSSHP
OH!
AME-MURA-SAN!
THAT TREE!
THAT'S PROBABLY IT!
LET'S RUN!
OKAY!
SPLASH
バシャ
HFF!
HUFF!
HURRY!
HURRY!
パチャ
SPLASH
HEH HEH!
HEH HEH HEH!
パチャ
SPLASH
AH HA HA!
パチャ
SPLASH
AH HA HA HA HA!
ザァァ
ZSSSSH

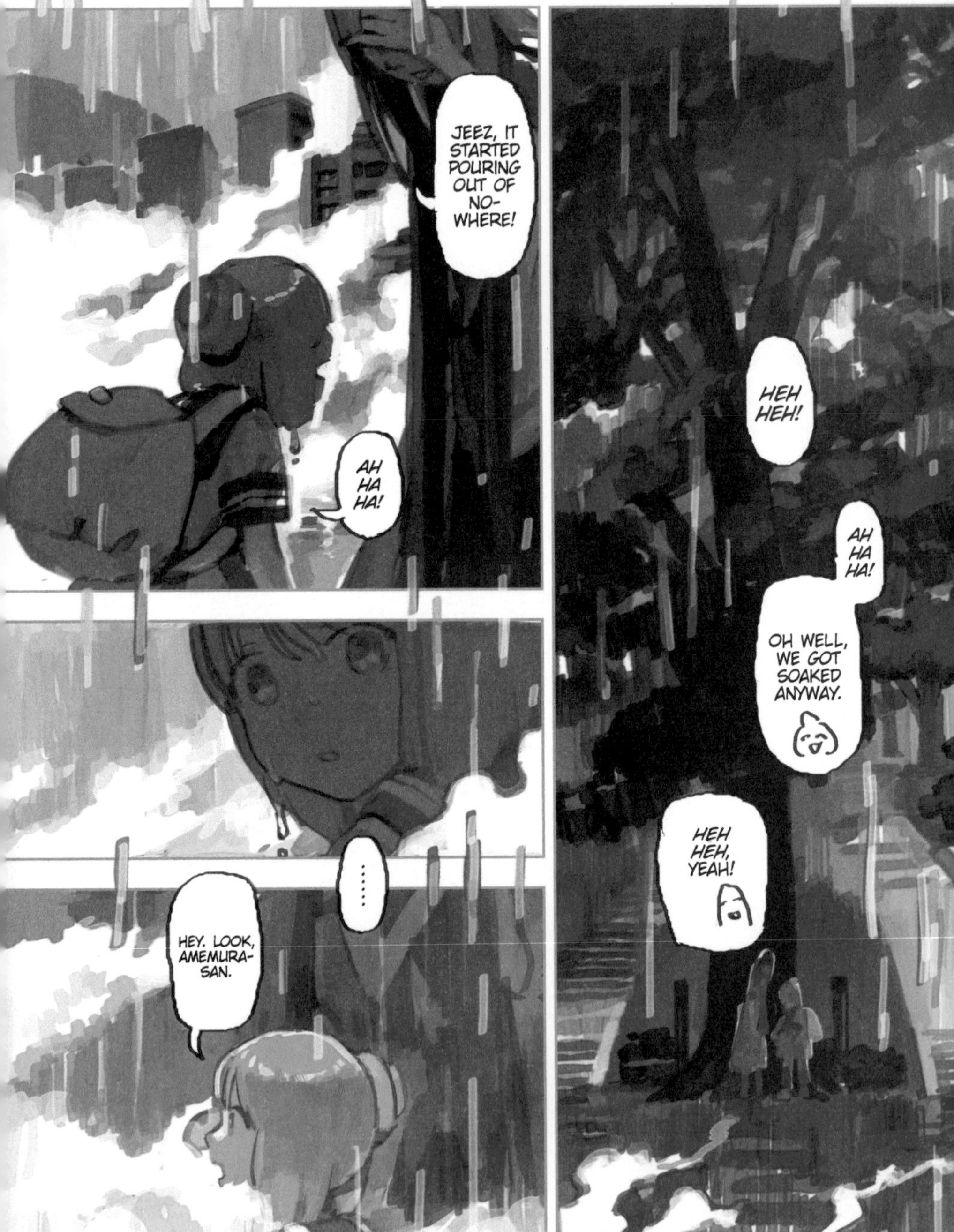
HEH HEH!
AH HA HA!
OH WELL, WE GOT SOAKED ANYWAY.
HEH HEH, YEAH!
JEEZ, IT STARTED POURING OUT OF NO-WHERE!
AH HA HA!
......
HEY. LOOK, AMEMURA-SAN.

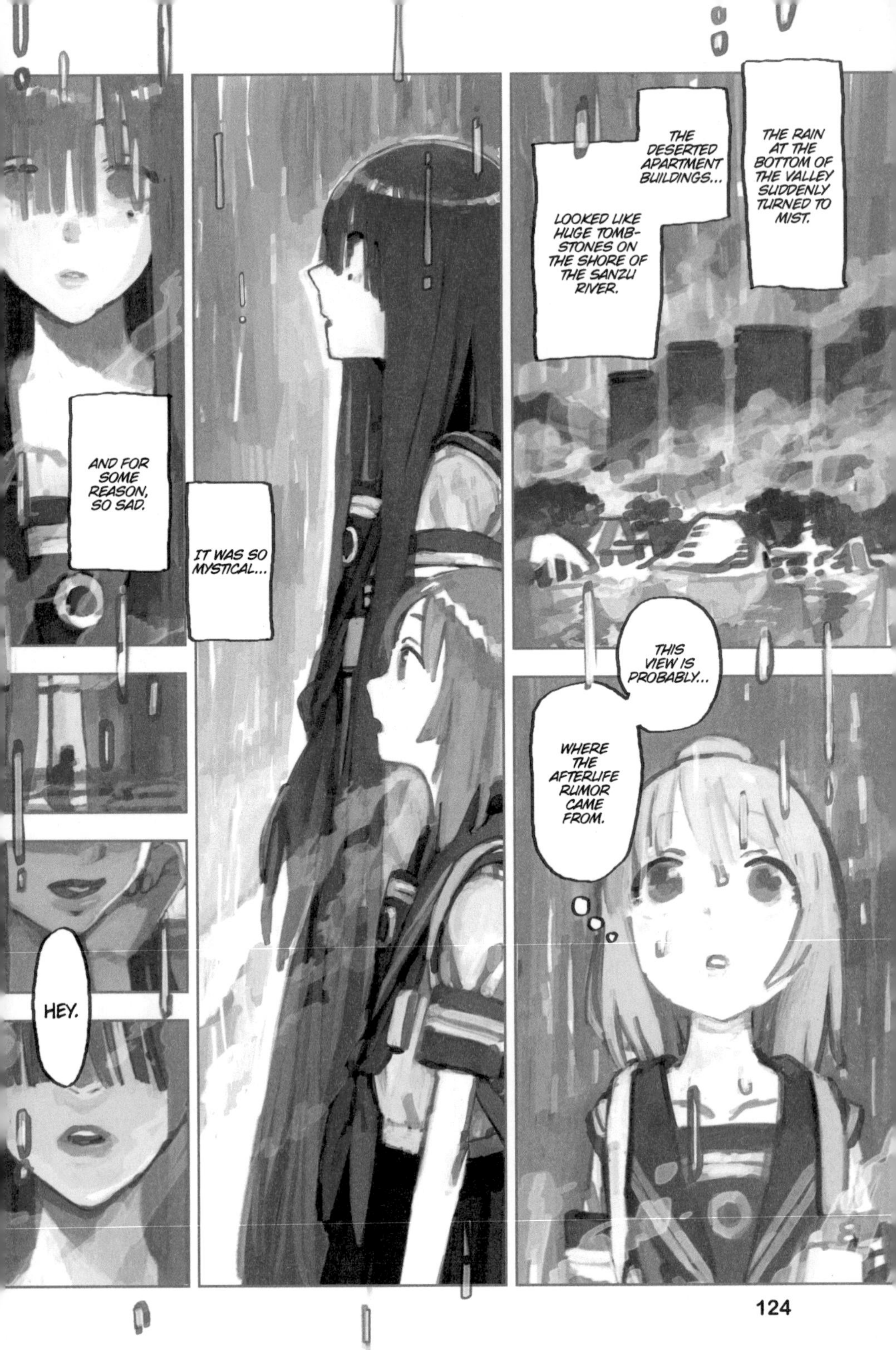
THE RAIN AT THE BOTTOM OF THE VALLEY SUDDENLY TURNED TO MIST.
THE DESERTED APARTMENT BUILDINGS...
LOOKED LIKE HUGE TOMB-STONES ON THE SHORE OF THE SANZU RIVER.
THIS VIEW IS PROBABLY...
WHERE THE AFTERLIFE RUMOR CAME FROM.
IT WAS SO MYSTICAL...
AND FOR SOME REASON, SO SAD.
HEY.

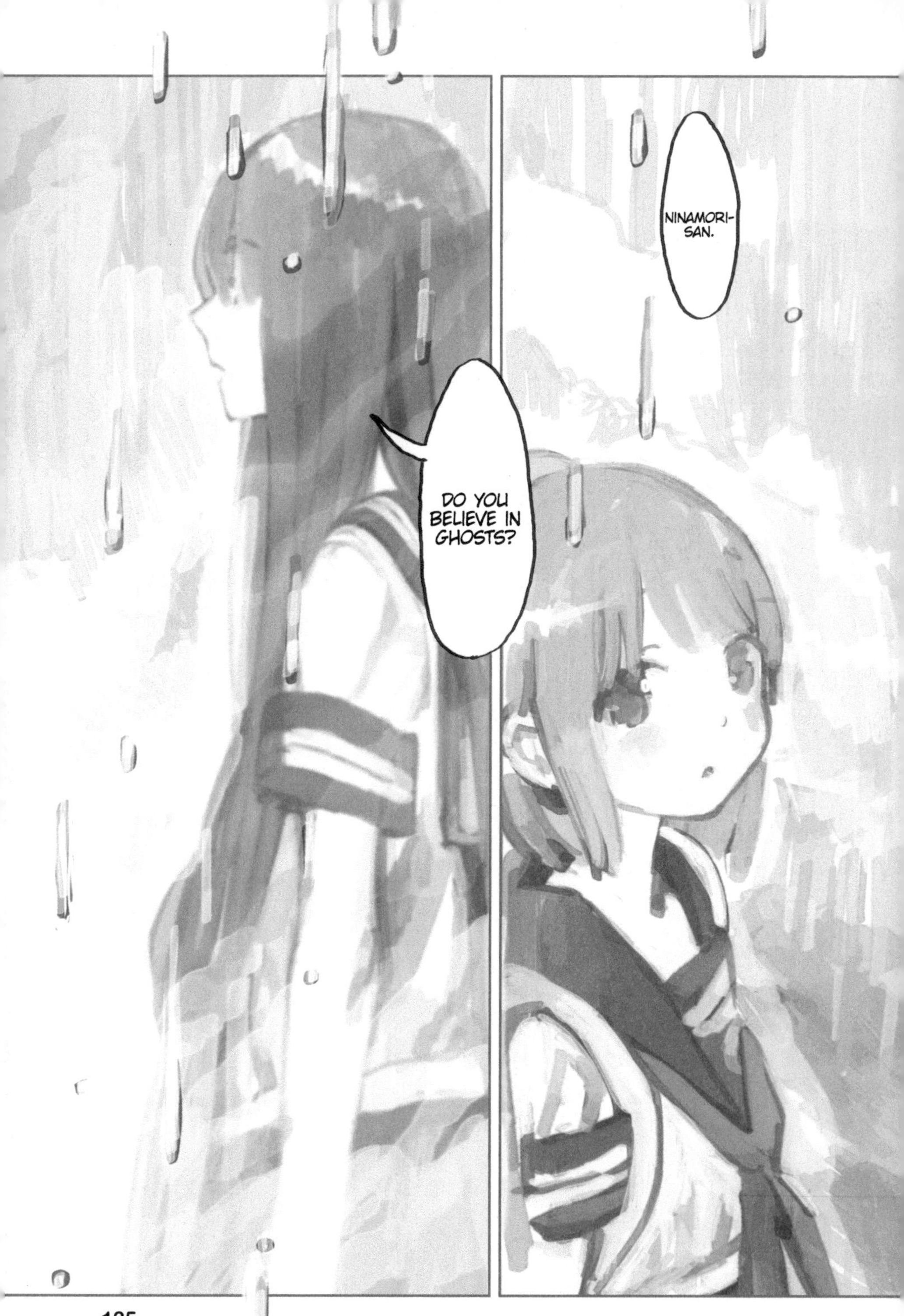
NINAMORI-SAN.
DO YOU BELIEVE IN GHOSTS?

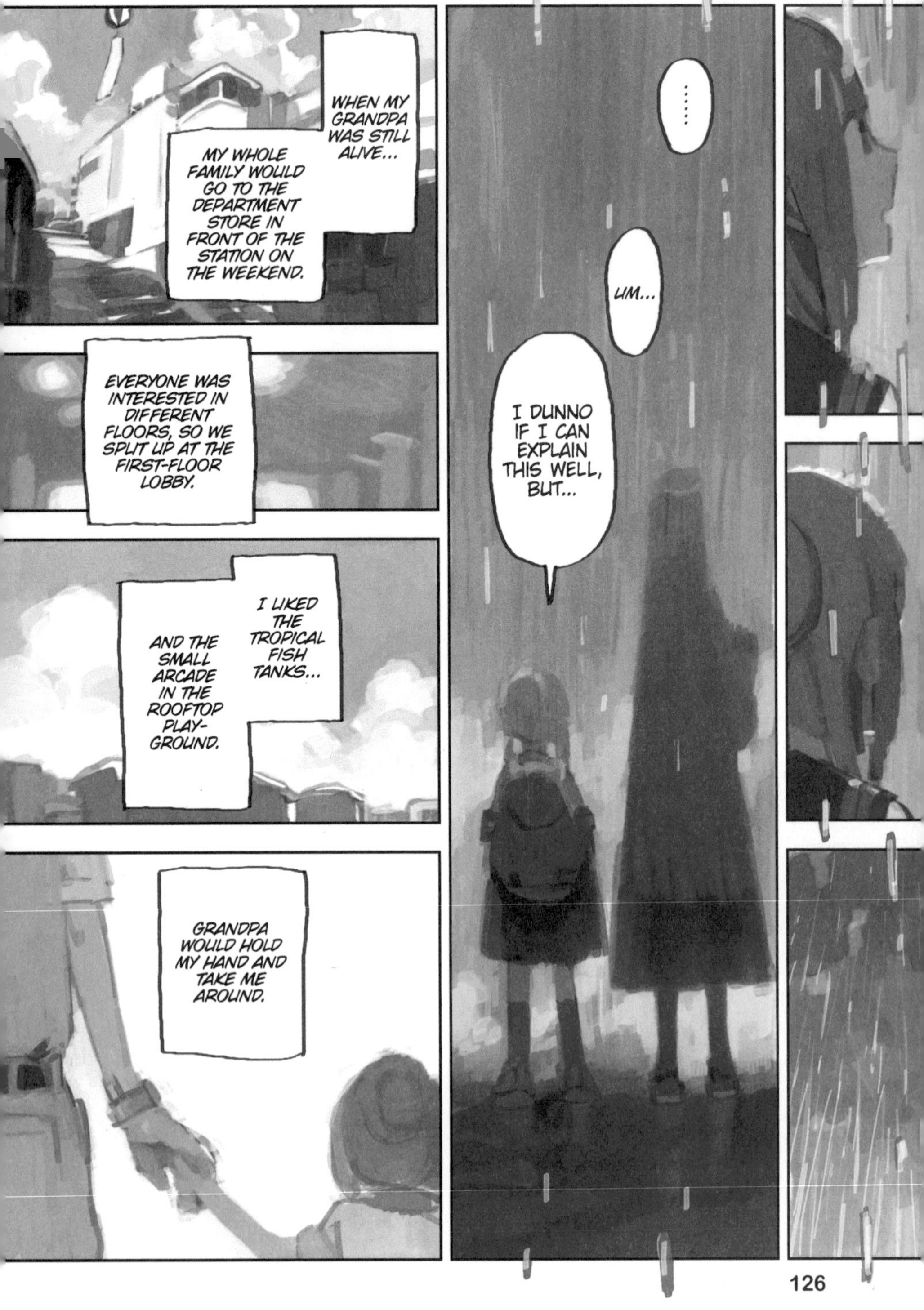
……
UM…
I DUNNO IF I CAN EXPLAIN THIS WELL, BUT…
WHEN MY GRANDPA WAS STILL ALIVE…
MY WHOLE FAMILY WOULD GO TO THE DEPARTMENT STORE IN FRONT OF THE STATION ON THE WEEKEND.
EVERYONE WAS INTERESTED IN DIFFERENT FLOORS, SO WE SPLIT UP AT THE FIRST-FLOOR LOBBY.
I LIKED THE TROPICAL FISH TANKS…
AND THE SMALL ARCADE IN THE ROOFTOP PLAY-GROUND.
GRANDPA WOULD HOLD MY HAND AND TAKE ME AROUND.

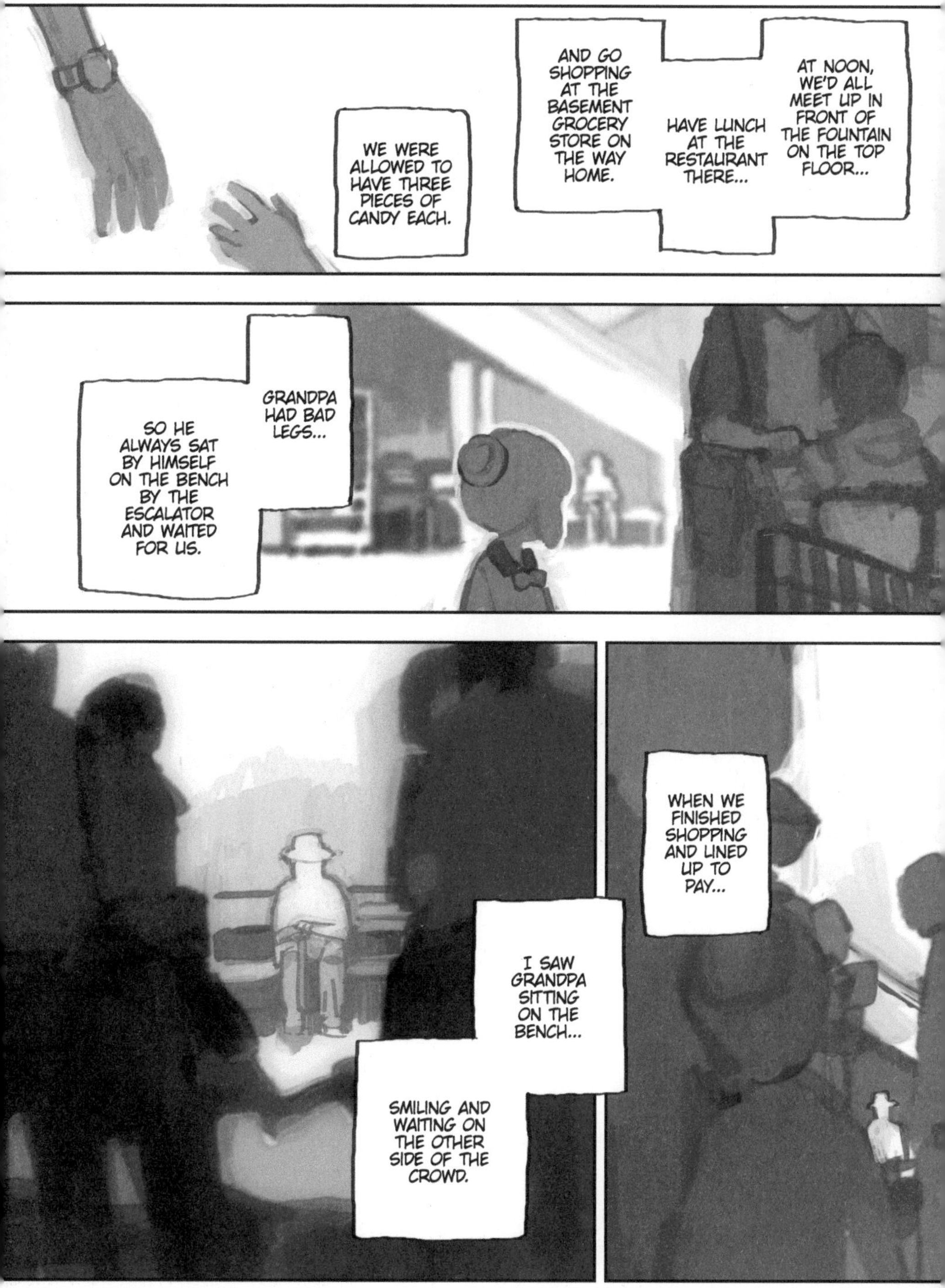
AT NOON, WE'D ALL MEET UP IN FRONT OF THE FOUNTAIN ON THE TOP FLOOR...
HAVE LUNCH AT THE RESTAURANT THERE...
AND GO SHOPPING AT THE BASEMENT GROCERY STORE ON THE WAY HOME.
WE WERE ALLOWED TO HAVE THREE PIECES OF CANDY EACH.
GRANDPA HAD BAD LEGS...
SO HE ALWAYS SAT BY HIMSELF ON THE BENCH BY THE ESCALATOR AND WAITED FOR US.
WHEN WE FINISHED SHOPPING AND LINED UP TO PAY...
I SAW GRANDPA SITTING ON THE BENCH...
SMILING AND WAITING ON THE OTHER SIDE OF THE CROWD.

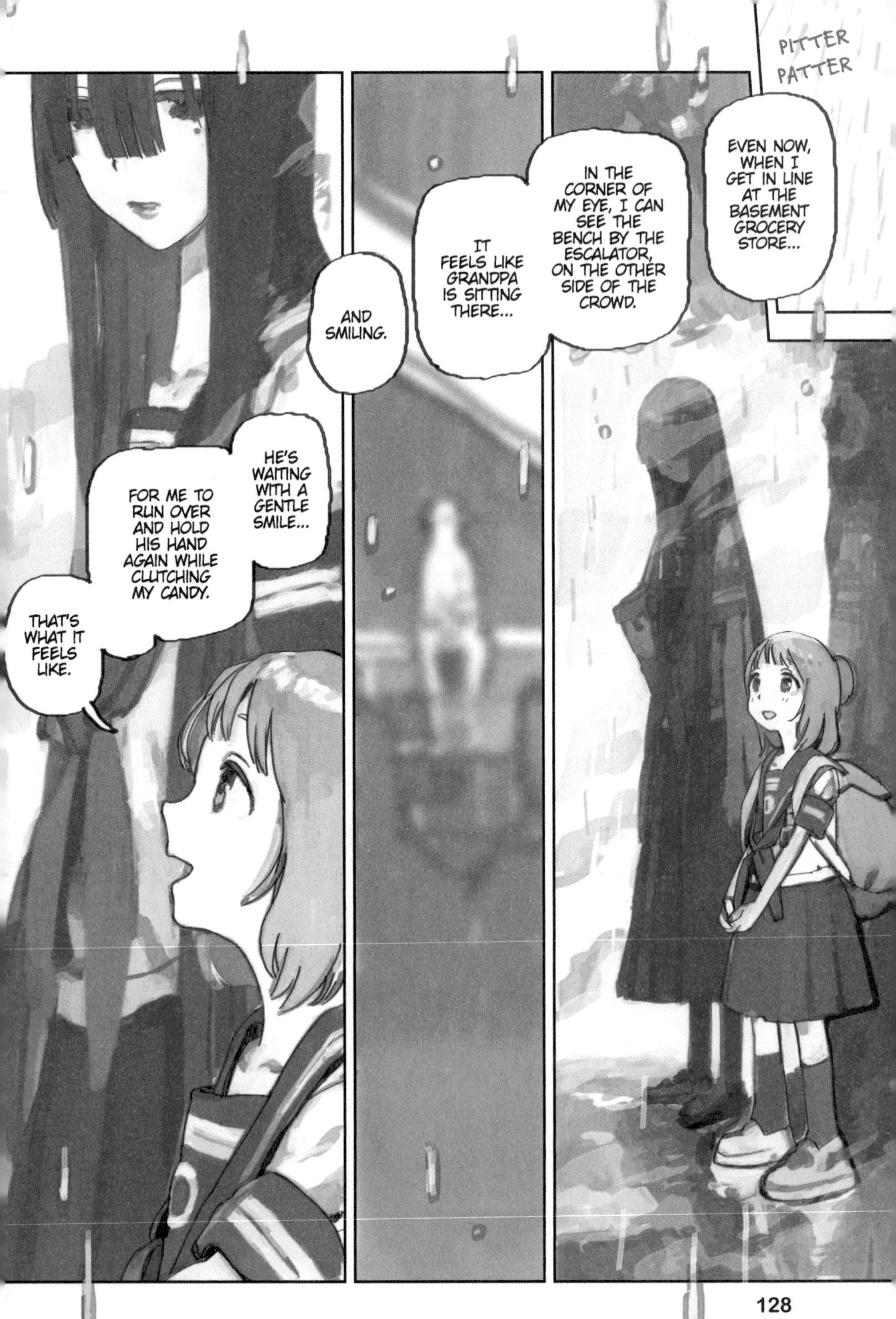
PITTER PATTER
EVEN NOW, WHEN I GET IN LINE AT THE BASEMENT GROCERY STORE...
IN THE CORNER OF MY EYE, I CAN SEE THE BENCH BY THE ESCALATOR, ON THE OTHER SIDE OF THE CROWD.
IT FEELS LIKE GRANDPA IS SITTING THERE...
AND SMILING.
HE'S WAITING WITH A GENTLE SMILE...
FOR ME TO RUN OVER AND HOLD HIS HAND AGAIN WHILE CLUTCHING MY CANDY.
THAT'S WHAT IT FEELS LIKE.

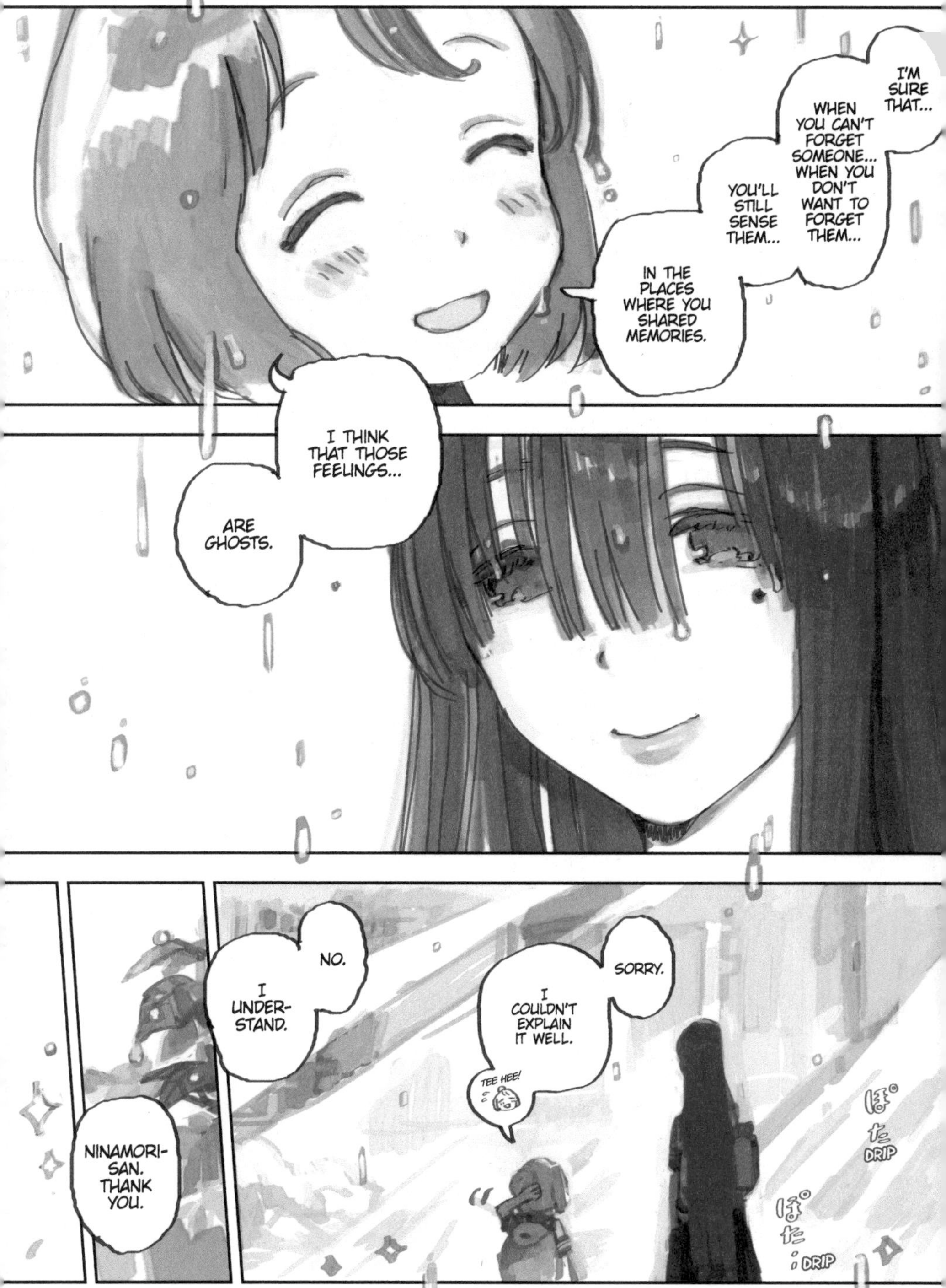
I'M SURE THAT...
WHEN YOU CAN'T FORGET SOMEONE... WHEN YOU DON'T WANT TO FORGET THEM...
YOU'LL STILL SENSE THEM...
IN THE PLACES WHERE YOU SHARED MEMORIES.
I THINK THAT THOSE FEELINGS...
ARE GHOSTS.
ぽた DRIP
ぽた DRIP
SORRY.
I COULDN'T EXPLAIN IT WELL.
TEE HEE!
NO.
I UNDER-STAND.
NINAMORI-SAN. THANK YOU.

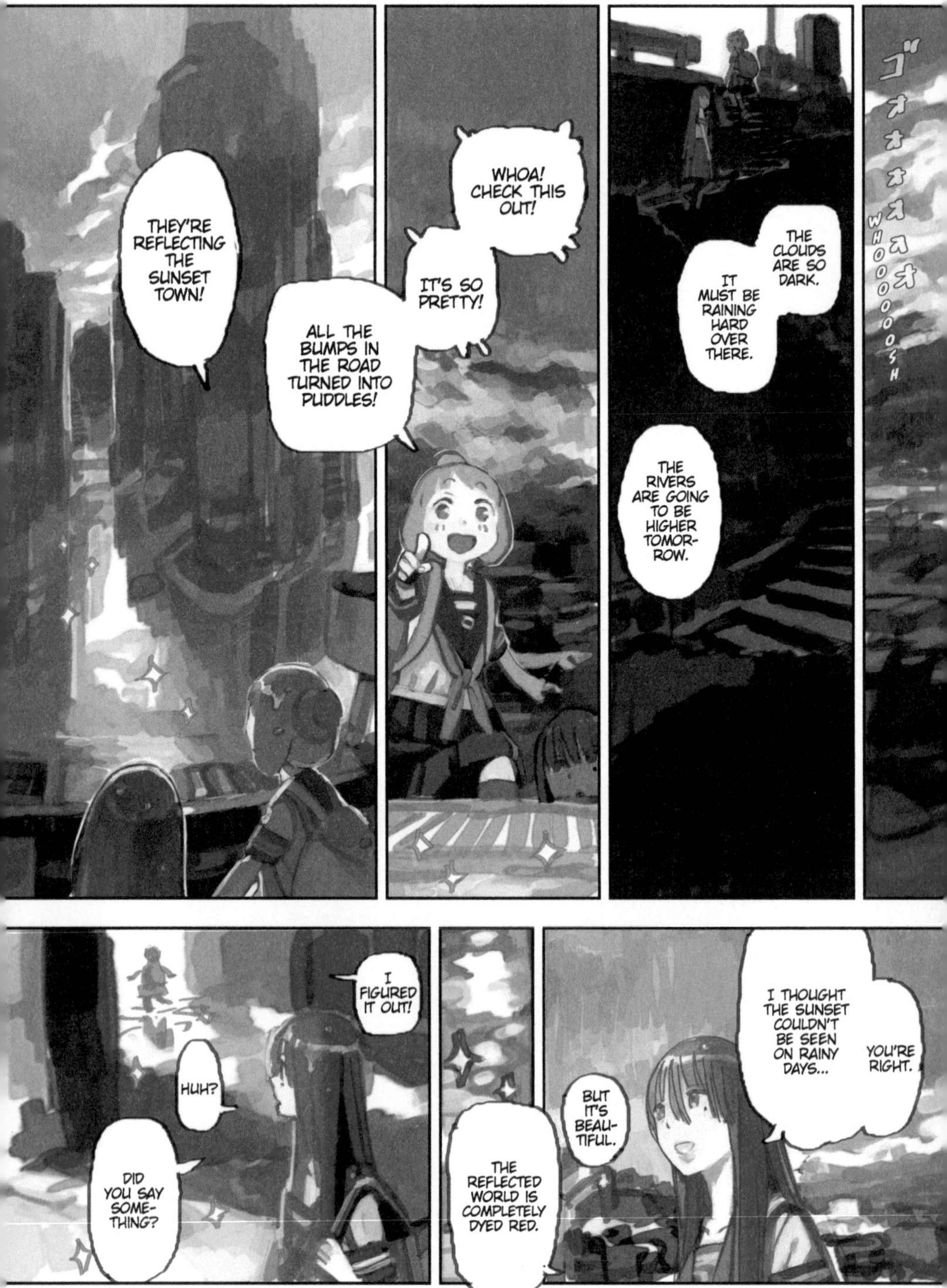

ゴオオオオオオ
WHOOOOOOOSH
THE CLOUDS ARE SO DARK.
IT MUST BE RAINING HARD OVER THERE.
THE RIVERS ARE GOING TO BE HIGHER TOMOR-ROW.
WHOA! CHECK THIS OUT!
IT'S SO PRETTY!
ALL THE BUMPS IN THE ROAD TURNED INTO PUDDLES!
THEY'RE REFLECTING THE SUNSET TOWN!
YOU'RE RIGHT.
I THOUGHT THE SUNSET COULDN'T BE SEEN ON RAINY DAYS...
BUT IT'S BEAU-TIFUL.
THE REFLECTED WORLD IS COMPLETELY DYED RED.
I FIGURED IT OUT!
HUH?
DID YOU SAY SOME-THING?

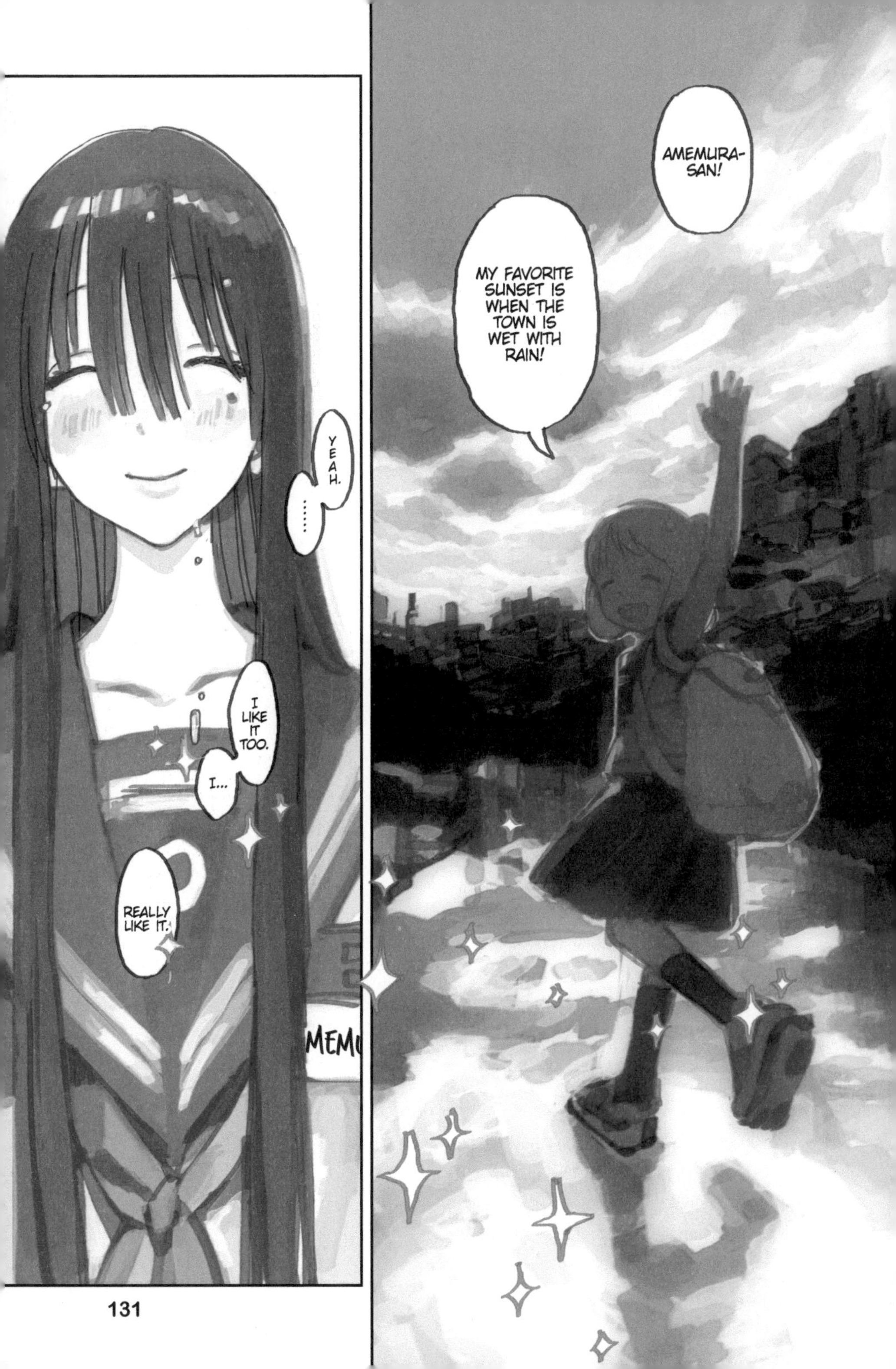

AMEMURA-SAN!
MY FAVORITE SUNSET IS WHEN THE TOWN IS WET WITH RAIN!
YEAH.
......
I LIKE IT TOO.
I...
REALLY LIKE IT.

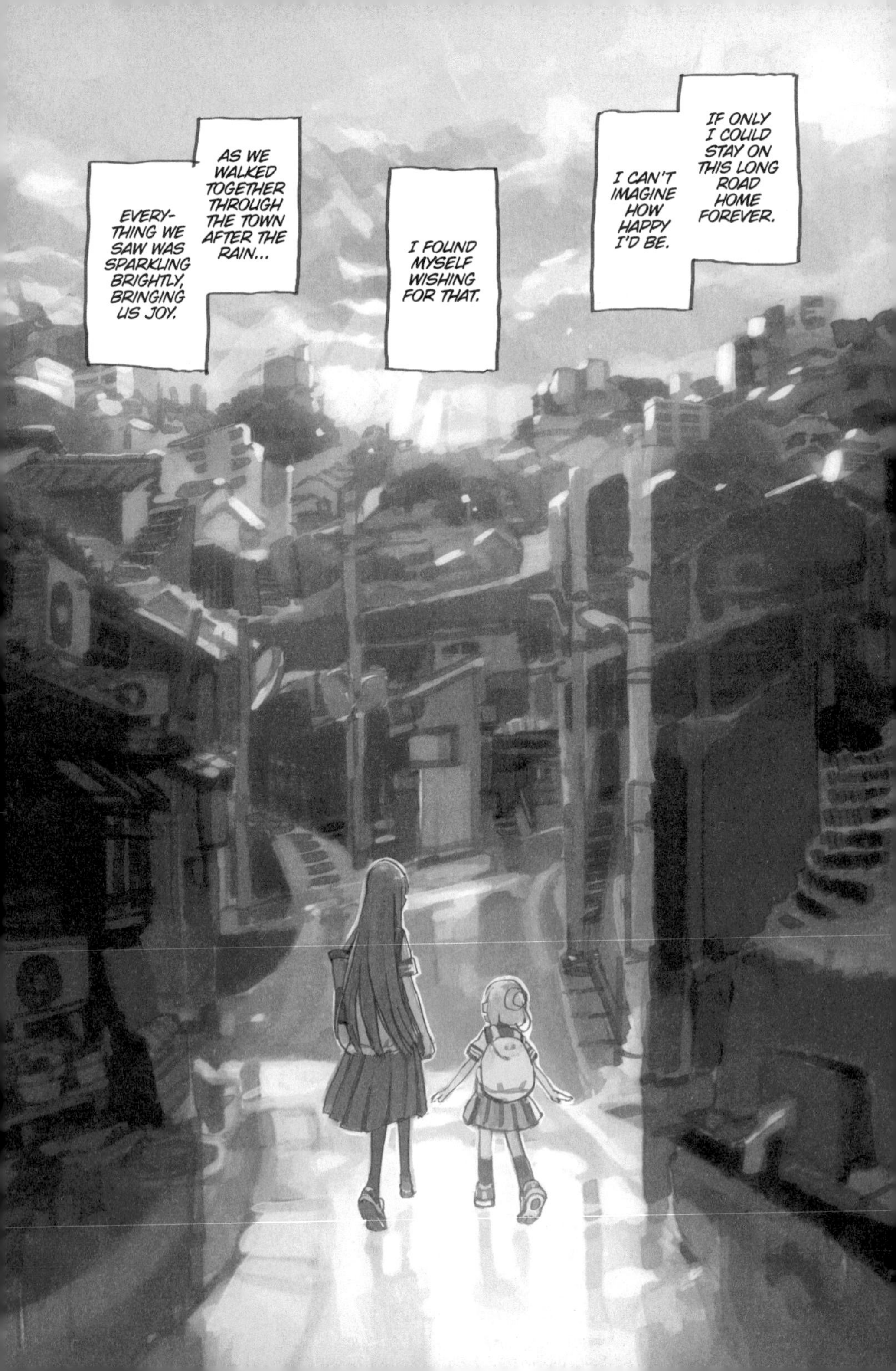
IF ONLY I COULD STAY ON THIS LONG ROAD HOME FOREVER.
I CAN'T IMAGINE HOW HAPPY I'D BE.
I FOUND MYSELF WISHING FOR THAT.
AS WE WALKED TOGETHER THROUGH THE TOWN AFTER THE RAIN...
EVERY-THING WE SAW WAS SPARKLING BRIGHTLY, BRINGING US JOY.

NIGHTFALL TRAVELERS

LEAVE ONLY FOOTPRINTS

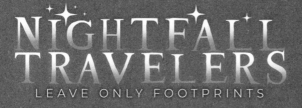

NIGHTFALL TRAVELERS

LEAVE ONLY FOOTPRINTS

Intermission: Good Night Akane-chan @ Coming Home After Chapter 6

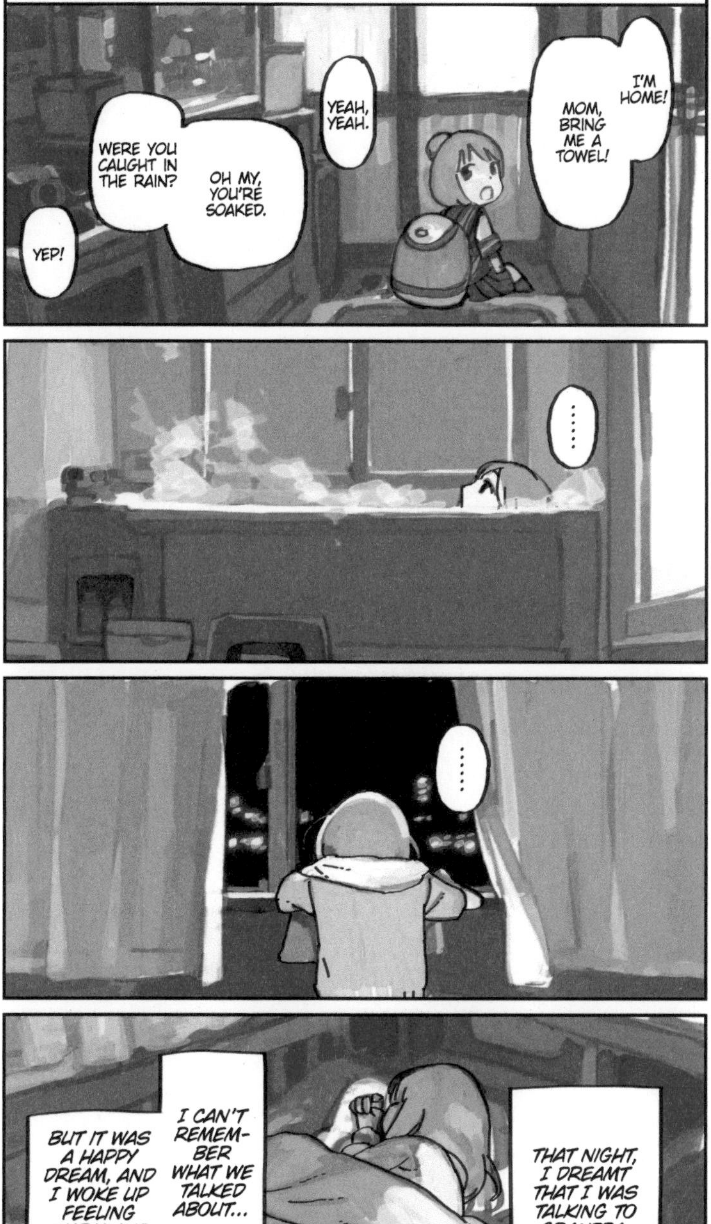
I'M HOME!
MOM, BRING ME A TOWEL!
YEAH, YEAH.
OH MY, YOU'RE SOAKED.
WERE YOU CAUGHT IN THE RAIN?
YEP!
......
......
THAT NIGHT, I DREAMT THAT I WAS TALKING TO GRANDPA.
I CAN'T REMEMBER WHAT WE TALKED ABOUT...
BUT IT WAS A HAPPY DREAM, AND I WOKE UP FEELING WARM AND FUZZY THE NEXT MORNING.

NIGHTFALL TRAVELERS
LEAVE ONLY FOOTPRINTS

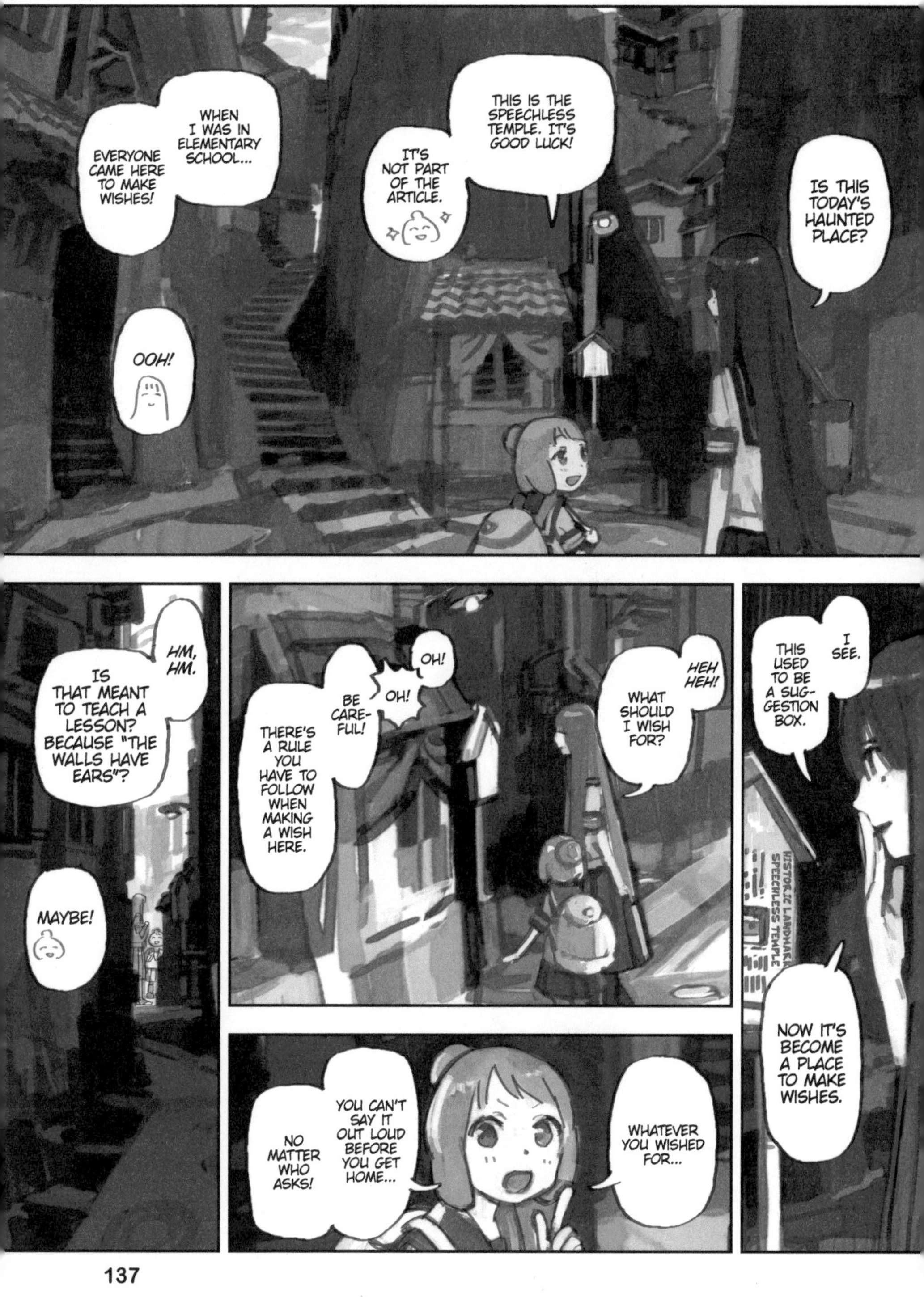
IS THIS TODAY'S HAUNTED PLACE?
THIS IS THE SPEECHLESS TEMPLE. IT'S GOOD LUCK!
IT'S NOT PART OF THE ARTICLE.
WHEN I WAS IN ELEMENTARY SCHOOL...
EVERYONE CAME HERE TO MAKE WISHES!
OOH!
I SEE.
THIS USED TO BE A SUG-GESTION BOX.
HISTORIC LANDMARK SPEECHLESS TEMPLE
NOW IT'S BECOME A PLACE TO MAKE WISHES.
HEH HEH!
WHAT SHOULD I WISH FOR?
OH!
OH!
BE CARE-FUL!
THERE'S A RULE YOU HAVE TO FOLLOW WHEN MAKING A WISH HERE.
WHATEVER YOU WISHED FOR...
YOU CAN'T SAY IT OUT LOUD BEFORE YOU GET HOME...
NO MATTER WHO ASKS!
HM, HM.
IS THAT MEANT TO TEACH A LESSON? BECAUSE "THE WALLS HAVE EARS"?
MAYBE!

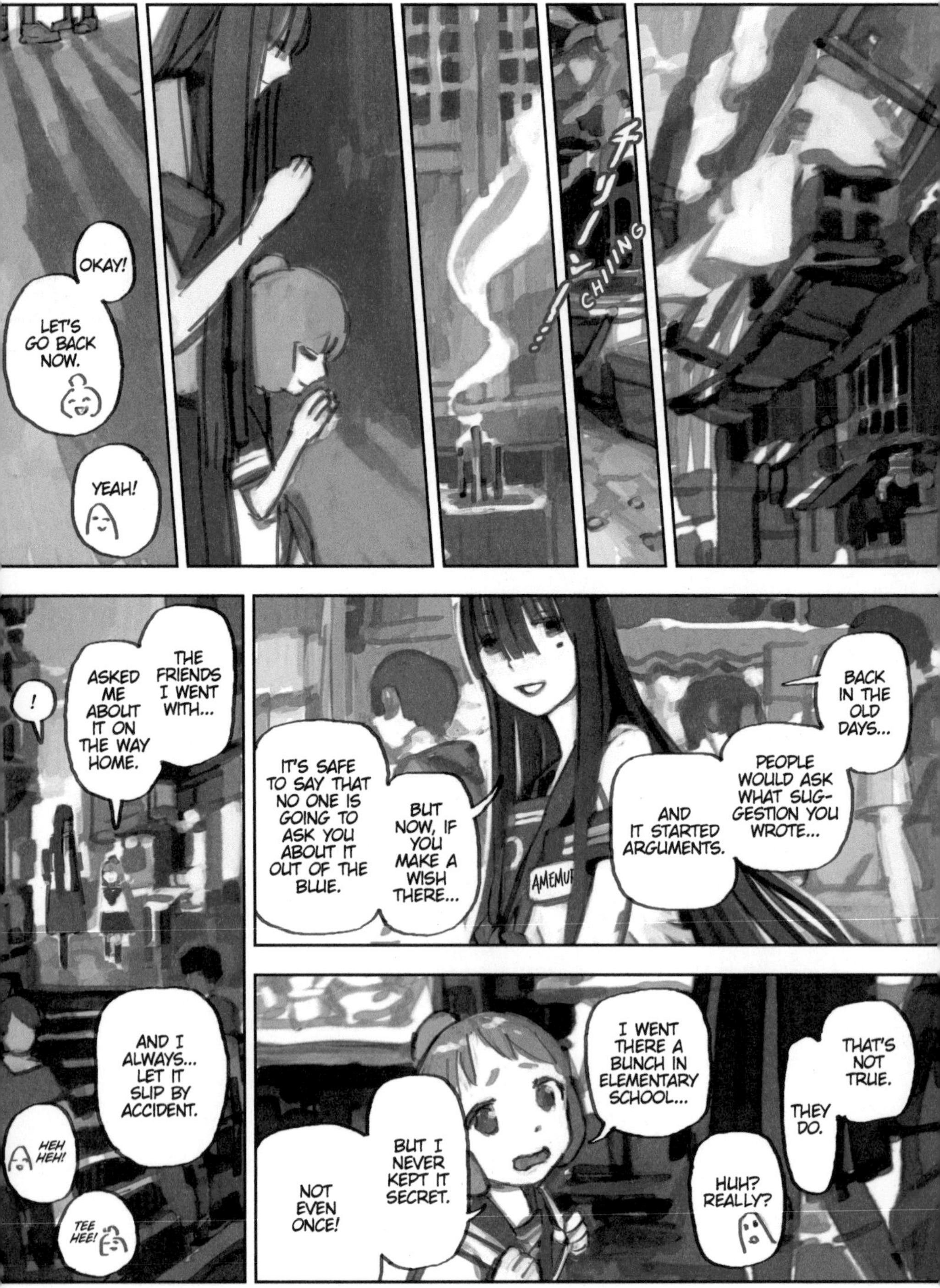
チリーン…
CHIIING
OKAY!
LET'S GO BACK NOW.
YEAH!
BACK IN THE OLD DAYS...
PEOPLE WOULD ASK WHAT SUG-GESTION YOU WROTE...
AND IT STARTED ARGUMENTS.
BUT NOW, IF YOU MAKE A WISH THERE...
IT'S SAFE TO SAY THAT NO ONE IS GOING TO ASK YOU ABOUT IT OUT OF THE BLUE.
THAT'S NOT TRUE.
THEY DO.
HUH? REALLY?
I WENT THERE A BUNCH IN ELEMENTARY SCHOOL...
BUT I NEVER KEPT IT SECRET.
NOT EVEN ONCE!
THE FRIENDS I WENT WITH...
ASKED ME ABOUT IT ON THE WAY HOME.
!
AND I ALWAYS... LET IT SLIP BY ACCIDENT.
HEH HEH!
TEE HEE!

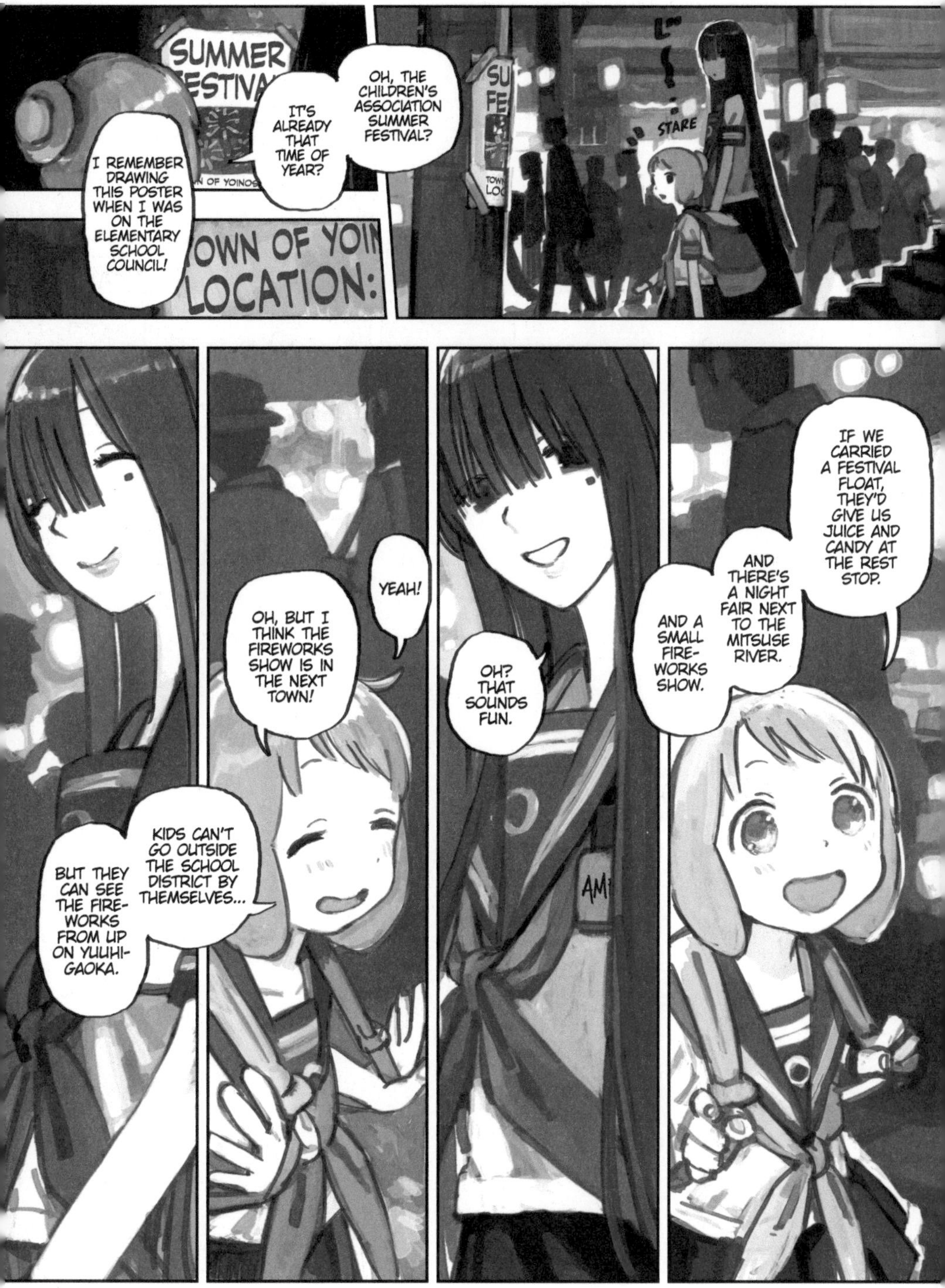
STARE
SUMMER
OH, THE CHILDREN'S ASSOCIATION SUMMER FESTIVAL?
IT'S ALREADY THAT TIME OF YEAR?
I REMEMBER DRAWING THIS POSTER WHEN I WAS ON THE ELEMENTARY SCHOOL COUNCIL!
TOWN OF YOIN
LOCATION:
IF WE CARRIED A FESTIVAL FLOAT, THEY'D GIVE US JUICE AND CANDY AT THE REST STOP.
AND THERE'S A NIGHT FAIR NEXT TO THE MITSUSE RIVER.
AND A SMALL FIRE-WORKS SHOW.
OH? THAT SOUNDS FUN.
YEAH!
OH, BUT I THINK THE FIREWORKS SHOW IS IN THE NEXT TOWN!
KIDS CAN'T GO OUTSIDE THE SCHOOL DISTRICT BY THEMSELVES...
BUT THEY CAN SEE THE FIRE-WORKS FROM UP ON YUUHI-GAOKA.

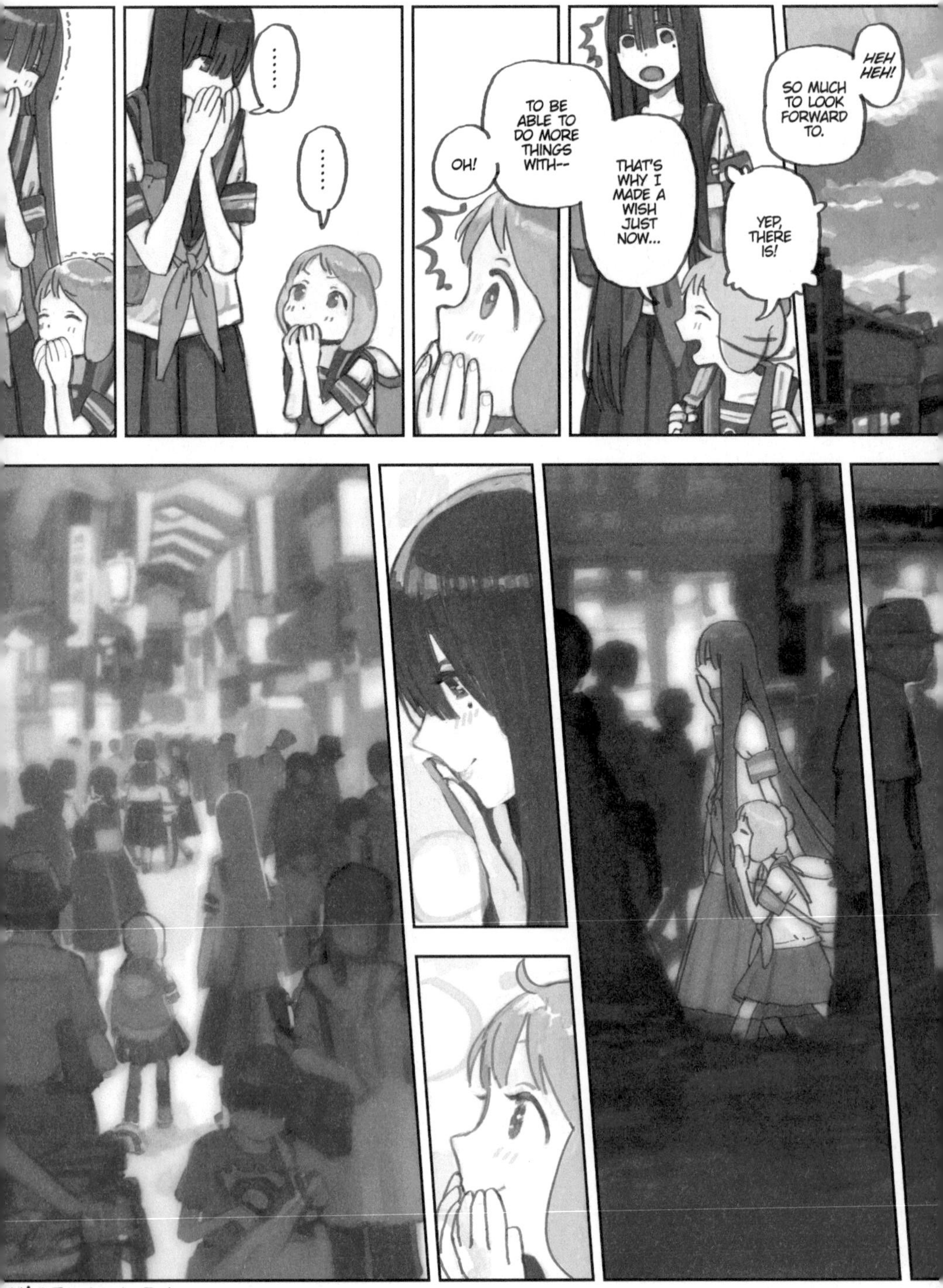
HEH HEH!
SO MUCH TO LOOK FORWARD TO.
YEP, THERE IS!
THAT'S WHY I MADE A WISH JUST NOW...
TO BE ABLE TO DO MORE THINGS WITH--
OH!
......
......

NIGHTFALL TRAVELERS

LEAVE ONLY FOOTPRINTS

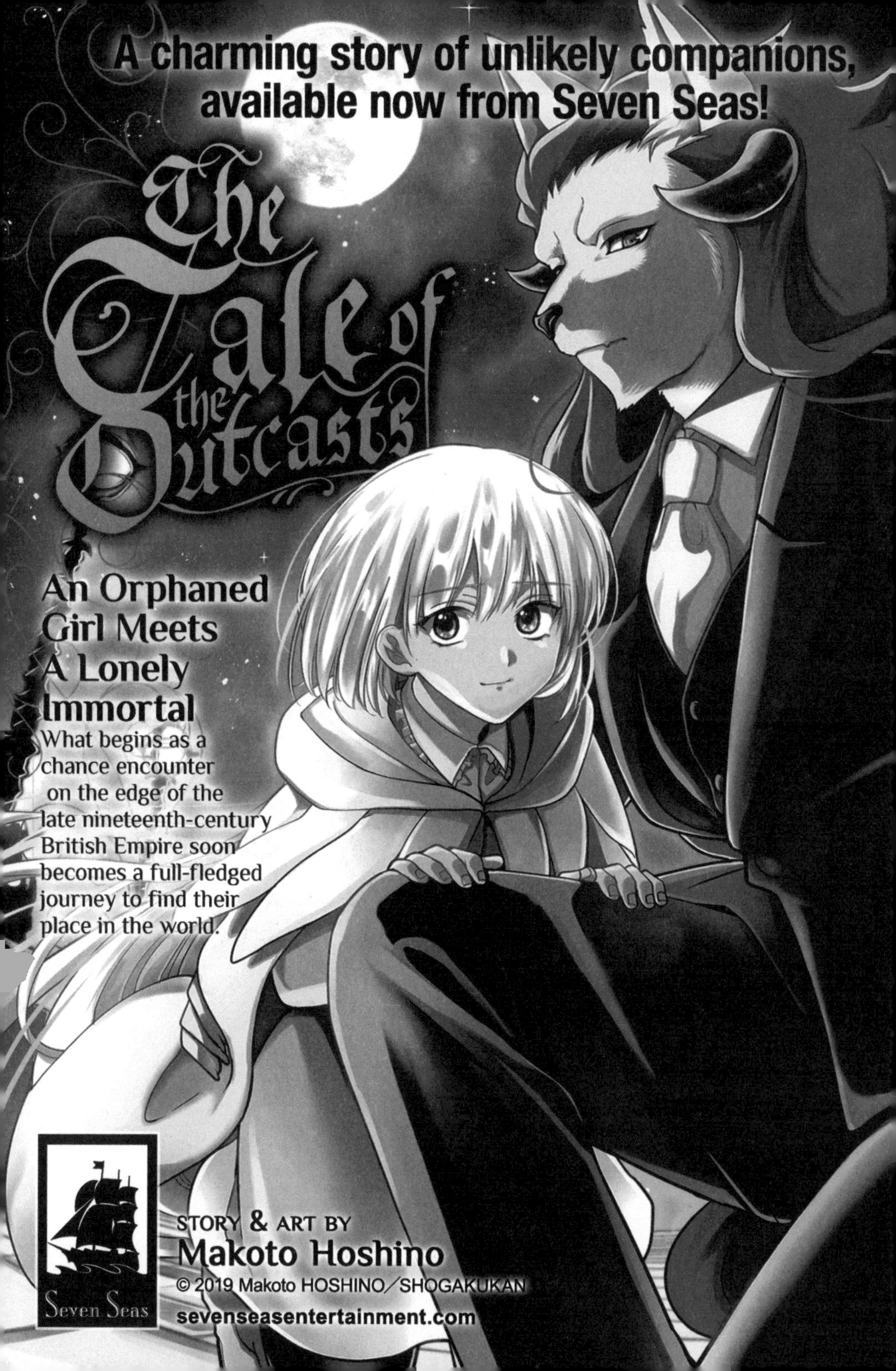
A charming story of unlikely companions, available now from Seven Seas!
The Tale of the Outcasts
An Orphaned Girl Meets A Lonely Immortal
What begins as a chance encounter on the edge of the late nineteenth-century British Empire soon becomes a full-fledged journey to find their place in the world.
Seven Seas
STORY & ART BY
Makoto Hoshino
© 2019 Makoto HOSHINO／SHOGAKUKAN
sevenseasentertainment.com

SEVEN SEAS ENTERTAINMENT PRESENTS

NIGHTFALL TRAVELERS
LEAVE ONLY FOOTPRINTS

story and art by TOMOHI

TRANSLATION
Minna Lin

LETTERING
Ochie Caraan

COVER DESIGN
Nicky Lim

LOGO DESIGN
George Panella

PROOFREADER
Krista Grandy

COPY EDITOR
Dawn Davis

EDITOR
Linda Lombardi

PRODUCTION DESIGNER
Christina McKenzie

PRODUCTION MANAGER
Lissa Pattillo

PREPRESS TECHNICIAN
Melanie Ujimori

PRINT MANAGER
Rhiannon Rasmussen-Silverstein

EDITOR-IN-CHIEF
Julie Davis

ASSOCIATE PUBLISHER
Adam Arnold

PUBLISHER
Jason DeAngelis

YUYAKE TRIP Volume1
©TOMOHI 2021
Originally published in Japan in 2021 by HOUBUNSHA CO., LTD., Tokyo.
English translation rights arranged with HOUBUNSHA CO., LTD., Tokyo,
through TOHAN CORPORATION, Tokyo.

Seven Seas press and purchase enquiries can be sent to Marketing Manager Lianne
Sentar at press@gomanga.com. Information regarding the distribution and purchase of
digital editions is available from Digital Manager CK Russell at digital@gomanga.com.

Seven Seas and the Seven Seas logo are trademarks of
Seven Seas Entertainment. All rights reserved.

ISBN: 978-1-63858-278-6
Printed in Canada
First Printing: May 2022
10 9 8 7 6 5 4 3 2 1

READING DIRECTIONS

This book reads from *right to left*,
Japanese style. If this is your first time
reading manga, you start reading from
the top right panel on each page and
take it from there. If you get lost, just
follow the numbered diagram here.
It may seem backwards at first,
but you'll get the hang of it! Have fun!!

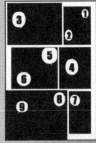

Follow us online: www.SevenSeasEntertainment.com